The
EIGHT ESSENTIAL
PEOPLE SKILLS
for
PROJECT
MANAGEMENT

Other Books by Zachary Wong

Human Factors in Project Management
Personal Effectiveness in Project Management

The
EIGHT ESSENTIAL
PEOPLE SKILLS
for
PROJECT
MANAGEMENT

Solving the Most Common
People Problems for Team Leaders

ZACHARY WONG, PhD

BK®

Berrett–Koehler Publishers. Inc.

Berrett-Koehler Publishers, Inc.
1333 Broadway, Suite 1000
Oakland, CA 94612-1921
Tel: (510) 817-2277 Fax: (510) 817-2278 www.bkconnection.com

Ordering Information
Quantity sales. Special discounts are available on quantity purchases by corporations, associations, and others. For details, contact the "Special Sales Department" at the Berrett-Koehler address above.
Individual sales. Berrett-Koehler publications are available through most bookstores. They can also be ordered directly from Berrett-Koehler:
Tel: (800) 929-2929; Fax: (802) 864-7626; www.bkconnection.com.
Orders for college textbook / course adoption use. Please contact
Berrett-Koehler: Tel: (800) 929-2929; Fax: (802) 864-7626.

Distributed to the U.S. trade and internationally by Penguin Random House Publisher Services.

Berrett-Koehler and the BK logo are registered trademarks of Berrett-Koehler Publishers, Inc.

Printed in the United States of America

Berrett-Koehler books are printed on long-lasting acid-free paper. When it is available, we choose paper that has been manufactured by environmentally responsible processes. These may include using trees grown in sustainable forests, incorporating recycled paper, minimizing chlorine in bleaching, or recycling the energy produced at the paper mill.

Library of Congress Cataloging-in-Publication Data

Names: Wong, Zachary.
Title: The eight essential people skills for project management :
   solving the most common people problems for team leaders / Zachary Wong.
Description: First Edition. | Oakland : Berrett-Koehler Publishers, 2018.
Identifiers: LCCN 2018030047 | ISBN 9781523097937 (hardback)
Subjects: LCSH: Project management. | Personnel management. | BISAC: BUSINESS &
   ECONOMICS / Project Management. | BUSINESS & ECONOMICS / Management. |
   BUSINESS & ECONOMICS / Business Communication / General.
Classification: LCC HD69.P75 W655 2018 | DDC 658.4/04—dc23
LC record available at https://lccn.loc.gov/2018030047

First Edition
25 24 23 22 21 20 19 18   10 9 8 7 6 5 4 3 2 1
Book producer: Westchester Publishing Services
Cover designer: Adam Johnson
Cover art credit: Image by Rawpixel.com/Shutterstock

Dedicated to
Elaine,
the love of my heart

Amy and Sarah,
the heart of my happiness

Contents

Introduction

The Eight Essential People Skills were developed after decades of study, research, experience, and feedback from hundreds of team leaders from industry, government, and academia. These eight were identified as the most common, sought-after skills by project leaders for solving the toughest people problems in today's workplace, including how to diagnose and solve people problems, confront and correct bad behavior, reduce team dissatisfaction and disharmony, turn around difficult people and poor performers, get people to do what you want them to do, raise employee motivation and attitude, reduce change and risk aversion, and manage a difficult boss.

The purpose of this book is to give you models, tools, and insights to help you effectively diagnose and correct people problems. These Eight Essential People Skills are a set of practical strategies, methods, tips, and techniques to help you immediately improve as a project team leader. As one reader expressed, "I need this material—you don't learn this stuff in school or at work and it relates to the things we actually face in the real world."

If you are a current or prospective team leader, congratulations! You have one of the most challenging and rewarding jobs in today's workplace. Leading teams is a double-edged sword, as the joy and satisfaction of working with others are too frequently tempered by the heartaches and headaches of supervising personnel, resolving disagreements, and handling people problems. You're expected to be part supervisor, part counselor, part coach, part management, and part frustrated.

The Eight Skills are designed for individuals, team leaders, and managers who oversee and coordinate the daily performance of others. Most books on people management and leadership tend to preach certain practices and habits to improve one's people skills. Adopting a set of standard practices does not make you an effective leader. The best team leaders are *problem solvers* and *facilitators*, so this book is structured that way, giving you facilitative models, skills, and tools to diagnose people problems and then

1

offering you processes, options, and ideas that you can choose from to fit your situation and who you are.

Whether your background is in technology, social sciences, humanities, natural sciences, engineering, or other studies, it is unlikely that you were ever schooled in the principles and practices of leading and motivating a team. When it comes to learning people skills, you're pretty much left on your own, and nothing is harder than leading teams. To be successful, it takes a combination of supervisory, process, and communication skills; knowledge of human psychology, organizational behavior and human factors; and teamwork, integrity, and leadership. Given the breadth and depth of these subjects, it's certainly a tall order to expect project team leaders to be fluent in all of them and an even greater stretch to believe that project leaders can adeptly apply them to a diverse work team.

More than ever, people skills are in high demand, due to the continued rise in team-based projects and organizations, a more educated and collaborative workforce, employees wanting more authority and responsibility, the need for more innovation and productivity, and workers seeking more meaningful work. In short, people want to know more, do more, create more, and contribute more than ever before. People are more socially connected, tech savvy, and eager to make an impact. Never before have individual workers had more power, freedom, ability, and technology to make tremendous differences in their work teams, departments, companies, and industries, as well as the world. But are team leaders adequately equipped to serve this new avant-garde and take advantage of this tremendous brain trust and human resource? How do you facilitate and motivate people in this new global work environment? Because of changes in the demographics and culture of the workplace, project team leaders need a new set of skills, models, and tools to lead our changing workforce.

What Is a Project Team Leader?

A *project team leader* is someone who provides guidance, direction, facilitation, coaching, expertise, and motivation to a group of individuals who are working together to achieve a common goal, work product, or result. The Eight Skills are applicable to not only project management but all fields and workplaces where you find team leaders, such as team managers, group managers, supervisors, superintendents, coordinators, technical leads, and anyone who oversees the daily performance of others. These are people who have direct contact with their work team and are responsible for the work direction, productivity, and performance of their team.

What Are People Skills?

In this book, *people skills* are defined as the ability to understand, facilitate, communicate, and work with people on an individual, team, and organizational level to meet stakeholder expectations, motivate high employee performance, and achieve team success. It's imperative for today's project team leaders to possess strong knowledge of and skills in working with people, building an effective team, and solving people problems. People skills in project management is a huge topic that is immensely important for today's project team leaders. Although the task may seem daunting, the objective of this book is to try to condense this vast subject down to the few critical skills that project leaders need and want in managing team performance today.

The Most Important Challenges for Today's Project Team Leaders

Managing Multiple Roles: Increased Expectations and Demands on Team Leaders

In the past, most large organizations had layers upon layers of management and supervisors. This was required to achieve a hierarchy of power, authority, knowledge, control, and communication. But with increased efficiency, productivity, and information technology, as well as faster product cycles, communications, and work processes, organizations have delayered and decentralized to create a more flexible, agile, collaborative, self-managed organizational structure with highly competent project team leaders. With a more capable, educated, and sophisticated workforce, the "do more with less" movement has redefined the functions of the project leader. Being an expert in your field or knowing the work better than anyone else doesn't cut it anymore. Today's project leaders have more functional, supervisory, and leadership responsibilities than did preceding generations. The job description demands a strong and competent team leader.

In managing projects, project team leaders not only deal with executing complex work plans, budgets, and processes but also handling a wide range of people problems, work conflicts, performance issues, and difficult behaviors. When there's a gripe or problem, the team leader is the go-to person and the first line of authority. Because the workforce is more diverse, better educated, and more self-determined, the project leader is no longer an authoritarian but rather a multiskilled, facilitative leader who is expected to enable, influence, and motivate high employee performance. Also, as the complexity, pace, growth, and diversity of the workforce increase, a more robust set of people skills is required.

With more responsibilities, you would think that project team leaders would be given more time and space to operate in. No such luck—you're left between a rock and a hard place; you are expected to serve both management (rock) *and* your team (hard place). Also, you're expected to be both caring and tough at the same time in handling people problems. Let's face it: project leaders have numerous roles and responsibilities and are required to do the following:

- ▲ Meet or exceed the expectations of your team *and* the expectations of your boss and management.
- ▲ Keep one eye on the daily tactical work *and* your other eye on the strategic "big picture."
- ▲ Respect each person as an individual *and* do what's best for the organization.
- ▲ Be empathetic, caring, and concerned *and* be firm, decisive, and tough.
- ▲ Think outside the box, be a risk taker, and lead change *and* get the project done on time, execute with excellence, *and* complete all required administrative tasks ("get the wash out") error-free.

Project team leaders now live in an *and* world, not an *or* world—you have fewer options and more demands. You're expected to bridge the divide between your management (your boss) and your work team by connecting company strategies with action plans, management initiatives with work directives, and business objectives with individual performance goals. No doubt, bridging the gap between management and your work team can feel like a no-win, "can't please everyone" experience. Yet you remain enslaved to two masters, and that's a scary spot to be in.

For this first challenge, the most common questions from team leaders are the following: What are my key roles as a team leader in serving both management and my team members? What is the best strategy for leading people in this softer, faster-paced work environment? How do I ensure I'm working on the right problem in the right way? Autocracy is gone, so how do I effectively maintain control and influence as a facilitative leader? How do I balance the interests of individuals, my team, and management? How do I avoid being too soft or too hard when dealing with people problems? How do I address tough people problems without getting hurt emotionally?

You can find the answers to these important questions in the following chapters:

▲ **Skill One: How to Diagnose and Correct People Problems**
▲ **Skill Two: How to Be Tough on People Problems without Being Tough on People**

Motivating Higher Performance in Others: Increased Need for More Skills in Managing Individual and Team Behavior

What makes or breaks a team is not process, skills, or experience but team behavior. How well a project leader motivates and manages team behavior will determine the success of the project. The most important behaviors for a team include trust, communication, feedback, recognition, interdependence, valuing individuality, transparency, and accountability. In the past, project leaders were primarily focused on project objectives, goals, work plans, budgets, and deliverables. Today, project leaders must be competent in understanding team behavior and knowing how to facilitate, not dictate, the "right" behaviors. You do not *manage* people; you *lead* people. As a team leader, your job is to *manage performance*, which requires managing *behavior*. This requires knowledge of human factors and skills in behavioral management, which are not easy to come by. These fields are so abstract that it seems farfetched to try to apply them to such a practical discipline as project management. That's why they have been ignored for so long in the discipline.

The world has moved from baby boomers to millennials, analog to digital, print to social media, company loyalty to career loyalty, individual- to team-based culture, "scare and conform" to "care and concern," delayed to instant gratification, annual performance reviews to daily feedback, and linear to agile management. With these changes in the workplace and demographics, we're seeing a change in the organizational structure and a corresponding need to change the way we motivate and manage team performance. The role requires greater partnership, collaboration, and facilitation.

Solving people problems often means correcting undesirable behaviors, poor performance, and conflicts. How do team leaders typically deal with these challenges? The most popular strategy is avoidance—you go inactive and don't address the problem with the employee. You fear negative backlash, being branded as a harsh boss, lowering morale, or, worse yet, the employee filing a complaint with Human Resources. But inaction has consequences. Instead of taking care of the problem, most team leaders simply live with it, try to compensate for it, and hope it will resolve itself or be transferred to someone else. Deep inside, you know you're procrastinating, and the mess only gets messier. Confronting difficult and low-performing employees is a tough task for any project leader. It doesn't matter how seasoned you are, it's a situation that nobody likes to face, and it's one of the key reasons why so many people are reluctant to be team leaders—it's simply not worth the headache.

For this second challenge, the most popular questions from team leaders are the following: What are the key behaviors for highly successful teams? How do I motivate and facilitate these key team behaviors? How do I keep people happy and satisfied with their work? How do I increase and sustain high team performance? What are the specific steps and techniques for effectively correcting difficult people and underperformers? What are the secrets to getting people to do what I want them to do? What are the critical root drivers of interpersonal conflicts and behavior?

You can find the answers to these common questions in the following chapters:

▲ **Skill Three: How to Build Highly Successful Teams**
▲ **Skill Four: How to Boost People's Attitudes, Happiness, and Performance**
▲ **Skill Five: How to Turn Around Difficult People and Underperformers**
▲ **Skill Six: How to Motivate the Right Team Behaviors**

Striving for Greater Impact: Leading Change, Solving Problems, Taking on New Challenges, and Influencing Your Boss

Today's team leaders have to contend with constant change and challenges in managing projects and leading people. The most challenging aspect of project management is the uncertainty and unpredictability in the execution of strategies, work plans, processes, technology, procurement, cost management, and systems control. To succeed in project management, team leaders and project teams must be good in dealing with uncertainty and risks. You can't achieve and do great things without taking some risks. You have to be a good risk taker to lead new projects successfully, implement new technologies, make changes, improve work processes, solve tough problems, and make a greater impact. However, when the time comes to try new things, people tend to wait, hesitate, analyze, and talk themselves out of it. Risk aversion is a major barrier in project management, and it's a behavior that prevails in many organizations. Team leaders need new and better skills to help teams overcome the fear, reluctance, and discomfort of risk taking. You can increase your success and make a bigger impact by improving your team leadership in risk taking.

The second major people skill that is essential for making a greater impact is your ability to "manage up" and establish a strong working relationship with your boss. Your boss is your most critical resource for the authority, support, and freedom necessary to accomplish your goals and ambitions. Also, having a good relationship with your boss is important for your happiness and well-being. Your boss can be a great enabler or disabler in your job, and there is nothing better or worse than having a good or bad boss, respectively. In order to be successful, you need the knowledge and skills to effectively manage up and gain greater influence and favor from your boss.

For this third challenge, the most frequent questions from team leaders are the following: What are the key behaviors needed to improve my ability to deal with uncertainty and risks? What are the keys to overcoming risk aversion and resistance to change? How do I build greater confidence and willingness to challenge myself and my team to try new things? How do I help move my team forward when facing new and difficult changes, problems, and challenges? What are the best ways to manage up and gain greater influence with my boss? What are the best ways to increase my value and opportunities and get what I want from my boss?

You can find the answers to these frequent questions in the following chapters:

▲ **Skill Seven: How to Succeed When Faced with Change, Problems, and New Challenges**
▲ **Skill Eight: How to Gain Favor and Influence with Your Boss**

This book was written to give you the essential strategies, skills, and tools for solving the most common and toughest people problems as a team leader. The material has been structured so that it is easy to relate to and learn. To accommodate different learning preferences, every chapter contains a well-balanced mix of concepts, strategies, stories, examples, processes, tools, and techniques, along with illustrations, graphics, tables, and other visuals. Throughout the book, case studies and stories are provided to introduce the core concepts of each skill, followed by case-in-point examples to help reinforce and clarify key ideas. Also, at the end of each chapter, a memory card and skill summary are included to help you review, remember, and reference the most important learnings.

Leading people is a personalized art that requires extensive practice and experience. If you are a seasoned project manager, this book will likely explain a lot of the gut feelings and experiences that you have had in your job. *These skills will affirm, change, and challenge your current thinking about leading teams and managing people's performance.*

This book represents some of the best knowledge that I have been fortunate to acquire through my teaching, research, and consulting. The Eight Skills were derived from the many questions and problems that my students and clients voiced as project leaders. This enabled me to reflect on, draw up, and develop useful solutions based on my forty years of experience. In this process, I have discovered not only that my past learnings are valuable to others but also that I could further improve them by testing and honing them in a wide variety of organizations and circumstances. This process continues even today, and I am grateful to have had the opportunity to learn so much.

As a way of paying it forward, it is my goal to share these valuable learnings with as many people as possible in hopes that this knowledge continues to spread and improve. I hope the Eight Skills will serve you well in your career, as well as in your personal life.

SKILL ONE

How to Diagnose and Correct People Problems
The Wedge

The New Organizational Wedge Model—
No More Pyramids

Diagnosing and solving people problems begin by understanding the basic configuration of today's organizations. Historically, the classic model for organizational structures has been the pyramid, where a small number of executives resided at the pinnacle, senior managers sat just below that, a slew of middle managers populated the midsection, and the widest, biggest, and lowest tier represented the employee base (Figure 1.1, left-hand side). It was top-down management, and the hierarchy represented the relative distribution of authority, decision-making, knowledge, and pay. The higher you were, the more you had, and the people below served the people above. The bulk of the employees resided in the lower half of the pyramid and had limited power, control, and access to information. Also, moving up the hierarchy in terms of advancement and internal communications was a steep climb. However, over time the assumption that workers are laborers who require close supervision and a "command and control" structure has become more obsolete.

In more recent years, another conceptual model was proposed called the inverted pyramid, which reversed the traditional model and tried to show the change in management behavior and the empowerment of employees to make decisions and changes (Figure 1.1, right-hand side) (1). In this new model, the executives serve and support the bulk of the organization and are responsive to the employee base. In practice, it's unclear whether organizations have truly adopted this bottom-up, worker-based, reverse

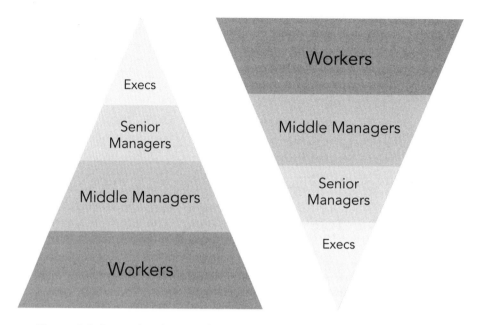

Figure 1.1 Pyramid and inverted pyramid models

hierarchy philosophy. Management and executives of most organizations certainly support their employees and want them to excel in their jobs; but do executives and management really serve the employee base, as the inverted pyramid implies, or do they serve the owners of the enterprise, which are usually shareholders, investors, financial institutions, and other equity stakeholders? Governmental organizations are charged with serving the interests of the taxpayers and their constituents; for nonprofits, it's their sponsors and supporters. Does your organization operate as a hierarchy pyramid or an inverted pyramid?

The inverted model seems to imply that workers are highly empowered—that the will of the workers prevail—which is certainly not the case. Clearly, organizational policies, rules, and authority are defined by the owners and management of the enterprise. Although management styles have greatly changed over the years, and there's definitely more employee empowerment and less autocracy, one can argue that in today's organizations, the operating model is probably somewhere between a pyramid and an inverted pyramid—a *horizontal pyramid* (Figure 1.2).

Furthermore, due to the characteristics of the new generation of workers and advances in skills, technology, education, and communications, organ-

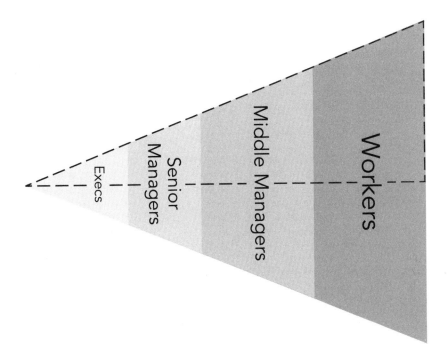

Figure 1.2 Transformation of the pyramid to a wedge

izations are much flatter, leaner, smarter, and more efficient, and therefore *the pyramid should be cut in half horizontally, resulting in a wedge structure* (Figure 1.2, dashed line). The old pyramid structures are too big, slow, and bottom-heavy for today's workplace. The new model needs to be horizontal, streamlined, and efficient.

The model also needs to be further updated to reflect the fact that work teams now dominate the landscape. We have shifted away from executives, middle managers, senior managers, and workers to a more team-based platform of management, work teams, and individual contributors. *Individual contributor* is more apropos in today's workplace, where employees possess much greater responsibility, power, and value. The label "individual contributor" recognizes that each employee is unique and can have a significant impact on the success of the team and organization. They are not workers but rather unique and valued contributors (Figure 1.3).

In addition, the size of each section depicted in the wedge should correspond not to the number of people at each level but rather to the relative power, scope, authority, and resources bestowed at each level. So the wedge

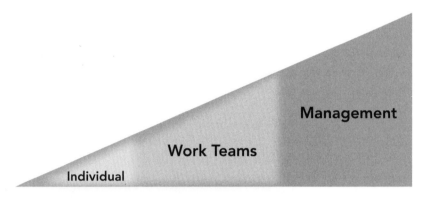

Figure 1.3 The wedge better reflects today's workplace

shows management at the top, commanding the greatest authority and influence in an organization, followed by work teams and individual contributors.

In today's organizations, the boundaries between levels are much less rigid in terms of teamwork, flexibility, and delegation of authority, which means we need to change the solid dividing lines in the pyramid to more seamless divisions in the wedge. More decisions are made in collaboration with teams of people, and the process is much more open and iterative than in the past. The project leader plays a critical role in facilitating, supervising, and leading teams, and they play a highly influential role in today's workplace. The "team leader" designation is missing from the wedge because team leaders today work fluidly between individual contributors and work teams and between work teams and management, so they operate across all three levels of an organization.

Finally, in these times of tighter budgets, cost reductions, outsourcing, faster cycle times, and less bureaucracy in organizations, the wedge also symbolizes the fact that organizations have established more *leveraged resources and processes* at all levels. For example, all services and functions that are considered a commodity or provide no competitive advantage (such as, customer service centers, maintenance, training, benefits, and accounting) are readily centralized, shared, or outsourced as a means of leveraging resources.

In short, due to changes in organizational management, personnel, technology, teamwork, communications, and leverage, I believe the wedge is a more accurate representation of how organizations are structured and operate today. Skill One will take a deeper look at the wedge model and how it can help you as a project team leader.

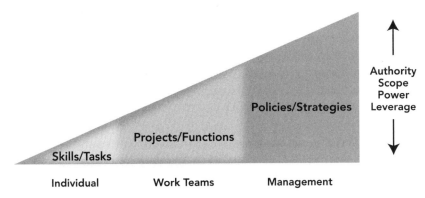

Figure 1.4 Relative roles, authority, scope, power, and leverage in the wedge

Roles and Responsibilities

Each level of the wedge plays a different role that carries a different level of power, scope, authority, leverage, and responsibility (Figure 1.4). I will discuss the significance of these attributes in more depth in Skill Two.

▲ Individual contributor: Skill and task oriented. Each employee brings unique talents, skills, experiences, and diversity to his or her work. Most employees have a relatively narrow scope, restricted authority, leverage, and limited power with responsibility for various work tasks, skills, and processes.

▲ Work team: Project and process oriented. This level typically has many different types of project and functional teams, which are led by team leaders, department managers, supervisors, superintendents, and coordinators. Compared to individual contributors, teams have more power, scope, leverage, and authority to make changes, decisions, and innovations.

▲ Management team: Policy and strategy oriented. The highest part of the wedge represents corporate departments and executives whose role is to lead and manage the organization. Management teams have the broadest scope, power, authority, leverage, and responsibilities for organization-wide planning, strategies, resource allocation, monitoring, control, and policies.

Leveraging the Power and Resources of Individuals, Teams, and Management

The wedge is a multifunctional model that serves as a *leadership, performance*, and *diagnostic tool* for solving people problems.

Use the Wedge to Better Understand Your Leadership Role

How does the wedge help you to understand your role as an organizational leader? From a leadership perspective, you have two key roles: creating organizational alignment and leveraging resources.

Organizational Alignment All team leaders are expected to lead, perform, and solve problems with excellence. You must be able to see the bigger picture and lead your team in working to meet organizational objectives and strategies. Linking organizational policies and strategies to team projects and processes, as well as individual skills and tasks, is a huge expectation for team leaders. As the wedge depicts, aligning your team's work upward to the management level and downward to individual contributors helps you to manage your resources effectively, achieve the right timing and priorities, apply the right strategies and focus for your team, and produce the most value for the organization. This is the essence of leading teams and projects. Organizational alignment is further discussed here and in Skill Two.

Leveraging Resources When it comes to leadership, leveraging and maximizing resources are critical to achieving organizational efficiency, profitability, growth, and sustainability. As a project leader, you are probably spread thin in terms of time, people, budget, and other resources. You have to strive continuously to do more with less but at the same time invest in long-term growth and development. The wedge symbolizes power and leverage, which increase as you go from individual to management level. *Leverage means using a modest amount of time, effort, and resources to yield a much bigger and sustainable result*—producing a *multiplier effect*, the biggest bang for your buck. In other words, you lead by leveraging individual and team resources to meet management-level expectations.

You are responsible for managing, aligning, and leveraging your team's resources. All your team's resources, including people's time, skills, knowledge, experience, ideas, and best practices, have limited value unless they are leveraged across the enterprise. The relative size of each level of the wedge reflects the proportional value of a single contributor (individual), many individuals working together on project and functional teams (work teams), and many teams working in alignment with the mission, strategies, policies, and goals of the organization (management).

What's the potential increase in productivity and efficiency of a team and organization over a group of individuals? One can surmise that sharing one person's skills, knowledge, and experiences with another person (such as in a mentor-mentee relationship or cross-training) could potentially double one's value by increasing the other party's knowledge and skills to the team and organization. But if we look at a *team* of people, where we can optimize and leverage the time, energy, ideas, skills, knowledge, and experiences across *many people*, the potential increase in productivity and efficiency would be even larger, say tenfold, than for a group of individuals working separately. This would come from not only cross-learning (such as mentoring, sharing information) but also team organization, processes, and coordination (such as communications, accountability, planning, scheduling); creativity (for example, team brainstorms, developing ideas together); decision-making and problem solving (such as more input and options); motivation (such as trust, camaraderie, team recognitions, peer pressure); and team values (consistent behaviors). No doubt a high-performing team has much more capability and value than a group of separate individuals.

Finally, leveraging the skills and experiences of *many teams* across an entire organization (such as matrix organizations, centers of excellence) can potentially result in a tremendous increase, perhaps a hundredfold or more, in efficiency and value compared to independent teams. This is often done with Management, Technology, Human Resources, Training and Development, Legal, Planning and Control, Procurement, Project Management, Recruitment, Employee Benefits, and many more. The hundredfold increase is also derived from leveraging financial resources, policies, strategies, goals, affiliations, and physical and intellectual assets.

> *"Leveraging the skills and experiences of many teams across an entire organization . . . can potentially result in a tremendous increase, perhaps a hundredfold or more, in efficiency and value."*

You can save significant time, energy, and money by better utilizing your organization's centers of expertise, services, and information. Whether it's a policy question regarding employee time off or you're looking for best practices in project management, these functions and services exist in a highly leveraged structure to assist you as a team leader. More importantly, it has broad, long-term, organization-wide precedents in policy administration.

Using the Wedge to Manage Performance and People Problems

In addition to helping you understand your organizational leadership role, the wedge is a model for visualizing and managing team performance and people problems.

Project leaders are expected to work seamlessly across all three levels of the wedge. You supervise a *team*, you're working one on one with *individual* employees, and you represent the policies and procedures of *management*. These responsibilities are implemented via key processes that are distributed in the wedge (Figure 1.5). You aren't expected to solve everything yourself. In order to manage performance effectively and solve people problems, you need to be aware of and use the best processes found within each level of the wedge. As a project leader, you have the responsibility for knowing and using these processes to support individual and team performance.

The wedge contains all the key human factors that determine employee, team, and management *performance*. Human factors are the underlying motivators of behavior and performance. Although you could probably think of hundreds of factors that affect performance, there are only a small number of factors that matter the most. These critical determinants, which I call *knobs*, regulate people's performance and are revealed later in this section. You want to use these knobs to *turn up and fine-tune performance*.

Finally, the wedge is a useful and powerful diagnostic tool for identifying and taking action on individual, team, and management performance *problems*. To be an effective problem solver, you must be competent in identifying the specific root problem first; otherwise you'll be wasting your time and effort trying to cure the symptom instead of the disease. More importantly, when trying to correct people's performance problems, use the level that gives you the best resources, expertise, and processes to

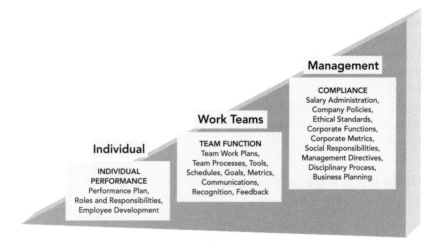

Figure 1.5 Key processes in the wedge

solve your problem. *When seeking to solve people problems, always act from a position that gives you the greatest strength and leverage.* But how do you do that? You use the *best leveraging factor* at each level of the wedge. I refer to these key leveraging factors as *levers* and they will be identified later in this chapter.

Diagnosing and Correcting People Problems

Using the wedge, the first step in diagnosing and correcting people problems is to determine whether the problem is an individual, team, or management issue. You take it to the right stakeholder and authority. For example, if the performance problem relates to compliance with laws, regulations, or company policies, such as employee discrimination, workplace hostility, employee harassment, fraud, or other such violations, take it promptly to the management level—Human Resources, Legal, Medical, Finance, Health, Environment and Safety, or others. As a policy, legal, or company-wide issue, your focus and action must be at the upper end of the wedge, where they have the subject-matter expertise, experience, precedence, authority, and responsibility to handle the issue effectively. *It's not your responsibility to try to interpret, judge, correct, or resolve the issue, because it has larger ramifications and precedence in terms of legal, policy, public relations, and other management-level concerns.* Of course, you will be involved in the process, but at this point it's *not a supervisory-level issue.* It's not a knock on your intelligence or ability; it's a matter that belongs to management. These types of issues require *maximum leverage* and attention—*wedge it up.*

Case in Point An employee on your team complains to you that she has been unable to complete her work assignments because a coworker has been repeatedly "yelling," making "negative remarks," and asserting that she "needs to work harder" in processing invoices so that he can approve payments. She feels "intimidated, demotivated, and stressed" to the point that her work output has gone down. She has asked him to stop being so aggressive toward her, but it hasn't worked. The coworker is a high performer, but his impatience gets the best of him.

Although your employee would like you to use your authority as team leader to correct the coworker's behavior, your first priority should be to ensure that she is safe and to temporarily restrict the coworker's contact with her until you and your organization have conducted a prompt review of the situation and allegations, including speaking in greater detail with her, other possible witnesses, and the coworker. But the problem that your employee has raised likely obligates you to report the problem to the management level because it has *potential legal and policy ramifications* (harassment, hostile work environment). Depending on applicable laws and company policy, once your employee reports such an incident, you may be warranted to seek counsel from Human Resources to ensure compliance with *company policies and procedures*. The point is that small incidents can have big implications, and certain people problems require prompt reporting to a higher level in the wedge so that you can enlist the most leveraged subject-matter expertise, experience, precedence, authority, and responsibility to assist you on the issue. It may be nothing, but it's best to take all such claims as real and serious and let management make the call. A more specific step-by-step process for diagnosing and correcting people problems will be covered in the next section.

Take the Problem to the Appropriate Level

If the employee problem pertains to the operation of the project team, such as project deadlines, violation of team ground rules, project implementation issues, team processes, or team conflicts, then the performance issue deserves to be taken to the work team level. Your team members are all stakeholders and have the best knowledge, skills, and experience to address the problem. Because the scope and ramifications of the problem affect the team, your perspective and action on the problem must be considered by the entire work team or representatives of the team.

As teams are in the middle of the wedge, it's not unusual to find that many team issues, such as inadequate resources, also require involvement from individuals or management. In this case, the problem first needs to be defined and analyzed and alternative solutions explored at the work team level. This could lead to changes in individual assignments or project budgets, which would concern management. The key is to know what skills, processes, authority, and responsibilities exist at each level and then process your problem in the right way, both up and down the wedge.

Finally, if the problem is clearly an individual performance issue, such as absenteeism, low productivity, poor work quality, inadequate work skills, poor communication, or bad behavior, the problem needs action at the individual level. In the next section, I will describe the tools and procedures in the wedge to diagnose and correct people performance problems, and I will reveal the key performance factors (knobs) and best leveraging points (levers) for boosting individual, team, and organizational performance.

Solving Individual Performance Problems

Step 1: **Determine the cause of the problem.** Getting to the root cause of an employee problem may sound like a daunting task given the endless possibilities, but it isn't that difficult. Simply apply ERAM to the problem. ERAM is an acronym for *expectations,*

resources, ability, and *motivation,* and they are the four *key performance factors* in determining employee behavior and success. Essentially all individual performance problems can be attributed

"ERAM is an effective tool for diagnosing the root cause of individual performance issues."

to one or more of these factors—each of these factors is a *knob* that regulates performance, and ERAM is an effective tool for diagnosing the root cause of individual performance issues.

> **Expectations:** Are the responsibilities and work assignments clear to the individual? What are the customer or sponsor expectations? Expectations may include the specific work task, content, purpose, priority, output, quality, format, timing, and behaviors. The individual may need more detailed guidance and clarity on work specifications or customer needs. Miscommunications and misunderstandings between employee and supervisor on expectations are common root causes of individual performance problems.

> **Resources:** Is the individual given adequate time, funding, equipment, materials, tools, technology, information, and support to complete the assignment successfully? The most common resource issues are lack of time, funding, and information. Make sure that you understand the employee's total workload and provide adequate time and support for the work.

> **Ability:** Does the individual have the right expertise, knowledge, skills, and experience to complete the work successfully? Ability includes both hard skills, such as technology, writing, and statistics, and soft skills, such as building positive relationships, leading others, and increasing self-confidence.

> **Motivation:** Is the individual reasonably applying himself or herself to complete the assignment successfully, demonstrating an appropriate level of commitment, effort, energy, and interest? If expectations, resources, and abilities are sufficient, then it comes down to motivation—"I didn't feel like doing it," "I didn't think it was important enough," or "I felt my effort was good enough." The motivation issue will be further discussed in this section and also in other chapters.

Step 2: **Verify the root cause for low performance by doing your own research.** Hopefully Step 1 (ERAM) enabled you to identify the likely cause for the performance problem. But before you try correcting it (unless it's obvious), be aware that the initial cause can often be inaccurate or incomplete. As a project team leader, trust your employees' explanations but always seek to verify the root cause of an individual's performance problem. What may sound like a reasonable excuse could be a cover-up for more serious problems of a personal, team, or organizational nature. Avoid making ERAM conclusions too quickly; make sure you get the whole story before proceeding. Not doing a thorough job in determining the root cause is probably one of the most common mistakes supervisors make in addressing employee problems.

Step 3: **After verifying the ERAM root cause, do a gap analysis of the current and desired ERAM for the individual.** Whether the problem is due to unclear direction, poor time management, or lack of motivation, it's important to reach agreement on the desired change, improvement, and result. Looking into the future, if the individual were to meet your expectations, what would his or her behaviors and outputs look like? Obtain a clear, shared agreement on the importance of the task, desired behaviors in performing the task, and specific deliverables. Immediately after the session, have the individual confirm in writing the agreed-on behaviors and results—remember, *what gets written gets understood.*

Step 4: **Have the individual write an action plan to close the gap on the ERAM element needing improvement.** Depending on the problem, this may take an additional meeting or two to agree on an action plan and specific expectations going forward. The key is to have the individual draft the action plan to ensure ownership; then you can provide feedback and suggested changes (the action plan can be combined with the written agreement from Step 3). Although some team leaders don't feel compelled to ask for a written plan, it will behoove you to have documentation—the more, the better. *A failure to maintain documentation on employee performance problems is one of the most common mistakes of team leaders.* And don't forget to include clear performance goals and metrics, as well as information on how you will assess the success of the work. Remember, *what gets measured gets done.* Depending on the seriousness of the performance issue, it may also be wise to state the consequences for both meeting and not meeting expectations.

Step 5: **Monitor individual performance and give feedback.** Set specific dates to review progress and provide ongoing feedback on the individual's performance. Don't wait too long after completion of the action plan to have your first follow-up review to ensure the individual is off to a good start and to send a signal that you are serious and care about the individual's performance. Feedback should include both things that are going well and things that need further improvement. Remember, *no feedback, no improvement.*

In all steps of this process, documentation is especially important and may be critical if the individual's performance requires disciplinary actions.

Which Human Factor Gives You the Greatest Leverage for *Individual* Performance? Of the four factors or knobs that drive performance (ERAM), motivation offers the greatest leverage for increasing individual performance. In addition to being a key knob or determinant of performance, motivation is also a key *lever* that you can use to substantially boost individual effort and results. When you instill motivation in people, they demonstrate a "want to" rather than a "have to" attitude. Motivation is an inner drive that raises your level of commitment, effort, ownership, persistence, ambition, initiative, and energy. It's a human factor that enables you to go *above and beyond* expectations and achieve goals that you have never achieved before.

Use all levels of the wedge to boost employee motivation by applying individual incentives, as well as using motivation from your work team and management levels. For example, employees who hear from their supervisor that they need improvement would be even more motivated if their fellow team members were also encouraging a change (peer pressure, mentor feedback) and even more so if they heard it from their customers (customer feedback). If individuals are asked to close performance gaps, they will be more motivated if they know their performance is also adversely affecting the team and organization.

The rule of thumb is the greater the gap, the greater the leverage required; also, the greater the gap, the greater the consequences that you would need to seek. For example, if the individual continues to struggle with absenteeism, you may need to "step it up" to a higher action or Human Resources. Higher management has greater leverage, power, and authority to administer stronger disciplinary actions. *When seeking to solve people problems, always act from a position of strength and leverage.* A more complete how-to discussion on motivating specific individual behavior is provided in Skill Six.

> **"The rule of thumb is the greater the gap, the greater the leverage required."**

Solving Work Team Performance Problems

The most common work team problems include interpersonal conflicts, missed deadlines, workload inequities, unproductive team meetings, unclear roles and responsibilities, difficult personalities, poor communications, lack of trust, lack of recognition, and low team output. Although humans are social by nature, this doesn't mean that everyone naturally gets along in a team. Teamwork is an organizational challenge in which you are trying to bring together a group of diverse individuals with different aspirations, work styles, personality types, and egos in order to achieve a common goal. Project leaders have to serve as the team's supervisor, referee, coach, mentor, and facilitator.

Team performance problems are different from individual employee problems. They involve a lot more people; it doesn't take much to start a problem; the problems can spread quickly; and you have people who work closely together, which make them susceptible to *aggregate toxicity* such as conflicts, excessive competition, jealousy, resentment, and other toxic behaviors. As a project leader, you must be on your toes and move swiftly to resolve any toxic problems.

For tackling team problems, the initial process is similar to the approach for individual performance problems—pinpoint the performance problem and then verify that the problem is a work team issue. Once this has been verified, then you can use the following procedure to fix the problem.

Determine the Cause for the Work Team Performance Problem ERAM is the most effective tool for diagnosing and solving individual problems. For work team performance problems, you need to use the CPB tool (2). CPB is an acronym for *content, process,* and *behavior,* the three *key performance factors* or knobs that drive *team* performance. Essentially all work team performance problems can be attributed to one or more of these elements.

Content: This is the purpose, objective, and goals of the team or
   project. When people aren't on the same page, team performance
   suffers. Team members who are uncommitted, have hidden agendas
   (ulterior motives), or are unclear on the objectives of the team are
   destined to fail. Content is the rallying point of the team, and when
   there is strong team ownership of a common goal, great things
   happen. Make sure everyone feels mutually accountable and
   committed to the goals of the team. The key is to ensure that
   everyone has a stake in the results; otherwise they will treat the
   project as a "have to" and not a "want to" project and team performance will likely disappoint.

Process: This refers to the team's planned procedures, work plan, schedules, methods, and tools. *Process operationalizes content,* which means team processes convert plans into action. Process is the most overlooked and underestimated factor in team performance. Without good processes, team members do not perform as well and do inconsistent and low-quality work. Process is the foundation of all high-performing teams and is a key driver of team behaviors. Work is more efficient when you have team ground rules, agendas, schedules, performance metrics, feedback, meeting facilitation, and other such team processes in place. In the absence of effective team processes, people will do their own thing and behave in a manner that suits them, not the team.

> *"In the absence of effective team processes, people will do their own thing and behave in a manner that suits them, not the team."*

Behavior: This is defined as the conduct and actions of people— what they do and say. *Of the three elements, behavior is the most important determinant of team project success.* Team behaviors are the interactions among team members, and they shape the dynamics and chemistry of a team. Some of the most important team behaviors include mutual trust, interdependence, accountability, transparency, valuing individuality, learning, and recognition. People's behaviors affect the attitude, motivation, and performance of a team.

Anytime you find a team struggling to work together, the problem is almost always related to either content, process, and/or behavior. Once you have identified the problem, you can then proceed to work with the team to clarify the *content,* improve team *processes,* or motivate the desired team *behavior* to get the job done. Your role as project leader is to facilitate improvements in content, process, and behavior. Facilitation is preferred over directing because it helps to ensure that the team retains ownership of any changes.

Which Human Factor Gives You the Greatest Leverage for *Team Performance?* Of the three factors or knobs that drive team performance (CPB), *process* offers the greatest strength and leverage for increasing team performance because *process drives team behaviors* and *team behaviors drive success.* Process is the key *lever* that you can use to substantially boost teamwork for three reasons: (1) when you have good team processes (such as work schedules, action plans, tools), you have more clarity, cooperation, and efficiency in planning and executing the work; (2) process depersonalizes the interactions among team members, thereby reducing emotional conflicts and other interpersonal problems; and (3) process facilitates desired behaviors. When it comes to team performance, process is a lever that has triple benefits for you.

Case in Point Team meetings often run long or get bogged down due to ineffective team decision-making. This is frequently caused by the lack of a clear process and method for reaching agreements. By default, most teams implicitly use consensus as their means for decision-making, which often leads to prolonged discussions and indecisiveness. Significant time would be saved if teams would make the effort upfront to clearly define their decision-making method either by: (1) using consensus but defining what it means (consensus usually means "you can live with it"), (2) choosing the most efficient decision-making process for the issue (such as, using "majority rules" for noncritical issues—not everything requires consensus), or (3) establishing a clear decision criterion (for example, "our decision will be based on lowest cost and easiest to do"). A good decision-making process drives good decision-making behavior.

Solving Management Performance Problems

Although everything starts from the top of the wedge, the organization is only as good as the performance of its employees and work teams. You have learned that the key tool for diagnosing and improving *individual* performance problems is ERAM (expectations, resources, ability, and motivation), of which *motivation* is the most important lever for raising individual performance. Similarly, the key tool for diagnosing and improving *work team* performance is CPB (content, process, and behavior), where team behavior is the key performance factor and *process* represents the best leveraging tool for boosting team results. The highest level of the wedge is management, where the top managers and executives of the organization reside. At this level, *organizational* behavior and performance problems are centered on two things: leadership and values.

In this context, *leadership is defined as the ability to motivate and inspire higher individual, team, and organizational performance.* There are innumerable leadership models available in the literature, and it is unlikely that you will find one model that fits all situations. The management model that is proposed here is one that works on the same platform and in alignment with work teams and individuals. To get sustained high performance, management must have the ability to *motivate employees to "want to" do their best* and *inspire team behaviors that create a culture of mutual support and inclusiveness.* What would such a leader look like?

▲ formulates and communicates a clear vision

▲ possesses high standards, character, and ethics

▲ defines clear and compelling organizational values

▲ inspires excellence and quality performance

▲ leads with great humility, gratitude, and kindness

▲ treats people with respect and trust, not fear and intimidation

▲ sets high goals and strategic direction

▲ strives to satisfy customers and stakeholders

▲ fosters confidence in others

▲ models desired behaviors—"walks the talk"

▲ builds consensus and acts decisively

▲ facilitates change as a collaborator and motivator

▲ encourages teamwork and positive team behaviors

▲ demonstrates personal accountability

▲ provides constructive feedback

▲ believes in continuous improvement and learning

▲ empowers individuals and work teams

Leadership is the key characteristic for the management level of the wedge, and just as we have diagnostic tools for the individual (ERAM) and team (CPB) levels, we also have a diagnostic tool for improving management-level performance: MVVOS—*mission, vision, values, objectives,* and *strategies.* Whether it's financial performance, competitiveness, market share, sales, or technology, the success of management is predicated on its ability to

> *"The success of management is predicated on its ability to define . . . and execute the organization's MVVOS."*

define, refine, communicate, resource, deploy, and execute the organization's MVVOS. These five components reflect the direction, trajectory, and growth of the organization. Success is dependent on getting these components right.

The management level is expected to demonstrate a strong belief in the *mission* of the organization, inspire a *vision* for long-term success, establish the right beliefs and behaviors through *values,* set clear and ambitious *objectives,* and execute plans and projects through powerful *strategies.* MVVOS ties the wedge together by providing a platform for managers and project leaders to align, cascade, and synchronize the organization to achieve its highest priorities and goals. In terms of people performance, MVVOS provides the overall priorities and direction of the organization, but the one key element that binds the motivation and behaviors of people is *values*. Values are the underlying beliefs, principles, and code of conduct for the organization.

At the highest level of the wedge, effective leadership is about more than just establishing clear values—it's about *operationalizing those values* that make the greatest difference. Management leadership is about visibly living and breathing the values of the organization, from decision-making, communications, accountability, prioritization, strategies, business plans, and resource allocation to personnel selections, human resources policies, and business codes of conduct. It all hinges on the ability of management to model the values of the organization in a manner that inspires employees along the entire wedge to do more, create more, and exceed expectations.

How MVVOS Can Help You with People Problems From the perspective of a project leader, the value of the MVVOS concept is in understanding that leadership is part of your job responsibility and that you are representing the interests and priorities of management, which are embodied in the organization's MVVOS. If those things aren't clear to you, then you owe it to yourself and the organization to give feedback and seek clarification. This knowledge will increase your ability to *motivate the right behaviors* in yourself and your employees and to resolve people issues for your team. And, as we have learned, *motivation* and *behavior* are two critical performance factors for individuals and teams.

As a team leader, your job is to ensure that the MVVOS of the organization gets translated, communicated, and deployed at the team and individual levels. MVVOS's elements are not just words but rather *mandates that require action*. Ideally, every project, work plan, goal, and performance plan should be tightly aligned with the MVVOS of your organization. You need to help your team and individual employees establish clear connections between their daily work, teamwork, and the MVVOS of

> "Ideally, every project, work plan, goal, and performance plan should be tightly aligned with the MVVOS of your organization."

management (Table 1.1). MVVOS represents your strongest authority for enacting individual and team plans, goals, processes, and performance metrics. Achieving alignment creates tremendous power and leverage for you.

Table 1.1 Achieving Alignment across the Wedge

Individual	Work Teams	Management
1. Employee Roles	1. Team Purpose	1. Company Mission/Vision
2. Individual Behaviors	2. Team Values/Behaviors	2. Values
3. Individual Goals	3. Team Strategies	3. Objectives
4. Work Tasks/Priorities	4. Team Goals/Processes	4. Strategies
5. Individual Metrics	5. Team Metrics	5. Company Metrics
6. Personal Preferences	6. Ground Rules	6. Policies
7. Perfomance Plan	7. Project Work Plan	7. Business Plan

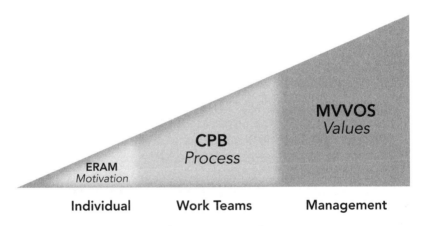

Individual   Work Teams   Management

Figure 1.6 Knobs and levers for managing performance

One method for creating an alignment mind-set in employees is to require that each employee identify at least one action that he or she will perform during the year to contribute to the success of each level in the wedge. For example, the employee can volunteer to serve as an emergency responder for the company (management level), identify a new software tool for tracking team action items (team level), and take a leadership course to improve one's competency (individual level).

Which Human Factor Gives You the Greatest Leverage for *Management* and *Organizational* Performance? Whereas *motivation* is the lever that drives individual behaviors and *process* leverages team behaviors, of the five performance factors that drive management and organizational performance (MVVOS), *values* offer the greatest leverage on organizational behaviors and results (Figure 1.6).

Case in Point We can draw from numerous examples of companies that have greatly enhanced their success through their effective leadership and deployment of organizational values, such as Apple (quality products), Nordstrom (customer service), Chevron (health and safety), and Southwest (customer service) (3, 4). But leverage cuts both ways, and companies can experience the opposite effect when either the wrong values are deployed or the right values are poorly implemented or sustained by management, as seen in companies such as Enron (financial fraud), Wells Fargo (false customer accounts), and Volkswagen (emissions fraud) (5). Also, values and organizational behavior require constant vigilance and renewal to stay current with internal and external challenges, such as experienced by Uber (work culture) (6) and BP (Deepwater Horizon oil spill) (5). You can't have a successful organization without a strong set of values to guide management, team, and individual behaviors.

The project leader's role in today's organization is immense, and expectations are high. Managing a project team can be very difficult, emotional, and stressful, but hopefully what you have learned about the wedge and what it contains—*knobs* (ERAM, CPB, and MVVOS) and *levers* (motivation, process, and values)—have made you feel more comfortable, confident, and skilled in proactively identifying and solving people problems. At the end of each skill, a memory card and skill summary are provided to give you quick access to the most important learnings of the Eight Essential People Skills for Project Management.

Skill One Summary

Due to advancements in technology, management, business, and workforce capabilities, the organizational structure is no longer a pyramid but rather a wedge. The wedge contains three organizational levels—individual contributors, work teams, and management—and each level has different responsibilities, power, authority, scope, processes, and leverage. The wedge is not only an organizational model but also a model for leading teams, managing performance, and solving people problems. Contained within each level of the wedge is a small number of key performance factors called knobs, which determine and regulate individual, team, and management performance, and specific levers, which can boost individual, team, and organizational success. The secret in solving people problems is to always act from a position of strength and leverage.

Getting to the root cause of an individual employee problem requires ERAM. ERAM is an acronym for *expectations, resources, ability*, and *motivation*, the four *key performance factors* in determining individual behavior and success. Essentially all individual performance problems can be attributed to one or more of these elements—they are the *knobs* for improving performance, and ERAM is an effective tool for diagnosing the root cause of individual performance problems.

For work team performance issues, you should use the CPB tool. CPB stands for *content, process*, and *behavior*, the three *key performance factors* or *knobs* for increasing team performance. Essentially all work team performance problems can be attributed to one or more of these elements.

The key performance factors or *knobs* for management are MVVOS: *mission, vision, values, objectives*, and *strategies*. Whether it's financial performance, competitiveness, market share, sales, or technology, management's success depends on its leadership and ability to define, refine, communicate, resource, deploy, and execute the organization's MVVOS.

Of the performance factors at each level, the key *levers* for boosting individual, team, and organizational performances are *motivation, process*, and *values*, respectively. Motivation is about maintaining a positive, productive, and collaborative attitude. Process facilitates team behaviors, and behavior is the key determinant of team success. Last, values are the core beliefs of the organization, and all workplace actions should be based on these values.

The more levels of the wedge that you can apply to the problem, the more likely you are to raise motivation and performance and operate from a position of greatest strength. To achieve sustained success, all levels must work together and be strategically aligned, mutually accountable, and interdependent. What works at the individual level must also work at the team and management levels. The wedge is an effective model and tool to help people leverage their individual power and abilities to solve problems and make a larger contribution to organizational success.

Skill One Memory Card

The Wedge
Always Act from a Position of Strength and Leverage

	Individual	Work Teams	Management
Key **ROLES**	Skills/Tasks	Project/Processes	Policies/Strategies
Performance Factors: **KNOBS**	**E:** Expectations **R:** Resources **A:** Ability **M:** Motivation	**C:** Content **P:** Process **B:** Behavior	**M:** Mission **V:** Vision **V:** Values **O:** Objectives **S:** Strategies
Leveraging Factors: **LEVERS**	**Motivation** Drives *Individual* Behavior	**Process** Drives *Team* Behavior	**Values** Drive *Organizational* Behavior

SKILL TWO

How to Be Tough on People Problems without Being Tough on People
The Three Hats

It was proposed in Skill One that project team leaders are now operating in a more horizontal, three-level, organizational structure that is shaped like a wedge, reflecting the relative distribution of power, authority, scope, responsibilities, and leverage. But as a team leader, how do you execute and use these principles on a day-to-day, face-to-face basis in the workplace? By virtue of your authority, power, and position, you have a captive audience of employees who report to you, and you are expected to use your power and authority to complete team projects successfully. As the person in charge, you are expected to handle tough problems, make tough decisions, and perform tough tasks in order to get things done. You're continuously tested, challenged, and placed in tough situations. To survive and succeed, it helps to be tough-minded, persistent, forceful, and decisive; but how do you do that without being autocratic, heavy-handed, and disliked by your employees? You want to be respected, not feared; be flexible, not permissive; and lead, not control; but how do you strike the right balance and yet fulfill your organizational roles and duties as a project team leader? You play different roles and wear different hats in your job—the key is to understand and master these roles and hats. In Skill Two, we're going to use three real-life cases to build on the concept of the wedge and introduce the concept of the *three hats*.

CASE 2.1: MANAGING TOUGH SITUATIONS—JUGGLING YOUR ROLES AS A TEAM LEADER

One evening, after a long day at the office, Robert, the team leader of Field Services, quickly loaded his laptop, cell phone, and work materials into his backpack and headed for his vehicle in the company's back parking lot. It was a cold, dark evening in December and the fog had already penetrated the night sky and indiscriminately settled around the company's property. Robert drove out of the parking lot in his company truck onto a long, narrow, winding, two-way street that was illuminated by overhead street lamps and some road reflectors dividing the incoming and outgoing lanes. There were no road signs or lights bordering the road, and in the foggy conditions he almost had to use his memory to navigate to the exit. The road was a bit icy and snowy—not too treacherous to require tire chains, but he had to drive carefully.

As Robert entered the second turn in the road, his car lights shone on what looked like a parked car just off the road. It appeared that the car was stuck in a shallow culvert among some piping, and there were no lights or indications that the car was running. Robert promptly stopped his car to see whether someone needed help or whether the car was abandoned, especially since it was sitting on company property. As Robert approached the car, the driver's door opened and someone started to get out of the car. To Robert's relief, it was Thomas, a longtime supervisor and mechanic who had worked at the company for over twenty years. Many years ago, before Robert was transferred to this facility, he had met Thomas at a project in Denver. Thomas was an outstanding mechanic, and he had taught Robert a lot about city permitting and regulations. Robert thought very highly of Thomas, and they got along well at work and occasionally saw each other at various community events.

As Robert approached the car, Thomas gave him a relieved smile while chewing a wad of gum and said, "Boy, am I glad it's you, Robert. I thought you were one of those dumb security guys." Robert replied, "No, I'm just one of your dumb managers." They exchanged a few barbs and Robert said, "So, what's your car doing in the muck?" Thomas quickly remarked, "It's so damn dark and foggy tonight; I usually take it slow, but I was anxious to get home, and the car just skidded off the road. There was nothing I could do. I think I hit a patch of ice. There's no damage. I was trying to call a tow service to pull me out, but I'm glad you're here with your truck and winch—do you have time to pull me out? It shouldn't take more than a few minutes." Thomas was right about it being a dark and foggy night, and the two were anxious to get home.

As Thomas was looking at Robert's truck, Robert turned to catch Thomas's attention and said, "Normally, I would be glad to pull you out, but you know it's company policy to report these accidents when they happen on company premises." Looking puzzled for a second, Thomas replied, "Of course, that's not a problem. As soon as I get home, I'll log on to the company's website and fill out a complete report, and I'll copy you on it too." That sounded good, but Robert responded, "I appreciate that, Thomas, but the process is to not move the vehicle unless it poses a hazard. I tell you what: I'll take you back to the office and help you fill out the report with security, and they will take you to the clinic down the street to make sure you're okay."

Before Robert could finish his description of the process, Thomas commented, "Hey, look, Robert, it's late, you're a busy guy, and I'm sure you have better things to do than to run me around tonight. I promise I will report it; I think the company would be satisfied with that. Many of these types of things don't get reported anyway, so I think we're way ahead of the game by reporting it." Robert responded, "I have nothing I need to rush off to. I would be remiss in my job if I didn't stay and ensure procedures are followed." Thomas interrupted again and said, "I understand it's your responsibility, but how about you pull me out, I'll drive up to security and do the paperwork and everything else, and you can go home to your family."

Robert remained silent and looked concerned. Breaking the silence, Thomas said, "Look, nothing wrong happened here; it was my personal car and not a company car, so we're okay. But if you get any complaints, which I doubt you will, just blame me. Hey, what are friends for?" To Thomas's annoyance, Robert said, "I like you, Thomas, and I just want to make sure we do what's right for both of us, so how about I drive you up and confirm you're all right, and we'll both be home in no time." Thomas was resigned at this point but gave it one more try, saying, "If I didn't know you better, I would think that you don't trust me." Robert calmly replied by saying, "I do trust you, and that's why you'll trust me by letting me help you with this." Finally, Thomas gave up and said, "Okay, I'll go, but can I grab my jacket first?" "Sure," said Robert.

After Thomas rummaged in his car for a few minutes and grabbed his water bottle and jacket, Robert drove him up to the security office, where they filled out a report and then completed a referral slip so that the clinic could examine him. After driving Thomas up to the office, Robert conferred with the senior security officer on company procedures and what authority and control he was giving the officer in this matter, and he left his cell number so that the officer could keep him informed. Then Robert signed off on the accident report and medical referral and told Thomas, "Thanks for doing this, Thomas; it's the right thing to do. You're in good hands here. They're going to take you to the clinic now, and I'll see you tomorrow. I'm sorry about your mishap. Take care."

Later that evening at home, Robert got a call from the senior security officer, who informed him that Thomas was tested at the clinic for drugs and alcohol and that his blood alcohol result was 0.12—well above the legal limit. They were calling a cab to take him home, and they would arrange a tow for his car. Robert thanked the officer for his help, and when Robert returned to work the next morning, he asked security to accompany him to Thomas's office. It didn't take them long to find two unmarked, silver flasks under his desk, one empty and the other half-full of alcohol. This was a clear violation of company policy, and Thomas had jeopardized his own safety and the safety of other people that day. Robert felt empathy and concern for Thomas and soon contacted Thomas to offer him help. He was relieved to hear that Thomas was safe and was amenable to going through the company process to resolve the matter. Robert also felt relieved about how he managed the entire incident.

Lessons from the Story

It was fortunate that Robert, the team leader, stuck to company procedures and did not relent to Thomas's suggestion to let him report the accident. If he had pulled Thomas's car out of the culvert and allowed him to drive home, who knows what could have happened that evening or in the future. This story is not unlike many encounters that team leaders have with their employees. You work together, you have nice work relationships and even good friendships, but these relationships are always tested—when the pressure is on and push comes to shove, will you stand on the side of the company or that of your employee? Sometimes you can't be on both sides. Where is your loyalty? Where is your compassion? You can pull rank one time and suddenly lose the trust of your employees. For a minor infraction or petty incident, a bad managerial decision can quickly lower team morale and reduce performance. What if Thomas's drug and alcohol results came back negative? Would Robert's decision still be the right call?

Robert had to make a judgment on the spot. These decisions are never black and white, and yet in the pressure of friendship, it's easy to let things go. Every manager has had to make tough decisions about people, and it's easy to second-guess yourself. It's always a struggle to know when to go easy and when you need to be tough. How do you strike the right *"It's always a struggle to know when to go easy and when you need to be tough."* balance? There's no right answer per se, but this story illustrates eight important concepts about the roles you play as a team leader.

Team Leaders Wear Three Hats

Team leaders are expected to wear a lot of hats, meaning that they have many different roles and responsibilities in their jobs.

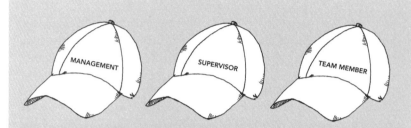

Figure 2.1 The three hats of team leaders

As a team leader, you wear three main hats—management, supervisor, and team member (Figure 2.1)—with each hat conferring a different level of power, authority, responsibility, and control. *Power* is the degree of influence you have over others; *authority* is the level of the organization that you represent and act in behalf of; *responsibility* is your set of duties and obligations; and *control* is the extent to which you define, direct, and execute process. Your skill in being tough on people problems without being tough on people depends on your ability to balance and execute these three roles.

Wear the Hat That Gives You the Best Strength and Leverage to Solve the Problem

Keeping in mind that each hat has a different level of power, authority, responsibility, and control and assumes a different perspective, the key is to wear the right hat for the situation. This means *wearing the hat that best fits the problem and puts you in the strongest position to effectively and efficiently solve the problem.*

▲ When you're wearing the *management hat*, you have the power and authority to *represent and administer company policies*, standards, procedures, and strategies—the *whats*. You control policy deployment and enforcement and are responsible for employee compliance, personnel, job performance, reporting, and budget control. You set goals, strategies, and work plans to meet organizational expectations. You have a broad, external, long-term, *strategic, organizational perspective* of the operation.

▲ When you're wearing the *supervisor hat*, you have the power and authority to *direct and control the deployment of pro-*

cess and how the work is conducted in accordance with management's plans, strategies, goals, policies, and priorities. You have the responsibility to ensure that the team's functions are completed efficiently and safely, employees are fit for duty, employee performance meets expectations, and your customers are satisfied with your team's work. You have a more focused, internal, short-term, *tactical, team perspective* of the operation.

▲ When you're wearing the *team member hat*, you have the power and authority to *execute and control your individual work tasks* and the responsibility to *demonstrate desired teamwork and partnership behaviors*, which include mutual trust, respect, collaboration, communications, learning, and support—having mutual care and concern. You have a *friendly, respectful, and interpersonal perspective*.

Have the Courage to Wear the Tough Hat

One of the most common mistakes of team leaders is not having the courage to wear the tougher management or supervisor hat when the situation calls for it. This arises from the fear of coming across too strongly and jeopardizing your good relationship with your employees. Avoid this mental trap by remembering that *your management and supervisor hats are worn to help, not punish, your employees.*

At the accident, Thomas was first testing to see whether Robert, his supervisor, would wear his team member hat and pull his car out of the culvert. Thomas has greater influence (power) when they relate as team members and less influence when Robert wears his supervisor or management hat. Thomas realized that Robert had his management hat on when Robert stated, "It's company *policy* to report these accidents when they happen on company premises." So Thomas tried to get Robert to replace his management hat (company policy) with his supervisor hat (control of process) by saying, "Of course, that's not a problem. As soon as I get home, I'll log on to the company's website and fill out a complete report, and I'll copy you on it too," hoping Robert would use his discretion as a supervisor to delegate control of the *process* to him.

When that failed, Thomas realized that Robert was sticking with company procedures and keeping his management hat on, so he tried to persuade Robert to at least switch to his supervisor hat by acknowledging his *process* obligations: "I understand it's your responsibility, but how about you pull me out, I'll drive up to security and do the paperwork and everything else, and you can go home to your family." Thomas then went as far as trying to get Robert to turn over his management and supervisor hats to him (policy interpretation and process responsibilities, respectively) and wear his team member hat by saying, "Look, nothing wrong happened here; it was my personal car and not a company car, so we're okay. But if you get any complaints, which I doubt you will, just blame me. Hey, what are friends for?" But Robert kept his management hat firmly on while also remaining friendly and caring to Thomas, saying, "I like you, Thomas, and I just want to make sure we do what's right for both of us, so how about I drive you up and confirm you're all right, and we'll both be home in no time."

Finally, Thomas tried a little reverse psychology on Robert by saying, "If I didn't know you better, I would think that you don't trust me," as one last attempt to appeal to Robert's friendship (team member hat). Robert stayed calm and echoed Thomas's strategy, saying, "I do trust you, and that's why you'll trust me by letting me help you with this." With no other options, Thomas complied, but before he left his car, he tried to buy more time by grabbing his jacket and drinking water to try to reduce his blood alcohol level. But he was caught anyway. Thomas was obviously hoping that Robert would wear his team member hat and give him a break on company protocol. Robert did a great job in not being afraid to wear his management hat *to help, not punish, his employee.* It's worthy of note that Robert's persistence and mental toughness in enforcing company procedures may have saved Thomas's life and those of others.

> *"Robert's persistence and mental toughness in enforcing company procedures may have saved Thomas's life."*

Avoid Relinquishing Control of Management and Policy Issues

In Robert's story, because the incident pertained to company policy, it would have been inappropriate for him, as the team leader, to relinquish power and authority to an employee for self-interpretation, self-administration, and self-enforcement of company policy, regardless of their relationship. Thomas attempted at least a couple of times to persuade Robert to relinquish his authority to him (management hat):

▲ "I promise I will report it; I think the company would be satisfied with that. Many of these types of things don't get reported anyway, so I think we're way ahead of the game by reporting it" (administration and enforcement).

▲ "Look, nothing wrong happened here; it was my personal car and not a company car, so we're okay" (policy interpretation).

Also, Thomas tried to assume Robert's control and responsibility of the process (supervisor hat):

▲ "As soon as I get home, I'll log on to the company's website and fill out a complete report, and I'll copy you on it too."

▲ "I understand it's your responsibility, but how about you pull me out, I'll drive up to security and do the paperwork and everything else, and you can go home to your family."

Robert maintained *control* of the process and used his discretion in delegating that control to a security person who was probably in a better position to escort Thomas safely to the clinic and home. Also, Robert kept his *authority* over the process (directing the formal course of action) and positional *power* (enabling him to override Thomas's suggestions). Robert had the inner strength to manage his power, authority, responsibility, and control correctly in this situation.

Be Friendly, Not Friends, at Work

Robert and Thomas knew each other from before and may have been friends outside work, but when it comes to work, you can't show favoritism or bias toward employees. You want to be a good supervisor and team member—friendly, polite, supportive, respectful, dignified, and encouraging to all your employees. But being friendly is not the same as being a friend. Friendliness is a behavior; friendship is a relationship. Friends hang out together, socialize, share secrets, do favors for each other, and protect each other.

"Friendliness is a behavior; friendship is a relationship."

Being both a friend and supervisor to subordinates can be a very awkward and difficult relationship to manage. Even in special circumstances, such as family businesses, your behaviors need to be clear. It's more effective to have a friendly supervisor-employee *partnership* than a friend-to-friend *relationship* at work.

Also, you can't be friendly and lenient to some and hard on others—that's being inconsistent and possibly discriminatory. *Everyone must see you wear the same supervisor hat and wear it the same way, rather than wearing different hats for different employees.* This doesn't mean you treat everyone the same; it means you make equitable decisions for all. Be consistent in how you wear your hats.

You Want Employees to Respect You, Not Like You

Knowing where to draw the line between being friendly and being a friend is not easy, and it's a common struggle for team leaders. It's human nature to want people to like you—it's the vanity of all team leaders. And let's face it: it's much easier to lead people who like you, trust you, and treat you as a friend—the camaraderie feels good and you're like a family. It would be great to have such close relationships with your coworkers, but your company is not a family, fraternity, or

"The key is not to confuse your need for respect with your need for social acceptance."

club—it's a business. The key is not to confuse your need for respect with your need for social acceptance. Seeking social acceptance will lead you down a risky path where you are apt to be more lenient, do personal favors, accept lower standards, and tolerate bad behaviors. Remember, you're a leader, not a buddy.

Be Hard on Policies and Standards, Not People

Regardless of the situation, it's important to show dignity, care, compassion, and respect to all employees. Being sensitive to others does not diminish your effectiveness as a team leader. *The key is to be hard on policies and standards, not people.* In other words, you want to be strict and rigorous with laws, regulations, company policies, standards, and procedures but not with people. As you saw in Robert's story, you can maintain a friendly and caring demeanor with people, but when it comes to work policies and procedures, they require your management and supervisor hats, respectively.

Empathy Connects You with Others

Like all effective leaders, Robert had the ability to show his feelings (emote) and understand the feelings of Thomas (empathy). Having the ability to emote is not a weakness but rather a strength. It means you are able to communicate your feelings and motives through emotions and not just through words. The vast majority of your communications with others are nonverbal, and your ability to emote your feelings and motives is tremendously important in leading others. Transparency builds employee trust, confidence, and loyalty.

Equally important to transparency is empathy. When you understand the feelings of your employees, you gain a deeper understanding of their concerns. You need empathy to know who your employees are and what they truly want. You can't fake emotions, so when you express your true feelings, employees will reciprocate. When this occurs, mutual trust and communication soar. You can't be a good people manager unless you have sensitivity and empathy for people.

Summary

In the end, Robert wore the *right hats* at the *right time*, in the *right way*, and for the *right reasons* in managing the situation (Figure 2.2).

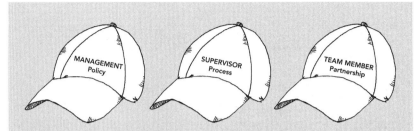

Figure 2.2 Roles and responsibilities of team leaders

▲ **Management hat:** Robert administered, enforced, and complied with company policies and procedures regarding vehicle accidents on company premises and employee health and safety. Management is focused on doing *what* is right.

▲ **Supervisor hat:** Thomas's car accident wasn't a clear-cut case, but Robert correctly followed company procedures and maintained his authority and responsibility in complying with the company's process. Supervisors are focused on *how* to do things right.

▲ **Team member hat:** Robert showed care and sensitivity toward Thomas (behavior), and more importantly, he may have saved Thomas's life. It might have been more comfortable for Robert to wear his softer team member hat, but for this situation, he realized he needed to show clearly that he was wearing his management hat. In good partnerships, team members are focused on *behaving* the right way in order to care for and support each other.

Robert's encounter with a late-night accident was a good example of how to balance the three hats and clearly wear the right hat for the situation. Now let's examine a second case in which the hats may not be as clear.

CASE 2.2: IT'S TOUGH TO LET GO—DELEGATING RESPONSIBILITIES TO OTHERS

Tony is a team leader of a construction project team that does contract jobs for small businesses. The team consists of Tony and nine other team members, including Greg and Val. On average, they work on two to four projects at a time, and the work pace can be very hectic and stressful. Today, Tony's work team was meeting to review the progress of their biggest project. Due to client design changes, they had to make decisions on modifying their work plan, budget, and schedule. The meeting was going well; the team was able to agree on needed changes, and everyone was satisfied with the new schedule. The last item on the agenda was to send an email to their client regarding budget changes and a new timeline. Here is how the conversation went:

Tony (team leader): We need to write an email to our client to advise them of our changes based on their needs and provide them with a breakdown of the new budget and schedule. I normally would do this, but I'm going to be tied up in meetings over the next couple of days and I will need someone to fill in. Any volunteers?

Greg: I'm willing to take a shot at it. When does it need to be sent?

Tony: No later than two days from today, which would be Thursday.

Greg: That's doable, but I'll probably need some help.

Val: I can help if you need it.

Greg: How about I draft it by tomorrow and send it to you, Val. Will you be available to review it?

Val: Yep. When are you going to send it to me?

Greg: Probably right after lunch.

Tony: Good, it's settled then—Greg drafts it, Val reviews it, and Greg will send it to me by midday Thursday for my review and release.

Greg drafts the email with all the necessary attachments and sends it to Val, who provides some edits and additions to the content. Greg receives the changes from Val, makes final changes, and forwards it to Tony. Tony makes a few more edits and sends it to their client on time, copying everyone on the team. Val reads the email but can't believe what she sees, so she heads to see Greg.

Val: Hey Greg, can I talk to you?

Greg: Sure, what's up?

Val: Well, it's about the client email you prepared.

Greg: Is there a problem?

Val: Yes! I spent an hour yesterday reviewing your draft email and provided a lot of good edits, but you didn't incorporate any of my important changes. I thought we were working together. I feel totally snubbed.

Greg: How so?

Val: For one, you left out my remarks about how the timeline could be accelerated to save on costs.

Greg: I didn't think the client needed to see that.

Val: That point was important—I wanted to show our client that we cared about controlling costs. Why didn't you talk to me about it?

Greg: I'm sorry, but we didn't have time. I sent Tony the draft and he took it and ran with it. I didn't send out the email, Tony did, so if you have a problem, you should really take it up with him, not me.

Val: Well, it's too late now—it's already gone out. Anyway, from now on, I'm just not going to review drafts anymore—it's a waste of time. Why ask for feedback when you're not going to use it?

Lessons from the Story

Val was obviously not pleased with the outcome, and Greg deflected the problem onto Tony; in the meantime, Tony assumed everything was good between Greg and Val. How can a routine task turn into a conflict between two coworkers? Whose fault was it for Val's discontent? This story illustrates three key concepts about the wedge and the three hats.

Use the Wedge to Diagnose Work Team Problems—
Content, Process, and Behavior

The preparation of a communiqué to their client was a team effort by Tony, Greg, and Val. As we learned in Skill One, team performance is determined by three knobs: content, process, and behavior (CPB). Which knob was most critical in this case—content, process, or behavior?

Clearly, the process could have been better—for example, Greg could have met with Val and made changes together, or Greg could have given Val a heads-up that he was short on time, appreciated her suggestions, and would get back to her later. However, this story is more about *behavior* than process—for example, was there mutual trust, respect, communication, and accountability among Tony, Greg, and Val? Were they working together or working apart? The work got done; it was a routine task, but Greg didn't demonstrate good collaboration, communication, or respect in his interactions with Val. More importantly, this conflict adversely affected Val's attitude toward Greg and her cooperation going forward. A team feedback process after the fact may help in these cases, but it's likely that Tony will never know what transpired between Greg and Val or be aware of the ensuing bad feelings. These types of team problems and their remedies will be covered in more depth in Skills Three and Five.

Your Hat (Power, Authority, and Control) Affects
People's Behaviors

Did Tony, the team leader, do everything right, or could he have done something that would have prevented the problem? Even though Tony delegated the work to Greg, Tony didn't make clear what authority and power Greg had in doing the work. Did Tony make it clear whether Greg and Val were working as equals (team member hats) or whether Greg was control-

"People's behaviors are affected by what power, authority, and control you delegate."

ling the content and process on behalf of Tony (supervisor hat) and Val was just providing input? People's behaviors are affected by what power, authority, and control you delegate. Greg thought that Tony gave him the *task, control* over the process, and the *power and authority* of authorship over Val (acting on Tony's behalf on the appropriate content), whereas Val obviously thought they were working together as equals and Greg had no right or authority to dismiss her input. This conflict could have been prevented if Tony had clarified what level of power, authority, and control he was delegating to Greg in order to manage team behaviors. How would the story have turned out differently if Tony had said in the meeting, "Thank you, Val, for agreeing to help Greg in reviewing the draft. Due to time constraints, let's be clear that Greg has my authority to author the draft as he sees fit. I'm going to need it back quickly, so I hope we can trust each other's roles [namely, Greg serving on behalf of his supervisor and appreciating Val's help, and Val understanding her role as a team member in providing input]."

Don't Hog the Hat: Build Trust by Delegating Authority, Power, and Control

In the car accident case (Case 2.1), Robert had to keep his management and supervisor hats tightly on to maintain *upward* control, power, and authority in administering and enforcing company policy. However, when team leaders delegate *downward*, as in Case 2.2 with Tony and Greg, there is a tendency for team leaders not to give up their hats. Project team leaders are apt to stay silent and be reluctant to delegate power and authority in order to maintain control. They want others to do the work, but they want to retain power, authority, and control and hog their hat. When you hog your hat, you are not only causing possible confusion but also promoting the wrong behaviors—control, fear, and distrust. *It's tough to let go and trust people to do things right.* However, people do their best work when they feel empowered, important, and trusted. This leads to positive and productive team behaviors. As a project leader, you're expected to delegate supervisory tasks and responsibilities to others, but it's important not to hog your hat.

Instead of saying, "Send [the email] to me . . . for my review and release," Tony could have let go and said, "Thank you, Val, for agreeing to help Greg in reviewing the draft. Let's be clear that

Greg has my authority to author the draft as he sees fit *and to release it on my behalf—Greg has my full trust, and I know you both will also trust and respect each other's roles."* When Tony acts with trust, others will likely follow suit—Val will trust Greg to choose the right edits. Remember, trust begets trust. You will find that people will do the right thing when they feel trusted.

Summary

These two cases perfectly illustrate the title of this skill: *be tough on people problems without being tough on people.* In the car accident case, Robert demonstrated that when you have a high-level issue, such as one concerning policy, procedures, standards, or regulations, you want to *tighten* your supervisor and management hats (*be tough on people problems*). In the case of Tony and Greg, we learned that when you delegate work downward, you want to *loosen* your management and supervisory hats, show good partnership (team member hat), and trust people (*without being tough on people*) in order to avoid people problems (Val's resentment and Greg's indifference).

As a team leader, your power, authority, and control will affect the behavior of your team. In this next case, we'll see how the power, authority, and control of your supervisory or management hat can have a profound effect on your own behaviors as a team leader.

CASE 2.3: BEING A TOUGH LEADER—DISPLAYING GENUINE LEADERSHIP

When it comes to job performance, Jean was one of the best laboratory technicians in a well-established, high-volume health services business near Silicon Valley in California. It took Jean only five years to work her way through the ranks and earn the title of team leader of Laboratory Services at the company. Her team worked the swing shift and had fifteen employees. About a year ago, Jean replaced the previous team leader, Elaine, a veteran of twenty years with the company who had moved up to become manager of business planning. Elaine handpicked Jean as her replacement based on her high performance, talents, and dedication as a technologist and felt confident that she would make a good team leader.

After eleven months in her new position, Jean struggled in leading her team. Early on, things were going well, but her interactions and communications with her team soon became more strained and the cooperation and camaraderie that she had previously enjoyed were no longer happening for her. At first, she didn't think much of it, as she expected her team to take some time to adjust to her new role. But it was apparent that team morale was low, and the team was not performing as well as she had hoped. Jean had some disagreements with certain employees regarding work schedules, individual work assignments, and overtime hours. Also, team meetings became more passive, less participative, and abbreviated. After many attempts to restore energy and productivity to the team, Jean was getting a bit frustrated and angry with her team and decided it was time to seek Elaine's help. She thought Elaine's experience with the team would give her some insights on what else she could do.

Jean made an appointment to see Elaine, and they met in Elaine's office, which was in the main office facility, separated from the laboratory. Elaine was excited to meet Jean again and to see how well she was faring as a team leader.

Elaine: Well, how do you like your new job so far?

Jean: It's going great. I love my job. I love all my jobs. I couldn't be happier.

Elaine: That's great to hear. I knew you would do well. You're such a hard worker and you know the operations so well. How are you getting along with your team? It can be tough transitioning from coworker to team leader.

Jean [*looking slightly worried*]: The team is working well, but the work is getting heavier and we lost two technicians. So I've been urging everyone to step it up, but it hasn't worked. But I know that's normal because people are sometimes lazy and don't want to work hard.

Elaine was puzzled. This didn't sound like the Jean she knew before.

Elaine: Who were the two who left the lab?

Jean: Wilson and Linda left the team a couple of months ago. They got new jobs across town at the new hospital. I wasn't surprised because they weren't happy here anyway.

Elaine was surprised that Wilson and Linda had left; they were both young, competent technicians who seemed to enjoy their positions.

Elaine: Why were they unhappy?

Jean: I think Wilson was mad I didn't give him time off for a last-minute vacation request that I couldn't afford since we were down personnel. I think Linda left because she was jealous that I got the position and she didn't like the work I gave her. You see, I put in a system where everyone is treated equally—everyone does his or her fair share of the grunt work—and I put in rules to improve efficiency and teamwork.

Elaine: And what are those rules?

Jean: Well, I put in specific rules on break times, vacation requests in advance, process times on samples, daily start-up meetings kept to ten minutes, and no socializing in the lab. This has really helped people focus on their jobs.

Elaine: Are they happy about this?

Jean [*speaking with a righteous tone*]: They pushed back in the beginning, but I told them that's what management wants and we need to do what management wants.

Elaine: Management wants these rules?

Jean: Yes, my manager says we need to cut costs and get more productive. My rules avoid wasting time and create more work hours. My job is to deliver what management wants.

Elaine: So how can I help you, Jean?

Jean: I don't think I'm clicking with the team, and you were always so well regarded by them and they listened to you.

I don't think they see me the same way. They don't listen to me. So I find it's best to leave them alone and not get into conflicts. [*Tears come to her eyes.*] How do I get tougher and get people to work for me?

Elaine: Being a team leader is hard, so don't be too hard on yourself. You're a good person, and your being here today shows that you care about your team, and that's important. When I first became a supervisor in my first job, I struggled the same way. You want to know what I learned that helped a lot?

Jean [*nodding*]: Yes, please.

Elaine: To be an effective leader, you have to be *yourself*. You can't just act tough—that wouldn't be who you are. For example, when you were a technician, you always supported more flexibility on the job and you wanted fewer rules, not more rules. What happened?

Jean: My manager said he thought the team could be more productive and warned me not to let people take advantage of me, being a former coworker and such. So I thought I had to show I was in charge and not let them think I was going to be a pushover. I was really sensitive about not showing any favoritism to my friends, so I set some clear rules to show I was fair and to get more work hours. But it's not working.

Elaine: Gee, Jean, when you were a technician, didn't you hate rigid rules? You see, when we treat everyone the same, we become unfair. Every person is unique; you and I are different, and we're motivated and demotivated by different things. Did you know that Wilson really wanted that vacation time to meet with his family, who were going through a difficult time? Having rules is fine, but not to the point of choking off communication, trust, compassion, care, and concern for others. I always thought those were your strong points.

Jean: Thank you, but I thought showing my emotions would make me look weak as a team leader.

Elaine: Showing others who you are, being transparent, welcoming their input, and being flexible is what a team leader is all about. If you're not yourself, then people can't see where you're coming from and they lose trust and confidence in you as a leader. Trust and sincerity earn you productivity and performance, not rules and control.

Jean: So rules destroy trust.

Elaine: Well, not all rules, but rules that demotivate or intimidate employees. I find that when team meetings are cut short, people's concerns are not heard, and when management is used to justify harsh rules, it makes people feel minimized and powerless.

Jean: What do you think I should do now?

Elaine: It's never too late to show yourself and regain trust. Think about it. And remember, you have a wonderful, hardworking team that wants to succeed, right?

Jean: Right, thanks so much, Elaine.

As Jean got up to leave, Elaine gave her a small gift: a white card on which she had written, "Be yourself."

Lessons from the Story

Jean is not alone in her struggles to find herself as a leader and to learn to wear the right hat. Too often, project leaders make the mistake of assuming a false persona when they're given leadership responsibilities. When Jean took on the challenge of being a team leader, she was suddenly expected to wear three hats —management, supervisor, and team member. But as a team leader, she made three false assumptions about her role.

Exerting More Power and Authority Will Yield
Better Results—False

Jean thought good leadership meant wearing the management hat and using its power and authority to get more work done. She became directive, inflexible, and controlling. It was likely that Jean wore her management hat to cover her discomfort in being a new team leader. She felt vulnerable in her new position and falsely believed that she needed the management hat to take command and control. Top-down management is rarely the best pathway to high team morale, motivation, and results. Jean relied too heavily on her management hat—"I told them that's what management wants and we need to do what management wants. . . . My job is to deliver what management wants"—which didn't go over well with her team. Unlike Robert's story in Case 2.1, this was an example of wearing the wrong hat, at the wrong time, in the wrong way, and for the wrong reasons.

Getting Tough on People Is a Sign of Strength as a Leader—False

Jean's concern about appearing weak drove her to be strict with people: "I had to show I was in charge and not let them think I was going to be a pushover." Getting tough on people's concerns was a misguided behavior that was rooted in fear and selfishness, not courage and empathy. Remember, it takes courage to wear your management and supervisor hats, and they're worn to motivate, facilitate, and help people succeed, not to intimidate and punish people. Empathizing and showing your care and concern for others are strengths, not weaknesses, as a leader. It demonstrates sensitivity, humility, kindness, inner strength, and self-assurance. These traits create genuine, positive work relationships.

> **"It takes courage to wear your management and supervisor hats, and they're worn to motivate, facilitate, and help people succeed, not to intimidate and punish people."**

Showing Your True Self Allows People to Take Advantage of You—False

This was Jean's biggest mistake. The less you show yourself, the less people will trust you. People believe in people who are genuine. No one likes a phony, especially as a leader. Leaders who are not afraid to show themselves are more confident, trusting, transparent, credible, open-minded, and accountable. These are the qualities that people look for in a leader.

Don't Let Your Role Define Who You Are

Jean favored her management hat, and when she wore it, she felt empowered, commanding, and in charge. It gave her a great sense of control and confidence. However, the hats represent a role you play, not the person you are. You can't assume a different demeanor or persona when you assume the role of a team leader. In other words, don't let the hat you wear change who you are or redefine your character. The three hats confer a level of authority, power, and responsibility, not your personality, values, conscience, emotions, common sense, feelings, and beliefs. These things are not contained in your hat but rather are found within your authentic self. Jean was so preoccupied in wearing her management and supervisor hats that she lost the person who was wearing the hat. She was not herself, and her employees knew it. Jean hid behind her management hat with tight rules and restrictions and wore her tough supervisor hat by demanding obedience to her new procedures.

Summary

As Jean discovered, when she acted more authoritative, empowered, and controlling while wearing her management or supervisor hat, the team's response was negative:

▲ The team's morale and productivity were low. Disingenuous people create distrust, uncertainty, and suspicion, which cause demotivation and low output in teams.

▲ The team experienced high stress and conflicts. The distrust and pressure of working with a phony team leader can cause stress, frustration, and anxiety for everyone. When your work environment is open and honest, work is easier, things are smoother, and people are happier.

▲ Leaders who use "management" to justify their tough acts tend to be insecure, defensive, and passive-aggressive. Blaming others, avoiding accountability, and hiding behind rules are not ingredients for high team performance. Effective team leaders always demonstrate responsibility for their actions.

The Toughest Challenge for a Team Leader

Low self-confidence and insecurity are probably the biggest reasons why people don't show their true selves. They believe that showing themselves would make them more vulnerable to potential criticism, negative feedback, ridicule, and manipulation. A person who bullies, intimidates, and gets tough on people is a person who has insecurities and self-doubt. As Jean put it, "I thought showing my emotions would make me look weak as a team leader." Many people mistakenly believe that their tough persona provides a protective shell, making them feel less exposed, less at risk, and more secure, when, in fact, it makes them more unstable and at risk for failure.

Like many new team leaders, Jean was worried that if she showed her true self, people would take advantage of her and challenge her authority. Jean's insecurity was driven by personal fear. People fear social rejection, criticism, failure, conflict, and inferiority. In Jean's case, her coping mechanism was to conceal herself behind her management hat. This is another paradox because *when you show less of yourself, you think less of yourself*, which weakens your self-confidence and raises self-doubt. This can become a vicious mental cycle—when you think less of yourself, you rely more on your hat to gain confidence, but this is a false confidence. Also, as your self-confidence goes down, so does your willingness to take on new challenges—you play it safe and don't expose yourself. Overly self-conscious leaders who worry about how they look to others and feel threatened by what others may think are ineffective, avoid accountability, and struggle with making decisions. Thus, a fake persona doesn't protect you; it actually weakens who you are.

"You are at your best when you are yourself, and your effectiveness diminishes when your authenticity diminishes."

The toughest challenge for a team leader is not as much in learning your new roles and responsibilities as it is in retaining the characteristics of what makes you an effective leader—your authenticity. It's true that nobody is 100 percent authentic or 100 percent fake. However, your success depends on the degree to which you express your authentic self. Simply put, you are at your best when you are yourself, and your effectiveness diminishes when your authenticity diminishes.

Effectively interacting with others is key to leading and motivating people. When you're leading others, you make a conscious choice to be honest or dishonest, genuine or disingenuous, receptive or deceptive, or somewhere in between. Your level of authenticity will determine your effectiveness as a manager, supervisor, and team member. Certainly, you can fake your leadership behavior, but it's not sustainable long term. Regardless of which hat you're wearing, your *true self*—feelings, conscience, common sense, intuition, and values—should never go away. These are the constants that maintain your sense of humanism and reality, which strengthen your leadership. *Remember that your hats are just costumes that allow you to play a role.* You can wear a hundred hats, but they shouldn't change who you are. And they shouldn't change how you treat others—hats cover your head, not your heart.

Six Ways to Bring Out Your Best

When you're authentic, it not only makes you more credible and trustworthy but also inspires others to do the same. One of the biggest opportunities for improving your creativity, intuition, decision-making, self-confidence, self-esteem, and leadership is to spend more time finding, understanding, and expressing your true self. These practices of introspection and self-awareness are valuable tools in becoming a more authentic team leader.

Here are six actions that you can take to become a more authentic team leader: increase transparency, express who you are, practice introspection, be comfortable in your own skin, show your pure self, and believe in yourself.

Increase Transparency

One of the best ways to show your authentic self and gain trust and credibility with your team is to be more transparent—letting people see your emotions, motives, and reasoning. This is a great way to learn how to better *align your inner motives with your outer behaviors.* Communicate the reasons behind your decisions, express honest thoughts about issues, clearly explain why you are making changes, and share your vision, strategies, and concerns. What's the alternative? Keeping things close to the vest, making people guess your intentions, and being evasive in addressing people's concerns are all pathways that lead to failure. Don't make people read between the lines. In the absence of knowing your true motives, people will assume a negative perception of your intentions.

Express Who You Are

Another great way to become more authentic is to express your genuine self by sharing your background; a valuable lesson, tip, or technique that you have learned; or a personal story that you cherish. Do activities that allow you to remove your hat and engage others—having coffee with your team, barbequing hamburgers for the crew, introducing your family to your workers, and sharing your hobbies or what you did over the weekend. These activities help to reveal a part of who you truly are. Giving work directions, setting work goals, doing performance reviews, and running meetings do not reveal who you are. Your ability to show yourself through personal interactions relates directly to your effectiveness in leading others. In a team environment, taking time to do things together as a team helps people to know one another. This results in not only better work relationships but also a much greater level of trust, understanding, and empathy for one another.

Practice Introspection

It's a healthy practice to periodically examine the *thinking and feelings* behind your decisions, actions, and behaviors, as well as your personal values and beliefs about an issue, conflict, or disagreement. Practicing self-inquiry is valuable for learning about yourself and improving your people skills. Try asking yourself insightful questions, such as, "What caused me to say that?" "How could I have said that better?" "What can I do to reduce my stress about this?" or "What did I learn about myself?" It's best *not* to ask yourself "*Why?*" questions, such as "Why did I say that?" or "Why did I spend so much time analyzing that?" because these questions elicit negativity and self-denigrating thoughts. Understanding your actions and reactions and consciously connecting your thinking, feelings, values, and behaviors are things that you can learn through meditation, mindfulness (7), positive psychology (8), and other practices.

Be Comfortable in Your Own Skin

Being comfortable in your own skin is about taking pride and joy in who you are. Reduce the strain and burden of excessive self-consciousness, competitiveness, and ego. Enjoy your imperfections and have realistic views and expectations of yourself. Recognize both your strengths and weaknesses and understand that *your strengths are your weaknesses and your weaknesses are your strengths.* For example, your confidence makes you decisive, but it can also make you arrogant, and your stubbornness weakens your openness but strengthens your persistence. It takes considerable experience, honesty, and introspection to find oneself. Your inner self is unique, and it's your uniqueness that makes you successful. The key is to practice being comfortable with yourself. Readily admit your mistakes, courageously face the consequences, and as soon as possible, take the necessary actions to fix your errors, recover, and learn from the experience. Taking responsibility for your mistakes and promptly correcting them are indicators of your maturity as a leader.

Show Your Pure Self

The purest expression of who you are occurs when you're having fun and showing your spirit, creativity, and passion. People like to work with people who are fun and enthusiastic about their work. In the throes of work, it takes great character and strength to not take things too seriously, laugh at yourself, be up when others are down, show genuine empathy when others are struggling, and not be afraid to show your feelings at work. It makes you authentic in the eyes of others. With that pure honesty comes mutual trust, confidence, and respect. Open, honest, unfiltered fun, enthusiasm, and positive interactions with others are pure moments that should be encouraged. In a given week, how many pure moments do you have at work?

Believe in Yourself

Confidence is a belief in your authentic self, which means that you trust who you are and your ability to make the right decisions. If you know who you are and know what you want, then it's a question of whether you believe strongly enough in yourself to take action. When you are confronted with a tough decision, how often do you trust yourself to do the right thing? Having the self-confidence to trust your instincts and decisions can improve your leadership and personal growth. People follow those who are believe in themselves and their work.

Skill Two Summary

Skill Two builds on the concept of the wedge, as team leaders are expected to work seamlessly across the three levels of the wedge while playing three roles or wearing three hats—individual contributor (team member hat), work teams (supervisor hat), and management (management hat)—with each hat conferring a different level of power, authority, responsibility, and control. Your ability to be tough on people problems without being tough on people depends on your ability to properly use and balance these three roles.

> **Management hat:** You have the *power and authority to represent, communicate, and administer company policies*, plans, goals, standards, procedures, and strategies. You are responsible for employee compliance, personnel management, strategic alignment, reporting, and budget control. You set goals, strategies, and work plans to meet organizational expectations.

> **Supervisor hat:** You have the *power and authority to deploy team processes and direct how the work is conducted* in accordance with management's policies, plans, strategies, goals, processes, and

priorities. You have the responsibility to ensure your team operates efficiently and safely, is fit for duty, meets performance expectations, and achieves high customer satisfaction.

Team member hat: You have the *power and authority to execute and control your individual work tasks* and the responsibility to demonstrate good partnership and teamwork, which includes trust, collaboration, communications, respect, compassion, and support—having mutual care and concern.

Your relationship with your employees is a complicated one in which you are representing *management* priorities, rules, and policies; serving as a *supervisor* in directing and assessing their work; and working together as a friendly, respectful, and supportive *team member*. But are you a team member, a supervisor, or management to your employees? Can you effectively wear three hats? It's clear that a team leader has many different roles and responsibilities, and it's tough to balance all three roles. A part of you wants to please management; a part of you wants your team to respect you as their leader; and you also want your employees to like you.

Skill Two presents three cases that illustrate important lessons for team leaders who play multiple roles in today's workplace. These lessons include the following:

▲ Understand that each hat carries a different level of power, authority, and control, as well as different responsibilities, expectations, and perspectives.

▲ Wear the hat that best fits the problem and puts you in the strongest position to effectively and efficiently solve the problem—*always act from a position of strength.*

▲ Have the courage to wear your management and supervisor hats during tough situations and use these hats to motivate, facilitate, and help people succeed, not to intimidate and punish people.

▲ Resist the temptation of relinquishing your management or supervisor hat to others in order to avoid conflict and employee discontent.

▲ You change people's behaviors when you delegate responsibilities. Be clear on what you are delegating in terms of expectations, power, authority, and control, and don't be afraid to empower and trust others.

▲ Correct common falsehoods. Exercising greater power and authority will *not* get you better results, getting tough on people is *not* a sign of strength as a leader, and showing your true self does *not* allow people to take advantage of you.

▲ Don't make the mistake of letting your hat define who you are. Assuming a fake persona as a leader will likely lead to failure. Rise up to the toughest challenge of being yourself. There are six actions that can help you increase your authenticity as a leader: increase transparency, express who you are, practice introspection, be comfortable in your own skin, show your pure self, and believe in yourself.

Skill Two is about wearing the right hat, at the right time, in the right way, and for the right reasons and situation. Hopefully your increased understanding of the roles and expectations of the three hats, as well as your awareness of the importance of being yourself, will greatly enhance your ability to handle tough people problems without being tough on people.

Skill Two Memory Card

Be Tough on People Problems, Not People
Wear the Right Hat and Be Yourself

Know Your Role	Be Authentic
1. Team leaders wear three hats—team member, supervisor, and management	1. Don't let the hat change who you are or your character—be yourself
2. Wear the hat that gives you the best strength and leverage to solve the problem	2. Increase transparency—align your inner motives with your outer behaviors
3. Have the courage to wear the tough hat when needed	3. Express who you are—put your hat away and engage others
4. Avoid relinquishing control of your management and policy responsibilities	4. Practice introspection—self-inquiry is essential in improving your people skills
5. Be friendly, not friends, at work	5. Be comfortable in your own skin— have the strength to be yourself
6. You want employees to respect you, not like you	6. Show your pure self—have fun, enjoy what you do
7. Be hard on policies and standards, not people	7. Believe in yourself—trust yourself and your instincts
8. Empathy connects you with others	
9. Don't hog your hat: delegate authority, power, and control to build mutual trust	

SKILL THREE

How to Build Highly Successful Teams
The Loop

The wedge and the three hats bring into context the multiple people skills required of team leaders today. Building on these concepts, the next essential skill for project leaders is knowing how to create a highly successful team, which is defined as a group of people working together with a shared purpose of meeting and exceeding stakeholder expectations through superior collaboration, team commitment, and selfless behavior.

Great team leaders do not manage people; they lead people. They don't tell people what to do; they motivate, facilitate, and inspire people to cooperate, collaborate, and support each other in achieving shared objectives, strategies, and goals. Also, great team leaders don't manage teams; they manage team performance and behavior, and team behavior is what makes and breaks team success. Therefore, building a highly successful team requires skills in managing team behavior, and the most essential behavior is team inclusiveness.

CASE 3.1: THE COMPANY MERGER—FORMING A NEW TEAM

It is a common strategy in business to seek greater profitability and earnings growth through mergers and acquisitions. Even in down market conditions where profits suffer, companies with strong balance sheets see potential opportunities to strategically buy out competitors, expand market share, and vertically integrate. It's a fast way to gain new earnings without

---

having to build new assets. However, company mergers and acquisitions are some of the most challenging experiences to go through. You're trying to integrate, consolidate, optimize, divest, and fit together two different companies as fast as you can. At the end of the process, you want to be a leaner, more robust company with better strategies, earnings growth, assets, technology, and people from both organizations.

During the merger of two large companies, one highly regarded human resources manager, Maria, was selected to run the corporate Employee Training and Development (ETD) Division of the newly merged company. Her former company was being acquired by a competitor, so she was being redeployed and relocated to the competitor's headquarters, where she was to consolidate and manage a staff of thirty-five employees drawn from both companies. About 20 percent of the new team would be composed of employees from her former company, and the remainder would be drawn from the acquiring company.

After thirteen hectic months of merging the ETD functions of both companies, which included the consolidation of policies, databases, training materials, resources, and supervisory and managerial training programs, the manager conducted a review of the division's progress and wanted to assess how well the people had weathered the change. Maria and two of her senior team leaders distributed an employee satisfaction survey and interviewed a representative cross section of employees currently working in ETD, as well as a few people who had left during the past year. Here are some of the major themes and representative findings from their review:

What Employees Liked

▲ Employees were glad to finally see things settled and operating more smoothly after a difficult period of consolidating records, reconfiguring processes, and onboarding a number of new employees from the acquired company.

▲ It was good news that the employee training and development program was retained in-house and not outsourced.

▲ Employees appreciated the efforts of management to keep people informed of the status and progress of the merger.

▲ People felt everyone worked together, supported each other, and tried to stay positive and optimistic during the transition period.

▲ Employees appreciated the frequent team meetings, which enabled people to meet each other.

▲ It was hoped that the work environment would stabilize soon and that management would refrain from making any more changes for a while.

What Needs Improvement

▲ Employees liked the opportunity to express their feelings and concerns about the transition period, but many expressed the view that it would have been better to seek feedback earlier than thirteen months after the merger.

▲ Although the company appeared sensitive to the needs of the employees, many still felt stressed and overloaded during the merger.

▲ Many major decisions were made by management that affected ETD operations, yet employees were not given a chance for input.

▲ Although employees from the acquired company were given a company-wide orientation, some employees expressed feelings such as, "I was treated more like a contractor than an employee," and, "I had to figure things out on my own, and there were many unwritten rules and company terms that I was unfamiliar with."

▲ The division still lacked documentation and standardized processes and methodologies. Employees didn't feel the new team was in sync yet.

▲ Staff wanted better communication and sharing within the division on what people were doing and why.

▲ Employees felt that the team was dominated by a few opinionated individuals from the acquiring company and that their ideas and issues were not being heard at times.

▲ The feedback from employees who had left the company included the following statements:

- "I hardly saw my supervisor."
- "I was given a *meets expectations* rating on my performance, which is my lowest ever, and I never got a good explanation. I don't think he liked me."
- "I chose to post out not because of the people but because I felt my responsibilities were being downgraded."
- "I couldn't see where I was going or what my role was going to be in this new group."
- "I never felt comfortable in the new company and decided to go back to school."

After reviewing the survey results, Maria had mixed feelings. She was pleased with the honesty of the remarks and appreciated knowing people's feelings. But she thought many of the comments were surprising and critical of her effectiveness as a manager. She didn't expect to get so much negative feedback and was disappointed that those who felt unjustly treated, overloaded, or uninformed didn't contact her. Maria had made it clear that her door was always open to anyone with concerns. Very few people took her up on that offer. Also, there were many group meetings where opinions could be expressed. Maria wondered whether the employees didn't know or trust her very well yet. She didn't know what more she could have done.

Lessons from the Story

These results are not uncommon for companies and teams who go through organizational restructuring, functional changes, or the formation of new project teams. You're trying to figure out logistics, communication, processes, roles and responsibilities, and work expectations. People are warned in advance that they should expect to receive extra work, encounter some conflicts, and feel uncomfortable. As a result, people issues are often neglected and treated as a cost that everyone is expected to pay. But in any restructuring or new project, the key to success is building a highly effective team. Everyone is in a rush to get the work done, but the work can't be done successfully without a committed, functioning team.

Looking back at Maria's feedback and experiences, what were her primary learnings? Is there a common thread or root cause for the disappointments that were felt by her team? Let's first discuss what compels a group of individuals to unify and work together as a team.

The Most Important Human Factor in Highly Successful Teams

The most important human factor in building highly successful teams is *team inclusiveness*, which means having a team that makes you feel accepted, included, respected, relevant, recognized, and valued. It's a feeling of being "in the loop" (Figure 3.1). The "loop" represents a place of acceptance, comfort, belonging, interconnection, and shared purpose. It is your home away from home. It's a place of safety, trust, fun, camaraderie, and support. The "loop" is a great model for learning the key concepts and skills of team inclusiveness.

Being in the loop satisfies two important human needs—purpose and peer acceptance. As illustrated in Figure 3.1, feeling in the loop comes from three

> *"Being in the loop satisfies two important human needs—purpose and peer acceptance."*

emotions: (1) you feel *accepted* by the team (Xs represent individuals in the team), (2) you feel a *belonging* to a *larger mission* (large surrounding circle), and (3) you feel a mutual

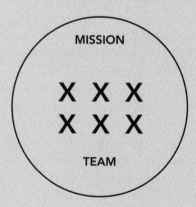

Figure 3.1 In the loop

connection with other team members (close alignment of Xs). In highly successful teams, team members believe in each other and are committed to the purpose of the team. As a project team leader, one of your most important responsibilities is to establish a clear and compelling mission, something that is much bigger in scope and meaning than the collective members of the team and inspires them to work for each other in achieving that mission. People are highly motivated by shared goals and team relationships. Inclusiveness comes from a shared belief that the team comes first and no one person is more important than the team—a "we over me" (we > me) attitude.

In the merger story, the positive feedback from the survey and interviews reflects the importance of inclusiveness to employees: the organization kept "people informed of the status and progress of the merger"; "everyone worked together, supported each other, and tried to stay positive and optimistic"; team meetings "enabled people to meet each other"; and employees liked the opportunity of "on-boarding a number of new employees."

Being in the loop makes you feel secure. But when you're out of the loop, you feel mentally disconnected from your team. It's a state of *exclusion* and you feel "out of it"—rejected, abandoned, disliked, or distrusted. You believe you are treated differently, you feel you are not privy to what's happening within the team, and you feel left out of the mission. In the merger, people felt *excluded* from the decision-making process ("employees were not given a chance for input"); they *didn't feel appreciated* when their feedback was not solicited for thirteen months; employees felt *stranded and alone*—"I had to figure things out on my own"; and they didn't feel informed on what others were doing—there was a lack of "sharing within the division on what people were doing and why." When people don't believe they're part of the larger mission, the loop is broken and so is their commitment.

> "When people don't believe they're part of the larger mission, the loop is broken and so is their commitment."

Self-Exclusion

In addition, the HR manager, Maria, may have felt excluded when the employees didn't share their concerns with her, and she questioned whether the employees trusted her. She felt as though she was out of the loop and not yet accepted by the team. It's important to note that everyone had some feelings of exclusion yet the problem was never anticipated, identified, or addressed. This is not an uncommon occurrence in the workplace, and it's most visible in times of stress, change, and conflict. However, most organizations fail to recognize the true cost of exclusion. *It's the biggest silent killer of projects and teamwork in an organization and exposes people to their greatest fears—peer rejection and feeling irrelevant.*

As the merger story illustrates, no one likes to be left out, uninformed, or rejected, but exclusion is not limited to peer rejection—it's also about self-exclusion. *Self-exclusion* is when people choose to mentally or physically disengage from their team, activity, or other interaction. They choose not to participate, connect or collaborate with others. Self-excluders prefer to be free, independent, and untethered from the obligations and hassles of having to work on a team.

Wanting to take a temporary break from a team is normal and healthy, but when self-exclusion becomes your preferred work style, it can quickly become a detriment to both you and the team. Disengaging yourself from others affects the dynamics of a team and also impacts your ability to work effectively with others and maintain good working relationships. When people don't understand your self-exclusion, they will usually assume the worst—"She doesn't care to interact with the team," "She doesn't want to work with us," or "She doesn't believe in what we are doing." *In short, feelings of exclusion can occur when others exclude you (social exclusion) or when you choose to exclude yourself (self-exclusion).*

Summary

In the story, feelings of exclusion caused people to feel out of the loop because they "never got a good explanation" on their mediocre performance rating, didn't feel valued—"I don't think he liked me"—or felt lost or abandoned—"I couldn't see where I was going or what my role was going to be." Exclusion was the common factor that caused discontent among the employees. Some chose to self-exclude themselves and leave, while others stayed but wished they could have been included more and kept in the loop. Self-exclusion is often considered a passive avoidance and self-centered, "me > we" behavior.

What Motivates and Demotivates People to Stay Engaged

You can't lead people without getting to know people. A great starting point in learning to understand people and fostering inclusiveness is recognizing the *personality types* of your team members. Without a doubt, knowing people's personality types is one of the most effective ways to understand people better. The idea that subpopulations of people share similar behavioral tendencies, work styles, motivations, personal preferences, personality traits, and temperaments has been around for a long time and has proved to be very valuable in understanding behavior. Research has shown that an individual's behavior and motivation can be in large part attributable to an inherent temperament or personality type (9, 10, 11). Personality type is not always predictive of people's behavior, but it does give you great insights into people's personal preferences and motivations. Although there are numerous models of personality types, the Myers-Briggs and Keirsey personality types are probably the most popular and simplest to learn and apply in the workplace—the four Keirsey temperament types are Rational, Guardian, Idealist, and Artisan (Table 3.1). As everyone is unique, probably no one is 100 percent one type or another, but it's likely that you will have one predominant personality type.

Rationals are thinkers who compete with others and are characteristically analytical, objective, logical, systematic, competent, and strategic. They

> "Without a doubt, knowing people's personality types is one of the most effective ways to understand people better."

Table 3.1 Basic Profiles of Personality Types

Keirsey Personality Types	Characteristics
Rational "Thinker"	Analytical Logical Competent Achievement seeker
Guardian "Supporter"	Cooperative Compliant Organized Security seeker
Idealist "Empathizer"	Thoughtful Feelingful Compassionate Identity seeker
Artisan "Risk Taker"	Expressive Nonconformist Resourceful Freedom seeker

are naturally attracted to sciences and technology such as math, chemistry, physics, engineering, computer sciences, and information technology. Rationals are critical thinkers, self-starters, and achievement seekers who strive to be mistake-free in everything they do.

Guardians are supporters who do for others and are known for their cooperation, teamwork, dedication, loyalty, strong work ethic, persistence, and sacrifice. They are attracted to authoritative, commercial, and service-oriented vocations such as government, military service, public service, education, politics, industry, and labor. Guardians are practical thinkers, hard workers, and security seekers who believe in getting the job done on time, every time.

Idealists are empathizers who care for others and are described as sensitive, thoughtful, selfless, ethical, genuine, compassionate, hopeful, sympathetic, collaborative, and visionary. They enjoy the humanities and engage in teaching, counseling, coaching, facilitating, preaching, leading, and healing. Idealists are romantic thinkers, consensus-builders, and identity seekers who want peace, harmony, and happy endings.

Artisans are risk takers who like to impress others with their cleverness, creativity, passion, resourcefulness, fun, persuasiveness, and boldness. They enjoy the arts, marketing, politics, media, entertainment, and hands-on activities and are not afraid to go on special adventures, pursue new opportunities, and change careers. Artisans are imaginative thinkers, self-promoters, and freedom seekers who want to be unique and do extraordinary things.

"In a team environment, Rationals want autonomy, Guardians appreciation, Idealists respect, and Artisans freedom."

In short, Rationals seek achievement, efficiency, competency, and autonomy; Guardians like security, responsibility, work, and stability; Idealists value harmony, honesty, respect, and compassion; and Artisans prefer independence, individuality, flexibility, and adaptability. In a team environment, Rationals want autonomy, Guardians appreciation, Idealists respect, and Artisans freedom. Rationals fear failure, Guardians hate rejection, Idealists dislike conflicts, and Artisans loathe criticism.

Besides using these descriptions, you can more accurately determine your personality type by taking any number of surveys that are readily available on the internet. Knowing personality types enables you to be much more skilled in fostering team inclusiveness. For each personality type, Table 3.2 shows what factors are inclusionary ("What Draws Me In") and what factors are exclusionary ("What Drives Me Out").

In general, all personality types are drawn into the loop by *respect, recognition*, and *relevance*. Furthermore, all personality types tend to leave the loop when they feel criticized, marginalized (belittled, relegated, put down), underutilized, undervalued, and unfairly treated. When pressures mount, personality types are apt to polarize—Rationals and Artisans go aggressive and dominate, whereas Guardians and Idealists go passive and withdraw. This polarization of aggressives and passives can cause team conflicts and animosity.

Keeping Your Team Together during Conflicts

During times of conflict, team members can become more self-centered, defensive, polarized, and exclusionary. When you feel rejected, your symptoms can range from mild, temporary irritation to severe, persistent depression. You can go through periods of sadness, inferiority, and victimization. It's important for team leaders to recognize that team exclusion and self-exclusion can have adverse consequences when feelings of rejection turn into feelings of victimization and are used as excuses for poor performance and other serious behaviors, such as hostility, sabotage, and even

Table 3.2 Inclusionary and Exclusionary Motivators for Personality Types

	Inclusion What Draws Me In ⟵— X	Exclusion What Drives Me Out ⟶ X
Rational "Thinker"	*Challenge*, analyses, problem-solving, strategic thinking, planning, systems, purpose, leadership, *impactful work*	*Incompetence*, inefficiency, emotional situations, illogic, unchallenging work, errors, failures, lack of results and goals
Guardian "Supporter"	*Appreciation*, security, teamwork, cooperation, projects, organization, responsibility, accountability, practicality, *stable work*	*Disorder*, instability, change, lack of direction, chaos, inequities, braggarts, loud mouths, bad leadership
Idealist "Empathizer"	*Respect*, fairness, care, compassion, inspiration, honesty, harmony, integrity, sensitivity, values, *meaningful work*	*Unethical behavior*, dishonesty, bullies, fakes, conflicts, meanness, pressure, insensitivity, injustice, stress, insincerity, manipulation
Artisan "Risk Taker"	*Freedom*, change, risks, thrills, action, creativity, openness, stimuli, enthusiasm, new opportunities, *exciting work*	*Boredom*, rules, restrictions, process, inaction, criticism, confinement, planning, structure, control, standard practices, mandates

violence. Feelings of exclusion don't just happen overnight—it usually takes a series of bad experiences to lose faith in the team; therefore, most incidents can be averted.

In the merger story, the manager thought the negative feedback appeared unjustified from her perspective. It may be true that employees' feelings of exclusion might be misguided, illogical, and unfounded. But people's perception is their reality. Exclusionary feelings are emotions, and whether they have a valid, logical basis is largely immaterial. Exclusion is a perception that surfaces when teams are exhibiting poor behaviors, such as lack of communication and accountability. People will drift away unless there are motivators to keep them in the loop; people will mentally depart if they don't feel wanted or have a relevant purpose that keeps them engaged with the team.

Inclusiveness requires a big commitment and extra effort. It's not something that happens naturally when people are brought together to work as a team. Although people enjoy socializing, it doesn't necessarily mean they like to work together. Socializing is not the same as teamwork, and teamwork is not the same as inclusiveness. Socializing occurs when people gather to chat, interact, and have fun. Teamwork occurs when a group of people work together in coordination with defined roles and responsibilities toward a shared goal. *Socializing and teamwork are behaviors, whereas inclusiveness is an attitude.* You can't have great teamwork without first having an inclusive mind-set. Inclusiveness is the "mental glue" that keeps a team together—acceptance, belonging, and connection. But to attain team inclusiveness ("we > me," the team comes first) requires a continuous, selfless effort from everyone. Without this effort, the team will naturally default to a "me > we" state. The true test of an inclusive team is in its ability to maintain a "we > me" attitude in times of conflict.

> **"The true test of an inclusive team is in its ability to maintain a 'we > me' attitude in times of conflict."**

CASE 3.2: THE TUNA FISH SANDWICH—PREVENTING CONFLICTS

One evening at home, Tom, an IT team leader, decides he will prepare a lunch in advance to give him more time to dress and eat breakfast the next morning. His favorite lunch is a tuna fish sandwich, which he has perfected over the years. He opens a can of premium tuna fish and empties half of it into a small bowl, where he chops it up finely and mixes it gently with some mayonnaise, mustard, chopped celery, a dash of dill, and a little relish in perfect proportions. He then spreads this blended mixture onto two slices of his favorite multigrain bread. To him, the secret is to get the right proportion of tuna fish to bread and layer the tuna fish evenly across the bread. Too much tuna and the bread gets soggy; too much bread and the tuna flavor is lost. No doubt, when it comes to making a tuna fish sandwich, Tom is a perfectionist.

After securing his sandwich in a ziplock bag, Tom covers the can of remaining tuna fish with plastic wrap in case his wife, Michelle, wants to make a sandwich too. From the kitchen, he shouts out to Michelle, who is watching television, "Hey, Michelle, I made a tuna fish sandwich. I have some extra; I'll leave it in the fridge for you, okay?" Michelle, who is distracted and not listening well, says, "Thanks a lot, honey." (Michelle thinks to herself, "That was nice of Tom to make *me* a sandwich.")

Next morning, Michelle gets up first as usual, prepares for work, and leaves right on time. Tom gets up, showers, shaves, gets dressed, and gulps down a cup of coffee and some yogurt. He grabs his backpack and heads into the kitchen to pick up his delicious tuna fish sandwich. As he scans the refrigerator shelf for his sandwich, it doesn't appear to be there. With great concern, he looks deeper into the refrigerator, thinking it must have been pushed farther back on the shelf. Not seeing it there, he searches more frantically on the other shelves—but no luck. He ponders, "Where did my sandwich go?"

On further inspection, he notices that the can of leftover tuna fish was untouched, and it suddenly dawns on him: "Oh my gosh, Michelle took my sandwich!" With that realization, Tom rushes to make another sandwich, but in his hurry, he puts in way too much mayonnaise and skips the other ingredients. He slaps it onto some bread and peels out for work. He is not happy. In fact, the rushing around in the morning makes him feel anxious and moody all morning. He feels robbed. He tries texting his wife several times, but there is no answer (it turns out that Michelle's smartphone wasn't charged). He doesn't deserve this. He worked so hard to fix his perfect, favorite sandwich and his wife just took it without a word to him. Tom feels he has a right to be angry.

After work, traffic is light and Tom gets home before Michelle. Michelle arrives home an hour later, and she asks him how his day went. Tom says, "My day was okay. By the way, did you take the sandwich that I had left in the fridge this morning?" Michelle replies, "Yes, thanks so much. I was running late, so having the sandwich ready to go was great! It was tasty, but I think tuna on sourdough is better." If you were Tom, what would be your response?

a. "I told you last night that I made a sandwich for myself and left extra in the can for you. You never listen to me! You know you were wrong; that's why you ignored my messages. You owe me a big apology!"

b. "That was my sandwich! Please ask me first next time instead of just running off with it."

c. "You took my sandwich and you ruined my morning; how would you feel if I took your sandwich?"

d. "You're too lazy to make your own sandwich, so you think it's okay to take mine?"

e. "Good, I'm glad the sandwich saved you time this morning. Actually, I had made that sandwich for myself, so I was bummed when I couldn't find it, but it's on me—I didn't make it clear. And sourdough does sound good—I'm going to make that for you next time!"

Which one represents your most likely response? Which answers are inclusionary, "we > me" (we before me; we come first), and which ones are exclusionary, "me > we" (me before we; I come first)?

Let's examine each answer:

a. "I told you . . . I made a sandwich for myself. . . . You never listen to me! You know you were wrong; that's why you ignored my messages. You owe me a big apology!" These remarks are accusatory, self-victimizing, and divisive. Tom feels he was wronged and deserves an apology. This is clearly a "me" (self-centered) response.

   Also, Michelle had misheard Tom and thought he had left a sandwich for her. Not knowing this fact (plus Michelle's not answering her phone), Tom assumes Michelle has negative intentions. As discussed previously, when people don't hear from you, they usually assume the worst.

b. "Please ask me first . . ." is a *controlling behavior*. No one likes to be controlled or told what to do. This is a "me > we" (self-centered) response.

c. "You ruined my morning; how would you feel if I took your sandwich?" is an *empathy-seeking question* ("Do you feel my injustice?"). However, it's also a "me > we" response, as Tom is blaming Michelle for ruining his morning, and his question may not get the empathy he is seeking and can often backfire on him. For example, Michelle could say, "It wouldn't bother me if you took my sandwich—it's not a big deal."

d. "You're too lazy . . ." is an accusatory, *judgmental* response that could inflame the conflict. No one likes to be accused or judged by others. It's a "me > we," scornful response.

e. This is a "we > me" response in which Tom is *empathetic*, stays *positive*, and avoids accusing, controlling, and judging Michelle.

   i. Tom starts with a positive, caring focus on Michelle, not himself: "Good, I'm glad the sandwich saved you time this morning."

   ii. He shares his honest feelings—"I had made that sandwich for myself, so I was bummed when I couldn't find it" (transparency).

   iii. He finishes with a forward-looking, inclusive, "we-building" comment—"And sourdough does sound good—I'm going to make that for you next time!"

This dialogue sequence is more than the old positive-negative-positive "sandwich" routine—the new and better sandwich (as outlined here) is to first empathize or recognize the other party (*you*); second, express your honest and personal views (*me*); and, last, close with a favorable, future, inclusive statement (*we*). It's not a tuna fish sandwich but a *"you-me-we" sandwich* that prevents a conflict and creates an inclusive relationship.

Also note in (e) that Tom takes personal responsibility for the miscommunication instead of blaming Michelle. To finish the story, it turns out that Tom says (e) and Michelle responds, "No, you made it clear—it was my fault for not listening. I'm sorry I took your sandwich. How about I make both of us a great sandwich for tomorrow!" This story illustrates that *a "we" ending is always better than a "me" ending.*

Lessons from the Story

Probably the most common reasons for poor teamwork and exclusionary behaviors are intrapersonal and interpersonal conflicts. Intrapersonal conflicts occur within an individual; examples include insecurity, self-criticism, low self-esteem, and internal value conflicts. Interpersonal conflicts are caused by team disagreements, a lack of cooperation, or the inability of team members to work together. In either case, conflicts drive people away (self-exclusion) or apart (social exclusion), and they typically occur when teams face tough problems, disruptive changes, and other difficult situations. Inclusiveness is the key determinant of how well a team survives and succeeds in overcoming these challenges. If a team can maintain a "we" over "me" mind-set, bad conflicts can be avoided and, if encountered, can actually strengthen a team. All team problems and interpersonal conflicts can either weaken or strengthen a team. It's a personal choice—is it about "me" or "we"?

The ability to consciously choose the team over oneself is not as much of an intellectual choice as it is an emotional one. Tom and Michelle's misunderstanding is not unlike the interpersonal conflicts that you sometimes encounter in the workplace when employees feel disrespected, minimized, taken advantage of, and ripped off by others and they demand justice. Responses (a) through (d) are all rooted in feelings of injustice, which creates an "I'm right, you're wrong" conflict. It's not unreasonable for Tom to feel wronged, and he needed to hear an apology to feel right again. Responses (a) through (d) are different ways of seeking justice, and Tom wanted an admission of guilt from his wife. In any conflict, incidents like this can become an emotional contest of who's right and who's wrong. Similarly, when team conflicts occur, people need an apology or atonement to feel right, and when that doesn't work, the usual reaction is to get even—"Since you wronged me, I have the right to wrong you." This vengeful mentality is commonly manifested in passive-aggressive behaviors in the workplace. When teams engage in this tit-for-tat exchange, it becomes a lose-lose proposition for both parties.

"Me" behaviors are divisive; "we" behaviors are unifying. "Me" thinking shrinks your perspective; "we" thinking enlarges your perspective, enabling you to see the broader picture, make a greater impact, and expand the team's loop. When you step back and look at the big picture, being right is important, but is it important enough to jeopardize your relationship with your wife? Do you want to

"Do you want to be right, or do you want to be married?"

be right, or do you want to be married? Is your sandwich more important than your relationship with your spouse? As a project leader, is being right more important than the success of the project? It's analogous to the classic question, "What's more important, winning the battle or winning the war?" Remember, you can't have a highly successful team unless you have an inclusive team and a unified purpose. When a "me" mentality prevails, the loop gets tight and exclusion takes place; when a "we" attitude is achieved, the loop gets bigger and there's room for everyone.

Summary

Tom and Michelle's story illustrates that choosing "we" over "me" is not about self-sacrifice ("I lose, you win") or competition ("You lose, I win"); it's about approaching things with a win-win, inclusive perspective. Fairness, respect, and justice are common personal values, and when they are violated, you can get very emotional, which often leads to negative behavior. We have to accept that *unfair things happen to everyone, and you have to keep small things small.* And you have to trust that *team success is more valuable than individual achievement, and inclusiveness is worth more than personal redemption.* It's a choice between the team and oneself, but it's also a choice between long-term sustainability (marriage, team success, inclusiveness) and short-term gratification (being personally right, successful, and redeemed).

Choosing between "We" and "Me"

One of the great challenges in managing teams is getting people to work effectively together while at the same time making each person feel individually valued. As much as we would like to think that no one is more important than the team and that the team always comes first, this is not the case in many workplaces. Do workers in your organization truly value and give priority to teamwork and inclusiveness ("we") over their individual performance and success ("me")? What prevails in your organization—"we" or "me"?

What are the main barriers to "we > me" in the workplace? There are numerous human factors that drive people to seek autonomy, self-satisfaction, and personal recognitions, but here are the main reasons:

▲ **Workers are rewarded based on individual performance.** In most organizations, compensation policies and systems are individual-based, rather than team-based. You are rewarded based on your individual skills, responsibilities, knowledge, experience, and performance. Good teamwork is regarded as a given; each member is expected to be a good team player, just as everyone is expected to work safely. It's not regarded as a differentiator of performance—it merely qualifies you to work.

▲ **Teams are too bureaucratic.** Nonteam advocates will argue that they work faster and make decisions quicker when they work alone. A team creates bureaucracy, invites conflicts, and drives people to the lowest denominator ("You're only as strong as the weakest link"). Not every problem and project requires a team effort. In certain cases, a team can be more of a hindrance than a solution. Also, having to support and accommodate each other and deal with interpersonal conflicts can be an emotional drain. That's why it's so important to reduce conflicts and bureaucracy as much as possible in your projects.

▲ **People like to be in control.** People want to be independent and accountable for their own work. It's more constraining and stressful to have to share responsibilities and accountability, collaborate and rely on others to get the project done —it's simpler just to do it yourself.

▲ **Egos need to be satisfied.** Your individual need to succeed is driven by ego, self-determination, and self-esteem. It's a matter of "I can't feel good about my team until I first feel good about myself." Although you would like people to check their egos at the door, reducing your ego may reduce your competitiveness and motivation, which are important to a team. It comes down to trying to balance the needs of the individual against the needs of the team.

Due to these reasons, establishing a "we" before "me" mind-set can be a tough challenge, but the payoffs can be tremendously rewarding. As a project leader, it's essential to continuously demonstrate the tangible benefits of great teamwork.

The Value of Good Teamwork

Despite the many factors that discourage individuals from working as a team, there is a lot to be said about good teamwork. There are very few projects and positions in the world that don't rely on some degree of teamwork to succeed. Even highly successful CEOs, inventors, and independent artists owe their success to their families, friends, teachers, colleagues, mentors, coaches, counselors, and other supporters. Projects succeed due to the collective efforts of people in some way, shape, or form. Many of your teamwork skills are derived from your circle of families and friends. You understand and appreciate the value of having positive relationships.

When teams are performing well together, the output is usually greater than the sum of the individual contributions; bringing together the right skills, talents, knowledge, and experiences inspires great creativity, effort, focus, and achievement. In terms of human factors, this undeniable success in teamwork may be attributable to camaraderie, peer pressure, social acceptance, mutual accountability, and fulfillment of certain human needs that can't be met alone—*peer acceptance*, *mutual respect*, and *a meaningful shared purpose*. In addition, there is a joy in working with other people that you can't get working alone.

It's clear that it's the human element that determines success (12). It all comes down to the collective motivation and behaviors of the team, and the team leader is critical in driving the right team behaviors. Good project leaders know that keeping a team motivated depends on melding the needs of the team with the needs of the individual to achieve a mind-set of "I succeed when the team succeeds"— the "we" mentality. As a team leader, it is essential to continue to reinforce the value of good teamwork and inclusiveness.

> *"'I succeed when the team succeeds'—the 'we' mentality."*

The Six Inclusive Behaviors of Highly Successful Teams

Building a highly successful team involves more than just bringing people together to work productively toward a common goal. Teams have to be able to manage change and not miss a beat in quality and output. Team members come and go as new opportunities occur. Also, team goals and projects will change over time. You don't want to start from scratch each time the team undergoes a change. Building a highly successful team is about more than goals and relationships; it's about building a *sustainable, inclusive team culture* that endures and strengthens over time (2). This sustainable culture is built on six critical "we > me" team behaviors: mutual trust, interdependence, accountability, transparency, learning, and valuing individuality.

People usually have a general idea of what these behaviors mean, but they're rarely well understood, especially in the context of a team. This section operationalizes these vital terms into actionable descriptions that you can use with your team. In practice, these behaviors are not independent but rather interrelated and codependent. You need all six working well—if one is compromised, the rest are compromised. As you go through each inclusive behavior, where do you think your team stands within the range provided?

Mutual Trust

Mutual trust is the belief that people are acting in the best interest of others—"We believe in each other." You trust that people will do what they say they're going to do, follow through on their promises, and respect each other's individuality and work preferences. It takes a leap of faith that each team member will do right by you and the team. In a highly inclusive team, when facts aren't known or when conflicts and miscommunications occur, team members *assume the best case, not the worst case,* and that *people's actions are made with good intentions, not bad intentions* (Figure 3.2).

Case in Point As illustrated in the previous case, when Tom couldn't find his sandwich and heard nothing from Michelle, he assumed that Michelle intentionally took his sandwich. Without knowing Michelle's side of the story, he assumed the worst case: that Michelle had *intended* to steal his sandwich and ignored his text messages. In fact, Michelle was very appreciative of Tom's generosity when she believed he had made her a sandwich. Michelle was operating with good intentions, not bad ones. In an inclusive team, people would unconditionally assume that Michelle was acting in good faith and not make harsh judgments.

In noninclusive teams, people are cautious, suspicious of people's true intentions, serve their own agendas, and are skeptical of people's trust. This distrustful attitude can be remedied by *increasing team transparency, accountability, and interdependence.*

Interdependence

Interdependence occurs when each team member's work is well integrated, coordinated, and mutually dependent. It's like the mechanisms of a watch.

Figure 3.2 Trust presumes good intentions

Figure 3.3 Interdependence outperforms independence

In order for the watch to work properly, all parts must be in sync; operate in unison with great precision; rely on each other to do their part; be focused on a single, clear purpose; and flawlessly perform their functions. When teams are interdependent, team members rely on, root for, and support each other to achieve a common goal (Figure 3.3). Your work depends on mutual expertise, cooperation, and communications.

Project team leaders often make the mistake of thinking that "divide and conquer" is the most efficient way to get the job done. That approach might work for certain projects, but in the long run, it's not sustainable. When your work is highly integrated and people are working closely with one another, you get improved communication, trust, accountability, mutual learning, and team problem solving and decision-making, and you get to know each other better. Dividing up work may be more convenient, but it rarely leads to high team success. Your goal is to build a highly successful team culture that supports and facilitates interdependence over independence.

In noninclusive teams, people work independently, focus on their own tasks, and only care about their part of the project. It's a *competitive* team environment where team members are vying for individual attention and achievement, and the team's loop becomes tighter and more stressful.

A good indicator of interdependence is the behavior of people in team meetings. Is there balanced participation, or are certain individuals dominating the discussion? Are people acknowledging each other's ideas, or are people talking over each other, not actively listening, or excessively judgmental? Are team members complimenting and recognizing one another? Are team members actively supporting or competing with one another? You can build greater team interdependence by demonstrating *mutual trust*, giving feedback, having *team learning* sessions, and reinforcing *team accountability*.

Case in Point Team leaders often run into a problem when team members are too busy on their own tasks and become less willing to help others. In a system that rewards individual performance, it's easy to creep into a "me > we" mode and become more independent and less interdependent. As a team leader, you're in the best position to mitigate this behavior in your team. You can help stave off excessive independence by asking every team member to contribute something to the improvement of the team every month or quarter, such as improving a team process, mentoring others, facilitating a meeting, giving a training session, or arranging a team luncheon or other team-building activity. It sends the message that "we're in this together," working as a single unit, and that all team members are in the loop. When every team member is regularly contributing something for the greater good, it becomes a habit, and that behavior carries over to team projects and tasks. You shape the behavior by practicing the behavior on a regular basis.

Accountability

Accountability is one of the most misused words in the workplace. It has always carried a negative connotation—"You will be held accountable for any problems!" Certainly, accountability means taking responsibility for your actions, owning up to your mistakes, and not making excuses, but when it comes to creating an inclusive team, *accountability* takes on a much broader definition. Each person is indeed held accountable for his or her roles and responsibilities on a team, but in the context of this skill, it's about team accountability, not individual accountability. Team accountability means that when one person's part of the project is failing, *everybody* on the team has a responsibility to fix it. In other words, *your failure is my failure*, and, conversely, *your success is my success* (Figure 3.4). When one team member succeeds, everyone deserves some credit because, directly or indirectly, that success was likely enabled by others. One person may be assigned and trusted to complete a task, but everyone takes responsibility for the outcome. When you have true team accountability, excessive competition and the blame game disappear and instead the energy is devoted to more productive things. This builds from the previous discussion on interdependence. Furthermore, when a gap in performance occurs during a project, others will automatically step up to fill the void.

> *"Team accountability means that when one person's part of the project is failing, everybody on the team has a responsibility to fix it."*

Figure 3.4 Team accountability means everyone is responsible for everybody

In noninclusive teams, team members avoid accountability by shunning project responsibilities, hiding mistakes, and blaming each other for failures. No one wants to be caught doing things wrong. It's a *fearful culture*, and when you mess up, no one comes to your aid. You're on your own—"your mistake, your problem"—and team members won't step in to help unless the boss makes them do so. It's a competition to see who makes the fewest mistakes, finishes first, and gets all the accolades. You can build more team accountability by encouraging your team to have a mutually responsible mindset and help others in time of need instead of assuming a "me" mind-set.

Case in Point   Nothing rallies a team together more than having shared goals, and goal setting is a common and important team process that motivates accountability. Unfortunately, team goals are usually content-focused—complete the project "on time, on spec, and on budget," and team leaders fail to recognize that project success depends on people's behaviors. So why don't project leaders set behavior-based goals and hold people accountable for their team behaviors rather than just focus on the endpoints of their collective work? When the focus is only on content outcomes, people tend to feel only partially accountable or accountable for just their part of the project. Set behavior-based goals and people will feel accountable to *support and help others throughout the project* to achieve the desired outcomes.

For example, avoid having only content or endpoint goals (such as deadlines, deliverables, milestones); include *behavior-based* goals that motivate team accountability, such as by assigning "cochampions" for each major task to increase mentorship, partnership, and interdependence; set goals that are more fun and exciting to accomplish (for example, number of success stories on teamwork, number of new ideas proposed, most creative solution to a problem); and recognize team members who exhibit team accountability behaviors (for example, checked in with others to offer their assistance; took prompt action to correct mistakes; promptly sought solutions rather than blame; helped cover responsibilities for absent team members). It takes some creativity and extra work to create a culture of team accountability. When team accountability increases, team performance increases.

Transparency

The quickest way to gain trust, respect, and confidence from others is to be more transparent. It's a vital ingredient in forming highly inclusive teams. Transparency means expressing the true motives, intentions, and feelings behind your actions. It's an act of overt honesty. It's a behavior that sounds simple, but it's tough to do. Honesty can make a person feel vulnerable to

Figure 3.5 Be transparent for the benefit of the team

criticism and judgment. You have to feel secure about yourself and have some courage in order to be transparent with others.

In this context, *transparency* refers to team transparency, which means that the behavior is practiced by all and has a team purpose, not an individual one (Figure 3.5). Team transparency works when it is used to increase team trust, learning, and accountability. It's not a license to spill your guts, speak whatever's on your mind, and say spiteful things to your team. It's a "we" behavior, not a "me" behavior. You're sharing your true motives and feelings to help the team, project, or organization succeed. *Transparency should be done with clear purpose and respect for the team.*

Case in Point When a team member arrives late to a team meeting, it's common for the person to apologize and then give a "transparent" justification—for example, "Sorry I'm late. I was on an important, long conference call; we covered a lot of critical topics and we were voting on a new proposal and I had to stay. I hope I didn't miss anything important. Where are you in the meeting?" Is this an inclusive, transparent behavior? As a meeting attendee, is this what you want to hear from a latecomer? Are these explanations for the benefit of the latecomer ("me") or the team ("we")? This behavior is almost always for the benefit of the latecomer—the latecomer wants you to forgive and excuse his or her lateness. Moreover, the latecomer wants you to stop everything and *help him or her catch up* on what was missed—"I hope I didn't miss anything. Where are you in the meeting?" This is a classic "me > we" behavior.

If latecomers truly cared more about the team, their transparency would be focused on helping the team, not themselves —for example, "Sorry I'm late—my bad. Please continue. I'll catch up, and to make up for my tardiness, I'll be glad to take any action items that nobody else wants." Wow! Instead of making *self-serving* excuses, this response is a transparent, accountable, inclusive, "we > me," *team-serving* behavior.

In noninclusive teams, it's common to see poor transparency— communication is a guessing game, and people say things they don't mean or say things to serve themselves and not the team. People spend their time looking for "hidden messages" and nonverbal cues. It becomes a mind game that creates distrust, fear, frustrations, and interpersonal conflicts.

For team transparency to work well, it requires a supportive team culture with team processes that facilitate transparency, such as team feedback, team decision-making, workload reviews, conflict resolution, and project lookbacks. It's critical for team members to feel safe to share their opinions and feelings openly with their team. Remember, team transparency is about keeping the discussion constructive. Use team processes to help depersonalize the interaction. For more on transparency, please see the case-in-point example for the next behavior.

Learning

It takes team discipline, transparency, accountability, and inclusiveness to learn together as a team in reviewing team projects, getting feedback, self-examining what's working and what needs improvement, and taking training together. However, one of the biggest opportunities to increase the value and productivity of your team is to *learn from each other by selflessly sharing information, knowledge, experiences, and skills.* Ideally, everyone should be motivated to share everything (Figure 3.6). This team behavior reduces internal competition, information hoarding, and power conflicts.

In "me > we," noninclusive teams, you don't see much sharing; project lookbacks are rarely conducted, and people are too busy to mentor, partner, coach, and share information with others. For some reason, it's just not in their culture, and leadership hasn't pushed for it. It's truly a missed opportunity. So much know-how is wasted when people leave their teams and take their learnings, expertise, and experiences with them. As a project leader, it is your responsibility to preserve, grow, and share skills and knowledge within your team.

Learning is a proactive behavior. You can facilitate interpersonal learning by establishing team learning processes, such as instituting mentor-mentee relationships and coaching systems, where a less experienced team member works alongside (shadows) a senior member; holding "best practices" sessions where you mutually share new tools and techniques; sharing notes from outside lectures, conferences, and webinars; and conducting team workshops to educate other groups. Team learning builds *interdepen-*

Figure 3.6 Learning requires active sharing

dence and *trust* among team members. These are good "we > me" activities that teach people to look beyond themselves, give to others, and seek to understand, support, and help others. Some of the best learnings are the learnings you get from others.

Case in Point Matt was an experienced, highly respected project manager who formed a new team about a year ago to develop a new capital project management process. He had a diverse team of seven people with different skill sets, experience, ethnicities, and personality types. This mix gave his team the skills, knowledge, and creativity to develop a viable capital project management system, and they were ready to launch it next month. The stress of the launch was showing in the team's behaviors—impatience, complaints, disagreements, and some mild interpersonal conflicts. After Matt conferred with a couple of his team members, it was apparent to him that misunderstandings and miscommunications were occurring among team members.

In that same week, Matt called a "timeout" on the project and scheduled an all-afternoon, "team communications" meeting for the next day. As prework for the meeting, he asked all team members to come prepared to share what they liked and enjoyed about the project so far, their biggest shortfalls or concerns, and what feedback they would like to hear from others about their personal interactions. It was to be a roundtable session where each team member would get a turn to share his or her views and receive feedback. At the meeting, Matt defined the process, set some ground rules, and even had the team do a practice run to ensure everyone understood the process; then he excused himself from the roundtable to give his team the room to speak honestly among themselves. He did join the team later to hear the outcome. However, the outcome is not the point of this case.

"Open and honest team feedback sessions are important for venting and reducing any team frustrations and problems."

In any project, it is normal to encounter occasional team misunderstandings, miscommunications, and mild conflicts; individually, each incident is usually not visibly detrimental, so they are often ignored or tolerated. But these little misunderstandings and miscommunications can accumulate and fester over time and the loop can slowly become pressurized. Your job is to keep these small problems from getting bigger, and that takes team *transparency* and *learning.* Open and honest team feedback sessions are important for venting and reducing any team frustrations and problems. They promote overt honesty and *transparency for the benefit of the team,* and at the same time, the team *learns together* through the process of relieving tension, stress, and pressure in the loop. You can kiddingly call this "group therapy," but it's a proven process for creating greater team trust, transparency, and inclusiveness.

Valuing Individuality

A team is a group of unique individuals working together toward a common goal. Inclusive teams recognize that teamwork requires shared values, processes, and behaviors, but that doesn't mean you should suppress individuality and independent thinking. The ultimate goal is that your personal interests ("me") and the interests of the team ("we") are consistent, and when the team wins, you win also—a win-win relationship.

To achieve a win-win relationship in your team, it's important to understand the values, diversity, motivations, demotivations, likes, and dislikes of your team members (Figure 3.7). As previously discussed, a great place to start is by understanding the different personality types of your team members.

Case in Point A business owner hired a local contractor to update his lighting system in his office. He wanted to install recessed LED lighting over his work area. The contractor was to install the new lighting while the business owner was away on a business trip. The following week, the owner returned from his trip and met with his contractor at the office to receive a briefing on the new lighting system. The contractor proudly showed off his craftsmanship and the great improvements to the office. When the business owner went to turn the lights on over his work area, he couldn't find the light switch. The contractor gave the owner a wry smile and said he had relocated the switch to a "better" spot on the wall. When the owner questioned the new location, the contractor said, "Trust me, this is a better spot. You know, I treat all my jobs as though they are my own office. That's how much I care about my work." The owner took a deep breath and said, "I appreciate your consideration, but I'm the person who works in this office, and I would much rather have the light switch here [pointing to the original location]. When do you think you can move it back?"

This case is about valuing individuality—what makes sense to you may not make sense to others, and what you believe is right may not be right for

Figure 3.7 Treat others as *they* would like to be treated

the other person. Valuing individuality is not about treating people the way *you* want to be treated; it's about treating people the way *they* want to be treated. Inclusive teams that value individuality will calibrate their behaviors to the preferences of others, not vice versa.

In "me > we" teams, people don't make the effort to learn how others like to be treated or aren't interested in adjusting their behaviors to accommodate the other party. The mentality is more one of, "I live by the golden rule—I treat people the way *I* want to be treated," or "If you don't like how I behave toward you, then that's your problem, not mine."

What Does a Highly Inclusive Team Culture Look Like?

You'll know whether your effort to build an inclusive team culture is successful by observing the interactions of your team, especially during times of disruption and change. You should be able to hear, see, and sense the team's mutual honesty, respect, care, motivation, and confidence. Also evident would be the team's demonstration of the six inclusive behaviors—mutual trust, interdependence, accountability, transparency, learning, and valuing individuality. These six critical behaviors are *team behaviors* that motivate members to think of others first and require everyone to practice them together.

People are attracted to teams for the fun and camaraderie (acceptance and belonging), well-being (comfort and happiness), and support (structure and stability), but what motivates an individual to stay in the loop is a belief that working together will also fulfill one's ambitions. It's a "we > me"

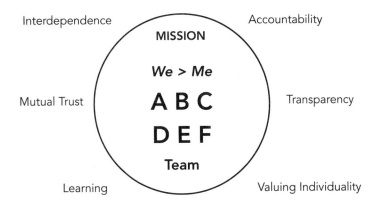

Team members: A, B, C, D, E, F

Figure 3.8 Model for creating highly successful teams

attitude with a "win-win" goal—both the team and individual team members are getting what they want. A highly inclusive team recognizes that team members are not simply workers who should think, act, and be treated the same way. In fact, treating everyone the same is exclusionary—you're not allowing people to express who they are. Let's not forget that each person is unique, with a different background and particular skills, knowledge, talents, and experiences. Thus, each team member is represented by a different letter in our final model of a highly successful team (Figure 3.8).

To some, the team loop and the six inclusive behaviors may seem idealistic and a stretch to apply to your workplace; however, the point of this chapter is to demonstrate what can be possible and to inspire you to move toward the "high" behavior, knowing that it represents the ultimate standard in building a highly successful team.

Skill Three Summary

Skill Three is about building a highly successful team, which is defined as a group of people working together with a common purpose of meeting and exceeding stakeholder expectations through superior collaboration, team commitment, and selfless behavior.

The most important human factor in building highly successful teams is team inclusiveness, which means having a team that makes each member feel accepted, included, respected, relevant, recognized, and valued. It's a state of being in the loop and feeling connected, informed, valued, and motivated. No one likes to feel rejected, disliked, or inferior, yet it happens frequently in the workplace. Exclusion is probably the single greatest cause of people's unhappiness at work and is considered a silent killer of team effectiveness.

The loop represents a place of team acceptance, belonging, interconnection, and shared purpose. It's like a second home—a place of safety, sharing, trust, fun, camaraderie, and support. Inclusiveness comes from a shared belief that the team comes first, we work for each other, and no one person is more important than the team—a "we over me" (we > me) attitude. To attain team inclusiveness, it requires a continuous, selfless effort toward a shared goal. You can't have a highly successful team unless you have an inclusive team with a unified purpose.

Inclusiveness requires extra effort and energy, and it's not something that happens naturally when people are brought together as a team. A team is a true melting pot of different people, ideas, and styles. As a team leader, your job is to consolidate the diverse backgrounds, skills, talents, and ambitions of individuals and create a single, sharply focused team with shared beliefs and goals.

Clearly, the ultimate challenge of project team leadership is to build an inclusive team culture and spirit where "we" prevails over "me" and individual and team success are truly tied together (win-win). It takes six key team behaviors to create an inclusive team culture: mutual trust, interdependence, accountability, transparency, learning, and valuing individuality.

Without a doubt, the resource that matters most in any organization is people. Whether you are managing a business, work team, or project, you want to maximize people's commitment, motivation, and output. The ideal state for a team is one in which everyone is performing at his or her highest level and feeling motivated, respected, recognized, and relevant. Achieving this state takes a lot of time, hard work, and sacrifice, but the one human factor that makes projects and teams successful is *team inclusiveness*.

Skill Three Memory Card

Building Highly Successful Teams
Create an Inclusive Loop

---

1. Establish "the Loop": Team acceptance, belonging, interconnection, and safety
2. Have a Team Mission: Establish a clear and inspiring shared purpose
3. Know People's Personality Types: Understand what drives people in and out of the loop
4. Foster a "We > Me" Culture: Team comes first—"we" is unifying, "me" divisive
5. Remember the Tuna Fish Sandwich: Inclusiveness prevents conflicts; use the "you-me-we" sandwich to build collaboration
6. Practice the Six Inclusive Behaviors:
   - *Mutual trust*—We presume everyone has good intentions and acts in the best interest of the team
   - *Interdependence*—We work together as a single unit, no one works alone
   - *Accountability*—A failing of one is a failing of all—we seek solutions, not blame
   - *Transparency*—We express the motives behind our actions for the benefit of the team, not ourselves
   - *Learning*—We glady share everything: information, knowledge, tools, and skills
   - *Valuing individuality*—We treat others as *they* want to be treated

SKILL FOUR

How to Boost People's Attitudes, Happiness, and Performance
The Ice Cream Cone

You can find pockets of highly functional work teams in any organization. With a combination of strong leadership, a compelling mission, good resources, effective processes, talented people, and inclusive behaviors, you have a great formula for generating excellent results. We have established that behavior drives team performance and that the six key team behaviors are mutual trust, interdependence, accountability, transparency, learning, and valuing individuality. These behaviors are important for preventing exclusion, reducing conflicts, and maintaining the loop, but how do you maximize people's performance? What is the secret for getting that extra, discretionary effort from people when you need it? Also, the new generation of workers wants much more than just challenging projects, team camaraderie and a biweekly paycheck. How do you keep people happy and satisfied with their work? How do you ensure continued high team commitment? All teams and individuals have their ups and downs—how do you invigorate a team when things get a bit dull? These are some of the questions we will be addressing in Skill Four.

**CASE 4.1: THE ICE CREAM CONE—THE IMPORTANCE
OF KEEPING A GOOD ATTITUDE**

This story is about a young boy named Charlie who loved ice cream. Charlie was in the fifth grade and attended a local grammar school that was close enough that he could walk to school each day. When Charlie behaved well at school and did his weekly chores at home, his mother would leave work early on Friday, drive to his school, and surprise him with an after-school trip to the toy store or ice cream shop. Charlie loved both places, but on a warm afternoon nothing was better than ice cream.

The neighborhood ice cream store was a small shop with a big glass front that attracted customers with its bright neon signs advertising ice cream, milk shakes, and malts, and its window panes were adorned with painted rainbows and balloons. Inside, the store owner always stood in the gangway between the back counter and the front ice cream cases and would serve up big scoops of ice cream while his customers watched. Behind the ice cream cases was a long counter packed with mixers, glassware, ice cream cones, silverware, and containers of chocolate syrup, nuts, cherries, crushed pineapple, bananas, and chocolate sprinkles. But the best thing about the ice cream store was not the decorations, the toppings, or even the ice cream; it was the *atmosphere*—the place was full of happiness, excitement, laughter, energy, and the aromas of candy, ice cream, hot fudge, and other sweet toppings that filled the shop's air. It was a joyful, sensational experience just to be there.

On this day, Charlie and his mother ordered their favorites—a big chocolate ice cream cone for him and a scoop of strawberry ice cream in a cup for his mom. The store owner skillfully placed a large scoop of chocolate ice cream onto a cone and handed the delight to the anxious boy. It felt great to get an ice cream cone. Regardless of your age, the process, anticipation, and joy of getting an ice cream cone makes it one of those pleasurable moments in life.

When Charlie received his ice cream, his mother told him, "Now, Charlie, go get a napkin before that ice cream gets on your clothes." The obedient son rushed over to the napkin dispenser, but as he pulled the napkin out with one hand, his other hand drooped, causing his scoop of ice cream to fall to the floor. In a panic, he dropped to the floor to retrieve his scoop, but his mom stopped him and said, "Don't touch that. We have to throw that away now." As the boy sadly looked at his empty cone, his mom said, "I'm sorry about your ice cream, but you should always remember to keep your cone up." Charlie tried to do the right thing, but he lost his ice cream. One moment he was happily holding an ice cream cone, and a second later, he was unhappy, disappointed, and frustrated and holding an empty cone.

Looking down at his fallen ice cream, the boy exclaimed, "It's not fair, Mom—you made me get a napkin and the ice cream fell off!" And as he angrily tried to throw his cone away, his mom stopped him and said, "Charlie, don't throw away your cone. If you do, you won't get any more ice cream. Don't you want ice cream?" Charlie quickly said, "What do you mean, Mom?" She replied, "Let's first clean up this ice cream and then you take your cone up to that nice man over there and tell him what happened." After wiping up the fallen ice cream, Charlie slowly walked to the counter and told his story to the owner. The store owner gave a sympathetic smile, thanked the boy for cleaning up the ice cream, and graciously topped off his empty cone with another scoop of chocolate. The boy felt relieved, restored, and happy again.

The mother thanked the kind owner, and as they were leaving the store, she said to her son, "Now, don't forget . . . ," but before she could finish, Charlie said, "I know Mom, *keep my cone up.*" The mother turned to her son and said, "That's right, Charlie. But more than that, whenever you lose your ice cream or something bad happens, don't get mad, blame other people,

> *"Don't behave badly when bad things happen. It only makes things worse. Do something good when bad things happen and it will turn out better for you."*

or throw your cone away—that's being bad. *Don't behave badly when bad things happen. It only makes things worse. Do something good when bad things happen and it will turn out better for you.* Thanks for being so good in cleaning up the ice cream and telling the man what happened." "And I got my ice cream!" replied Charlie. Smiling, his mother said, "Yes, you did Charlie. You did good."

Lessons from the Story

This story shows that people naturally have good and bad experiences, whether they're in an ice cream shop or at work, and the one human factor that determines how well people respond to good or bad things is their *attitude*. Attitude makes a big difference in people's performance; people carry their attitudes everywhere, and it shows in their behavior. Team leaders play a vital and influential role in managing employee attitude and motivation. Charlie's story embodies five key lessons about managing people's attitude and behaviors at work.

Everyone Likes to Be Rewarded with Ice Cream

Charlie was being rewarded with ice cream for his good behavior. Ice cream is a universal treat that is associated with happiness and fun. Everyone enjoys and longs for ice cream. In any workplace, you'll find people working hard, creating new ideas, and contributing to their teams and organization in hopes that their work will get noticed, praised, and *treated* with "ice cream." In this new model, *ice cream symbolizes praise, recognition, acknowledgment, encouragement, respect, gratitude, affirmation, and other positive feelings*. Charlie was given ice cream in more ways than one—he got his reward but he also got treated nicely by his mom and the ice cream store owner. Employee satisfaction is highly dependent on rewards, recognition, and how they are treated by their supervisor and others at work. As a team leader, treating people right and giving deserved recognition (ice cream) are effective ways to increase employee happiness, motivation, and team performance.

A great team leader is one who makes others feel good about themselves and their work. Charlie loved it when his mom left work early to surprise him and treat him to an ice cream cone for his good behavior. People feel good about themselves whenever they are rewarded with praise, appreciation, respect, and kindness (ice cream). What makes ice cream so motivating is not so much the ice cream per se but rather the excitement, process, and anticipation of receiving it. And those feelings of anticipation and excitement are reflected in people's attitudes; in this story, Charlie's feelings were reflected in his cone. *The cone symbolizes one's attitude.* Good things happened when Charlie kept his cone up, whereas bad things happened when he let it droop down. Everyone carries a cone

"A great team leader is one who makes others feel good about themselves and their work."

in life, hoping to get some ice cream, and when your cone gets filled with ice cream, it's very affirming, validating, and comforting. You feel well treated and happy.

Good Things Happen When You Keep Your Cone Up

As we saw with Charlie, when things go badly, you want to throw away or drop your cone (negative attitude) and you feel down, angry, frustrated, and sorry for yourself. When you keep your cone up (positive attitude), you are able to face your problem, see what went wrong, and learn from it. Moreover, it gives you *hope* that something good can still happen, that you're ready and able to accept something good or better— like another scoop of ice cream. Good things happen and you get better treatment when you keep your cone up. As a team leader, help employees keep their attitudes (cones) up even when bad things happen.

Stuff Happens—What You Do Afterward Is What Matters Most

Unfair things happen in the workplace, and employees can feel bitter, frustrated, and angry. And when employees feel victimized, it is not uncommon for them to lash out, get defensive, and seek blame. Charlie blamed his mishap on his mother, and he wanted to leave the ice cream on the floor, toss out his cone, and leave. In the workplace, these negative emotions can lead to avoidance, dissension, and passive-aggressive behaviors. Unjust things happen at work; however, *what matters most is not what happened but what happens afterward.* You can't always control the outcome of your actions, but you do have control over your subsequent attitude and behaviors. As a team leader, it's unlikely that you can prevent all circumstances leading to personal injustices, but you can have a bearing on the consequences and how employees respond to bad outcomes.

"Getting coned occurs when you do something good and expect to get rewarded, but the ice cream never arrives and you're left holding an empty cone." It's a choice: you can sulk, seek blame, and behave badly after bad things happen, or you can carry a positive attitude and behave productively and responsibly. As Charlie's mother puts it, *"Don't behave badly when bad things happen. It only makes things worse. Do something good when bad things happen and things will turn out better."*

People Feel Coned When Good Deeds Go Unrewarded

When Charlie drooped his cone and lost his ice cream, he was immediately sad; his attitude became negative, and he felt more punished than praised. He felt down, standing there with an empty cone with no ice cream—*Charlie got "coned."* Getting coned occurs when you do something good and expect to get rewarded, but the ice cream never arrives and you're left holding an empty cone, which makes you feel sad and disappointed.

Getting coned also happens at work. People do the right thing, follow instructions, and demonstrate the right behaviors, but due to misfortune or a blind eye, their good efforts go unnoticed or underappreciated. The lack of recognition and appreciation (getting coned) is one of the main reasons for people's dissatisfaction and discouragement at work.

Cases in Point Urgent report. Your project manager asks you to work extra hours over the weekend to complete an important report for a client, and on Monday morning, you email the finished ten-page report to him on time. After seeing no subsequent replies from your manager, you're anxious to know whether he received it and whether your hard work was appreciated. You text your manager, and he replies, "Yes, I got it. There's a bad typo on page six and several pages have the wrong header. Please correct asap." You just got coned— no ice cream for you.

Cost cutting. Your manager introduces a new cost-reduction initiative to save on travel expenses by having employees stay at lower-cost hotels. After three months, she wants to know how the new policy is working out and makes an appointment to meet with you. You gather feedback from your team and discover great unhappiness and discontent among your employees about the new travel policy—the discount hotels were more distant from their clients and the rooms were much noisier, which resulted in poor sleep and greater stress. Also, due to extra transportation costs and inconveniences, the cost savings were meager. At your meeting, you deliver the unfavorable news openly, honestly, and respectfully to your manager, who responds, "It always amazes me how spoiled you guys are. You make a good salary and are treated so well, yet when we ask for a little sacrifice for the good of the company, you whine about it. Why is the attitude so bad in your team?" Instead of appreciating your openness and good efforts, you get no ice cream and get coned as the messenger.

Training ideas. A team meeting is held to explore ideas to improve the training of new employees on the company's internal email and messaging system. Although most of your colleagues don't think it is worthwhile to draft and propose ideas, you take the extra initiative and time to research it, speak to experts in the area, and draft several ideas to share at the meeting. After you present your ideas, members of the team state that they think most of them are "way over the top," "probably too costly," and "off the mark." Just when you are about to explain your ideas, the project manager enters the room and announces, "Let's not waste our time on this; after giving further thought to the issue, I think I'm going to seek internal help from IT to develop the training program. What do you think?" The team praises their manager for the idea and everyone is happy but you. You're left holding an empty cone.

These short cases are sad but true. In the workplace, you can feel coned when your ideas are ignored, your work goes unnoticed, your achievements aren't recognized, you're passed over for new opportunities, or you feel unfairly treated. Perhaps it wasn't intentional, but you feel disappointed. Workers feel coned when they feel disrespected, betrayed, criticized, blamed, underappreciated, and micromanaged. It is well recognized that insensitivity, poor interpersonal behaviors, and bad treatment can take the joy and ice cream out of any job. It's not hard for employees to find reasons for feeling empty or coned at work. But as a team leader, you can play a vital role by motivating and recognizing employees with more ice cream (praise, respect, gratitude, acknowledgment, encouragement) and not leaving your employees feeling coned. In most workplaces, employees are holding their cones high, ready and hoping to get ice cream. Unfortunately, their cones don't get filled as often as they like. But you can learn to fill that void.

Reward the Behavior, Not the Outcome

Unhappy experiences can happen to good people in good places with good intentions. A boy dropping his ice cream while grabbing a napkin to please his mother is analogous to an employee getting reprimanded because he dropped a personal task in favor of solving a priority problem for a key customer. The employee believes that he was doing the right thing, but sometimes it results in an undesirable outcome. But as a team leader, you should *focus on the behavior, not the outcome*. You can control your own behaviors but not necessarily the outcome. Recognize good behaviors, even when there's a bad outcome, and *take responsibility, not blame*, when results are unfavorable. Charlie's mother had her son take responsibility by cleaning up the spilled ice cream instead of arguing about who was to blame. In the long run, keeping your cone up and doing the right thing increases your likelihood of a favorable treatment and outcome.

Summary

Charlie's story illustrates a number of principles about people's attitudes and motivations: everyone likes to be rewarded with ice cream; good things happen when you keep your cone up; stuff happens—what you do afterward is what matters most; people feel coned when good deeds go unrewarded; and recognize the behavior, not the outcome. We will now build on these concepts and show how you can apply them to raise people's attitudes in the workplace.

The Different Attitude Levels of People

It is essential for team leaders to understand the relationship between attitude and performance. In the following sections, we will use the ice cream cone model to help you visualize and recognize the different attitude levels of people, know what drives positive and negative attitudes and low and high performers, and learn how to improve people's attitudes, performance, and happiness. In our ice cream cone model (Figure 4.1), the cone is open and circular on top and gradually narrows and closes as you descend to the bottom of the cone. How you carry your cone—up, down, or in between—depends on your attitude. Of course, when you have ice cream loaded on top, you are apt to keep it upright in your hand. *How you carry your cone is a metaphor for your attitude.* Keeping your cone up is about maintaining a positive, confident, can-do attitude analogous to keeping your chin up. Feeling up or down is a conscious choice—you can change your attitude at any time.

The ice cream cone has three levels—the *lower cone*, the *upper cone*, and the *ice cream* on top—and each level represents a different aspect of your attitude:

▲ When you're mentally in your *upper cone*, you are carrying an "up," positive, can-do, open-minded, trusting, transparent, collaborative, and productive outlook. The openness in your thinking is symbolized by the large, open, upper part of the cone. This is a common characteristic of high performers.

▲ When you're mentally in your *lower cone* and feeling *down*, you are carrying a negative, "can't-do," closed-minded, doubtful, and exclusionary attitude. Closed-mindedness and a lack of transparency are common as you get further down in your attitude or cone. Exclusion and the lack of transparency are symbolized by the small, narrow, lower end of the cone. This is a common characteristic of low performers.

▲ When your cone is topped with ice cream, you are highly motivated. You feel praised, respected, and valued. You are accomplished, successful, and fulfilled. Having a full ice cream cone means you are being treated well and feeling satisfied and happy. You feel like a top performer.

Why is this ice cream cone model an essential people skill for team leaders? It is well recognized that attitude makes a big difference in how people work and interact with others. Attitude is a key human factor that

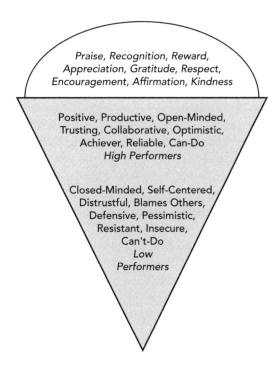

Praise, Recognition, Reward,
Appreciation, Gratitude, Respect,
Encouragement, Affirmation, Kindness

Positive, Productive, Open-Minded,
Trusting, Collaborative, Optimistic,
Achiever, Reliable, Can-Do
High Performers

Closed-Minded, Self-Centered,
Distrustful, Blames Others,
Defensive, Pessimistic,
Resistant, Insecure,
Can't-Do
Low
Performers

Figure 4.1 The ice cream cone model

is shaped by how you are treated by others, especially by your supervisor. How you treat an employee and what actions you take to sustain a desired behavior can quickly affect a person's attitude. The three levels of the ice cream cone are not separate but rather a continuum. Your mood and attitude can cycle up and down, as Charlie experienced when he received and dropped his ice cream, respectively. As we will further discuss in this model and later in Skill Five, you have to know what's keeping people down or up and work hard to keep everyone positive and motivated. Your challenge is to minimize the time people spend in their lower cone and maximize their time in the upper cone. This takes keen awareness and skill.

> *"Your challenge is to minimize the time people spend in their lower cone and maximize their time in the upper cone."*

What Drives Positive and Negative Attitudes

People perform at a higher level when they feel appreciated, accomplished, well treated, and happy. People have the ability to keep a positive, can-do attitude even when things aren't going well. *The ability and inability to maintain a positive attitude and also help others feel good about themselves and their work are the key differences between good and bad leaders and high- and low-performing teams.* That can-do, confident, collaborative, optimistic attitude comes from repeated, recognized achievements.

In contrast, when people feel that they are underachieving, unsuccessful, and unrecognized, they can become down, pessimistic, demotivated, insecure, and negative. As a result, they withdraw, get more narrow-minded and self-protective, and sink to the lower end of their cone. Without any ice cream, they become less interested in taking risks, trying new ideas, and making changes. When motivation drops, people tend to disengage. You can offset this decline by giving ice cream to your deserving employees—ice cream *psychologically moves people* to the top end of their cones (Figure 4.1).

It's important to recognize the characteristics of low versus high performers and how they carry their respective cones.

Low Performers

People with poor attitudes have lost their hunger for ice cream and their motivation for achievement. They accept the status quo and are content to do the minimum and blame their loss of appetite (enthusiasm) on outside factors, claiming, "The work is boring," "It's not worth it to put in extra effort," "No one listens to me anyway," and "What I say doesn't matter." They are your classic *low performers.* To make matters worse, low performers are known to be less tolerant and can easily have meltdowns and adversely affect others at work. The further down they go, the more they become discontent, disengaged, and difficult. They don't want to expose themselves, so they prefer to stay deep inside their cones.

A poor attitude is a learned behavior. When you run into people who possess a bad attitude, you often find that their attitude has been lowered by past disappointments and perceived poor treatment. It's likely that their enthusiasm toward work has been repeatedly coned along the way due to their own actions (resulting in mental baggage, regrets, bitterness) or due to other people's behaviors (such as excessive criticism, abusive boss). They have learned that it is safer to stay uninvolved and not take chances.

Low performers are not bad people, and they usually want to perform better. Project leaders can make a big difference and restore that motivation by creating a safe environment for down employees to come forward.

You can't read people's minds, but you can encourage employees to come forth when things aren't going well for them. If you're interested in knowing how to correct low performers, see Skill Five.

High Performers

Workers who have a good attitude are typically highly motivated, are confident, and want to do a good job. They work well with others, enjoy working in a team, and always meet your high expectations. They have a can-do, engaging attitude. Employees who are highly productive, strongly committed, collaborative, and open-minded and do high quality work are known as *high performers*. They are the mainstay of any organization and work hard every day to earn their ice cream, which energizes them to do even better work. You can't have enough high performers.

How to Improve the Attitude and Performance of Your Team

Being a good project leader is easy when things are going well and the work is successful; it's much tougher when expectations aren't being met and people feel overworked and discouraged. How often do you help people keep their cones up (good attitude and motivation), especially when the going gets tough? It sure feels nice when everyone is succeeding (lots of full cones), but when things go badly and people get stressed, they are at risk of dropping their cones and feeling down. Also, when things aren't going well, bad managers not only withhold ice cream; they knock people's cones down by criticizing, blaming, intimidating, and shaming people instead of giving encouragement.

> "When things aren't going well, bad managers not only withhold ice cream; they knock people's cones down by criticizing, blaming, intimidating, and shaming people."

Charlie's mom stepped in when Charlie had his mishap, and instead of scolding him for his inattentiveness, she helped him get back on a positive track, which paid off for everyone.

During stormy times at work, it's important for team leaders to help employees regain their self-confidence and motivation to move forward. When bad things happen to good people, good managers step in, encourage them, and help them restore their trust, confidence, and hope. If their cones are up, employees are more likely to continue contributing.

CASE 4.2: THE FINGER CUT—FOCUS ON THE BEHAVIOR, NOT THE OUTCOME

Susan is a junior member of the company's research and development (R&D) team, specializing in lubricants and greases. Her team runs a pilot plant that is located on the outskirts of their property, and one of Susan's responsibilities is running test samples back and forth between the research lab and the pilot plant. It's not the most exciting job, but Susan likes it and it shows—she is eager, enthusiastic, and energetic.

For the company, worker safety is considered a high priority. To support that priority, each year management gives out salary bonuses for teams with zero on-the-job injuries and auto accidents. It's almost the end of the year, and Susan's R&D team is on target to receive their zero-incident safety award. However, late in the day, while she is taking samples to the pilot plant, one of the sample jars is cracked and she cuts her finger while picking it up. It's a small cut, but she isn't able to stop the bleeding and goes to the nurse's office to get it treated. While there, she asks the nurse, "Is this cut reportable?" The nurse replies, "If it bleeds, it's reportable." Reluctantly, Susan fills out an injury incident form. When she returns to the lab and a couple of team members hear of the injury, they immediately express their disappointment and question Susan about her actions—"Why did you go to Medical?" "Why did you fill out the form?" "Do you know your actions just cost us our bonus pay?" Susan feels awful about it, apologizes, and just wants to head home. Before leaving, she thinks she'd better let her supervisor, Rod, know what happened. This is going to hurt more than the cut. Rod is as sharp and stern as they come, especially when it comes to safety.

Susan goes to Rod's office, meekly taps on the door, and says, "May I come in, Rod? There's something that you should know." Rod gestures her in and says, "Okay, what should I know?" Susan draws a deep breath and solemnly says, "I messed up, Rod. I did something awful, it was my fault, and I feel I have let everyone down." Rod interrupts, "So tell me what you did that was so bad." Her voice half-trembling, Susan looks contrite and says,

"I cut my finger on a bad sample jar and had to go to Medical to get it bandaged and it was reportable." Susan braces herself for the worst. Rod looks at Susan and immediately asks, "Is your finger okay?" "Well, the finger's fine, but I feel just terrible about the cut and then reporting it—that was dumb; it means we lose our bonus. I'm so sorry." Rod looks straight at Susan and says, "Susan, I'm glad your cut is minor. Please take care of it. And I know you're going to get some grumblings from your team about it, but they'll get over it. There's no reason for you to feel bad. You did the right thing and I fully support what you did." "Really?" said Susan. Rod continues, "You did good—you followed company procedures. Thank you. But please do me a favor and contact our safety officer to conduct a review of what happened and then share with us what you learned so that we can prevent this in the future." Susan walks out feeling 100 percent better than when she walked in.

Lessons from the Story

This story reinforces several key lessons regarding the importance of attitude:

▲ **Your attitude is like a cone.** Susan carried a good attitude, but just like in Charlie's story, it was suddenly changed when she "messed up" and "let everyone down" with her accident—she felt awful. No doubt, it affected her mood and behavior. Stuff happens to good people.

▲ **People feel coned when their good deeds go unrewarded.** The zero-injury, no accident bonus was a good incentive for safe behavior, but the team felt coned (no ice cream this year) and expressed their disappointment when Susan let them down.

▲ **Good things happen when you keep your cone up.** Susan wanted to escape from the situation but took a chance in reporting the incident to her supervisor. She was down, but she didn't hide from the incident—she could have concealed the injury and gone home, but she kept her cone up in reporting the accident to the company, her team, and her supervisor.

▲ **What you do afterward is what matters most—reward the behavior, not the outcome.** Rod didn't like that Susan was hurt and the outcome was not favorable for his team, but he kept his emphasis on her behavior after the injury, not the outcome. As Rod put it, "you did the right thing" and "followed company procedures." Was the accident preventable? Was Susan's handling of the sample jars unsafe? Rod refrained from judging Susan or the incident until a review was performed. Also, Rod understood that a lesser person might have tried to cover up the injury, but Susan responded in the right way—that's what matters most.

▲ **A successful team leader is one who makes others feel good about themselves.** Rod could have yelled, reprimanded Susan, and knocked her cone down for getting injured and reporting it, but he knew better. When bad things happen to good people, good managers step in, encourage them, and help them restore their trust, confidence, and hope.

Summary

Even though she lost her ice cream (no bonus) and let her team down, Susan kept her cone up and, like Charlie, was subsequently rewarded and received a special type of ice cream (reassurance, positive feedback, and kindness) from her supervisor. Sometimes the best ice cream that you can give someone is your encouragement, patience, listening, and forgiveness. Susan felt uplifted after her meeting with Rod, but more importantly, the memory and feelings of Rod's encouragement and support will stick with her much longer than the loss of the bonus. People always remember how they were treated during difficult times. Remember, *stuff happens. What matters most is what happens afterward*—both Susan and Rod acted admirably after the accident.

"Sometimes the best ice cream that you can give someone is your encouragement, patience, listening, and forgiveness."

Empowerment Raises People's Attitudes

You can help people keep their cones up by giving four empowerments: *responsibility, opportunity, encouragement,* and *recognition.* Preferably, providing new responsibilities and opportunities to employees is what you do *before* the work is performed; encouraging employees is what you do *during* the work; and giving recognition is what you do *during and after* the work is performed.

- ▲ **Responsibility:** People need to feel important, involved, and challenged. Giving people meaningful work helps them feel valued, relevant, and purposeful, which raises their self-esteem. When you give employees responsibility, it builds accountability and sends a strong message of trust.

- ▲ **Opportunity:** Everyone seeks continuous opportunities to learn, grow, and develop. New opportunities require your support in helping people see the potential benefits for them, the team, and organization, otherwise people won't be motivated to take the risk. A lack of opportunities causes people to settle gradually into the lower "comfort zone" of their cone. Their work becomes hopelessly routine. Opportunity creates *hope,* which is one of the most powerful motivators of performance.

- ▲ **Encouragement:** The hardest part of any project occurs in the middle of the game. This is where you often encounter bottlenecks and problems, and it takes the right skills, knowledge, experience, and, most importantly, encouragement to solve those problems. You essentially have to be a coach, trainer, mentor, counselor, and cheerleader to help the team move forward. As in Susan's story, *it's amazing what an encouraging word at the right time can mean to an employee who is struggling.* However, keep in mind that encouragement does not only mean giving pep talks; it also necessitates giving constructive feedback on what the employee is specifically doing well and what opportunities you see for improvement.

- ▲ **Recognition:** Giving employees affirmations, praise, and rewards is a powerful way to increase motivation. People have a basic need to feel accepted, wanted, and valued. They will keep their cones up as long as they have faith that their efforts will be rewarded. For the project leader, recognition serves to reinforce desired behaviors— *what gets recognized gets repeated.* This subject will be further discussed in Skill Six.

How to Treat People the Right Way for Maximum Impact

Have you ever given ice cream to your employees at work? Of course, the ice cream cone is only a metaphor and the thought of passing out ice cream at work sounds corny, but the challenging question to you as a team leader is, how often do you give recognition to your employees? Giving ice cream is another *triple winner* (like team processes in Skill One) because it keeps people's cones up (anticipation and attitude), it's an action that everyone wants (joy of receiving ice cream), and it reinforces people's hopes, ambitions, and commitment (to work for more).

To increase employee and team performance and reinforce desired behaviors, give more ice cream at work. There are many different types of ice cream that you can regularly give to your employees (Table 4.1).

All ice creams—whether it's getting a promotion, added responsibilities, or a pat on the back—may seem great for a while, but they will eventually melt away, often too quickly. Good leaders are mindful of the attitudes of their workers and are great at spotting "melt offs" and replenishing people's ice cream cones with different types and flavors. Also, people's motivation, energy, and enthusiasm will wane from time to time. As in Susan's story, everyone has good, great, and bad days at work. It's the role of project leaders to help keep their employees' cones filled and give people added incentives when needed.

Table 4.1 Ice Creams You Can Serve at Work

On-the-Spot	Individuals	Teams	Special
• "Thank you" Gift Cards: "Let me buy you lunch today!"; "Dinner is on me!"; "Enjoy a dessert!"; "Time for a shopping spree!" • Appreciation Gift: Vouchers for movies, museums, a day at the spa, lunch with coworkers, free ice cream • "Gift of Time" Pass: "Work-from-home day," "Leave work early day," "Take a break day," "Take a road trip"	• Priceless: Treat people with praise, respect, compliments, positive feedback, listening, encouragement, patience, empathy • Customized Gift: Give recognitions that fit the person's interests • Celebratory Gift: Chocolates, fruit, flowers, special lunch • Experiential Reward: Travel voucher, guided tour, sporting event, dining experience • Privilege: Reserved parking place, gym membership, company car, company credit card	• Celebratory: Special team luncheon, BBQ, picnic, food truck event, ice cream social • Team Recognition: Shout-outs at team meetings; managment-to-team, customer-to-team, peer-to-peer recognitions • Community Service Project: Fund-raiser, food bank, toy drive, park clean-up, support schools • Fun Team Outing: Trip to zoo, aquarium, museum, sport event, concert, show • Learn Together: Fitness, cooking class, dance class, yoga • Do Something Outrageous: Costume party, karaoke, treasure hunt	• Monetary: Bonuses and salary increases • Status: Job promotion, increases in authority or responsibility, lead a new project • Benefits: More vacation days, flexible work days or hours, business travel • Career Enhancement: Attend professional conference/lecture, learn new skills, leadership development, cross-training oppurtunity, mentoring
Types of Ice Cream to Avoid			
Trinkets, humorous certificates, generic plaques, obnoxious T-shirts, office paraphernalia, belated recognitions, cheap rewards, insincere praise, sarcasm, backhanded compliments			

The Right Way to Give Ice Cream

There's more to serving ice cream than just giving it out. If you have ever visited a great ice cream parlor, you know that there are skills and techniques involved in serving ice cream that create a wonderful customer experience. Giving recognition is like serving ice cream—it requires good skills and techniques.

In a 2011 American Psychological Association survey of 1,546 U.S. workers, more than two-thirds (69 percent) of employed adults were satisfied with their jobs (13). However, less than half of the workers (46 percent) were satisfied with the recognition practices of their employers. Also, it has been observed that supervisors commonly overestimate the frequency with which they recognize their employees and their effectiveness in doing so. It's not that supervisors don't recognize and reward employees—they just don't do it well.

The key to giving effective employee recognition is to SCOOP your ice cream: *sincerity, consistency, on time, on values,* and *personalized.*

- ▲ **Sincerity:** Fear of appearing disingenuous is a common barrier to recognizing employees—"I don't like to give recognition because it often appears patronizing or phony," or, "If I give too much recognition, it'll dilute its value." What many team leaders don't realize is that their concerns are likely excuses for their apparent insecurity and lack of skill in giving recognition. The secret to sincerity is this: *be specific to be sincere.* You need to pinpoint exactly what you liked about the employee's work. Don't just say, "Nice job," or, "Thank you for your presentation." These are vague, low-value acknowledgments. It's more effective to say, "In your presentation, I liked your creative graphics, the overall data summaries, and your six conclusions. You spoke clearly and at a good pace and finished on time—well done!"

- ▲ **Consistency:** When it comes to giving rewards and recognitions, employees pay close attention and remember how you treated them and others. You can't play favorites, give different benefits or monetary values for the same value of work, or reward only a few of those who contributed to the accomplishment. You must be consistent in the eyes of your employees. Also, you can't be inconsistent with other team leaders.

- ▲ **On time:** The effectiveness and sincerity of your recognition are reduced when you fail to give ice cream promptly. The best rule of thumb is to give your recognition no later than twenty-four hours after the event or accomplishment, but preferably on the spot.

Building on the previous example, you could say, "Thank you for your excellent presentation *this morning*. I especially liked your creative graphics, the high-grade data summaries, and your six conclusions. You spoke clearly and at a good pace and finished on time—well done!"

▲ **On values:** The best time to speak about team values is when you give rewards and recognition. Relating specific values and desired behaviors to high performance is a powerful way to operationalize your organizational values. It brings your values to life. Values don't appear to matter until they are utilized. Fundamentally, your team's values should serve as the basis for all rewards and recognition in your organization. Values evolve and become part of your culture when they are remembered in success stories and team accomplishments.

> *"Your team's values should serve as the basis for all rewards and recognition."*

▲ **Personalized:** Being more personal with your recognition makes the biggest difference in improving the impact of your recognitions. One of the main reasons that project leaders are ineffective in giving recognition is that employees feel the reward is not personally meaningful to them. Unlike monetary rewards, you can personalize your recognitions and still be consistent. Use these two approaches:

– **Personalize the type of recognition to the employee:** You can improve your recognition by ensuring that the type of recognition is truly valued by the employee and provides what the employee wants. How do you find out? It's simple—ask your employee. When employees join your team, ask them how they prefer to be recognized, what gives them the greatest satisfaction, and what form of recognition means the most to them. Be prepared to provide some specific examples.

Some employees prefer recognition in private, whereas others like to celebrate their good fortune with others. Employees may prefer a formal recognition (letter to the file, performance reviews), extra time off, peer recognition (verbal recognition in front of their team), symbolic award (plaque, certificate of accomplishment), appreciation award (flowers, bottle of wine), or a quiet, personal recognition (handwritten note). Personalizing your recognition sends a strong message that the award is about them and not about you. *Too often, giving recognition is more about the awarder than the awardee.*

- **Personalize the recognition by expressing how the employee's work helped you:** People take great pride in knowing that their hard work made a difference to others and had a positive impact on the organization. It's a shout-out that says, "Your work matters!" Adding this to our ongoing example, you would say, "Thank you for your excellent presentation this morning. Your creative graphics and project data summaries *will help me make improvements to our team communications,* and I agree with your six top conclusions, *which I plan to use in our business plan.* You spoke clearly and at a good pace and finished on time—well done!"

Skill Four Summary

Employee satisfaction is highly dependent on rewards, recognition, and how people are treated by their supervisor and others at work. As a team leader, treating people right and giving deserved recognition (ice cream) are effective ways to increase employee happiness, motivation, and team performance.

Skill Four introduces the important concept of the "ice cream cone" in managing people's attitudes and motivation. The cone represents your attitude, outlook, and mood, and the ice cream symbolizes praise, recognition, rewards, affirmation, respect, kindness, appreciation, and other positive feelings. Everyone carries a cone in life, and you want to fill your employees' cones with ice cream when they work hard and demonstrate desired behaviors. People are at their best when they feel appreciated, valued, and recognized.

Everyone has good and bad days at work, and it's the role of the project leader to help keep everyone positive and motivated, especially during bad times. Managing people is easy when things are going well; it's much tougher when expectations aren't being met and people feel overworked and underappreciated and have a lousy attitude. Attitude is one of the most important human factors in determining team success.

In leading teams, it's important to understand the different attitude levels of people, know what drives positive and negative attitudes, maintain a positive attitude in yourself and your team, and treat people the right way for maximum impact. This skill uses the ice cream cone as a visual model to enhance your understanding of how best to achieve a positive team attitude. It's your job as a team leader to help people keep their cones up.

To increase employee performance, give more ice cream at work. It's not the giving of ice cream that's important but rather the manner and context in which you deliver it. SCOOP your ice cream—give recognition that is *sincere, consistent, on time, on values,* and *personalized.* Ice cream is your best tool for keeping the spirit, camaraderie, and fun in the workplace. However, work stress, interpersonal conflicts, and disappointments can take the joy and ice cream out of any job. Workers feel "coned" when they feel disrespected, betrayed, criticized, unfairly treated, and underappreciated.

When bad things happen and people are feeling down and discouraged, good managers step in and take positive actions to restore trust, confidence, and hope. As a team leader, you want to create a positive and rewarding work environment where people are excited to come to work and, most importantly, where they feel recognized and receive their favorite ice cream. The most successful team leaders are those who make others feel good about themselves and their work.

Skill Four Memory Card

Boost People's Attitudes, Happiness, and Performance
Treat People with Ice Cream

1. Everyone carries an "ice cream cone" that reflects one's attitude, mood, and outlook
2. Good things happen when you "keep your cone up"
3. Ice cream symbolizes praise, recognition, respect, encouragement, gratitude, and affirmation
4. A great team leader is one who makes others feel good about themselves and their work
5. People feel "coned" when their work goes unrecognized or they feel unfairly treated
6. Recognize the behavior, not the outcome
7. Bad stuff happens; what you do afterward is what matters most
8. Raise your team's attitude by empowering people with responsibility, opportunity, encouragement, and recognition
9. When giving ice cream, SCOOP it:
   - Sincerity: Be specific to be sincere
   - Consistency: Don't play favorites or give unequal rewards
   - On Time: Give recognition promptly
   - On Values: Use team values as the key criteria for recognition
   - Personalized: Make sure the recipient feels valued

How to Turn Around Difficult People and Underperformers
Roll the Ball Forward

In the previous skill, the ice cream cone and finger injury cases served as valuable testimonies that attitude is a key determinant of motivation, happiness, and performance. But unfortunately, ice cream is not the solution for all people problems, and not everyone's attitude can be improved with a pat on the back. It's not uncommon to encounter employees who underperform, carry a less than desirable attitude, and make minimal contributions yet they see no problems with their performance or behaviors. These individuals are known as difficult people and underperformers, and it takes a special set of skills to understand and correct these low performers. Difficult and underperforming behaviors are probably the toughest people problems to solve because your options are few and far between. You can't excuse it and reward bad behaviors. You know that doing nothing can be a slow death for your project, so you're left with the unenviable task of confronting the problem employee. Confronting poor performers is a process that most project leaders don't like face, but Skill Five offers a new and effective model for addressing and turning around difficult people and underperformers.

CASE 5.1: WHY WE DON'T CONFRONT POOR PERFORMERS

In 2012, university researchers conducted a survey with a group of sixty-eight local municipal and county supervisors (14). The survey takers were city and county managers, assistant managers, department heads, line managers, and other city and county officials across the state. Survey participants were asked to identify possible reasons that would dissuade them from confronting poor performers. They were also asked to rate the severity of each reason that may preclude supervisors from having performance discussions with low-performing employees. In addition, they were given a scenario of a good worker whose performance had recently slipped and were asked to identify their top reasons for not having a corrective conversation with the employee.

The survey results of the top barriers for supervisors to confront poor performers (and the response rates) were as follows:

▲ I dislike and avoid confrontation. (59 percent)

▲ I have no skills in having difficult conversations. (49 percent)

▲ I do not want to be perceived as tough. (43 percent)

▲ I am not trained to deal with performance issues. (42 percent)

▲ I do not want to get employees in trouble. (41 percent)

▲ Employees actively avoid feedback. (39 percent)

▲ Supervisors fear creating a negative work environment. (32 percent)

▲ Laws place unreasonable restrictions. (32 percent)

The top two reasons that respondents gave for not confronting a normally good employee whose performance had started to decline were the following:

▲ I did not want to create a negative work environment. (55 percent)

▲ Confrontation makes me uncomfortable. (47 percent)

Lessons from the Story

Because supervisors worry that corrective feedback can be very unsettling to employees and can provoke backlash (anger, complaints, resentment), they avoid the confrontation. However, what they may not realize is that inaction has its own consequences and passivity usually makes the problem worse. And when the problem gets too severe, team leaders are known to switch from passive to clever and take the ultimate escape route—transferring the problem employee to another supervisor.

People problems are like land mines—no one wants to go there. Most team leaders dread facing interpersonal conflicts. They have more excuses for deferring actions on problem employees than any other workplace issue, and it's a behavior that is prevalent in almost every organization.

Summary

It's clear from the results that these supervisors disliked and avoided delivering disappointing news to their employees and feared creating a negative work environment, and their reluctance appeared to be due to their lack of skills in confronting and having corrective discussions with low performers. Although this survey was only a small cohort, the conclusions were clear—there are many barriers that preclude supervisors from taking action to correct low-performing employees.

The Ten Toughest People to Work With

At the University of California at Berkeley, a group of thirty-two experienced project managers convened to discuss current issues in project leadership, and one of the activities was to list the most challenging types of people to supervise. In no time, they were throwing out descriptions and names of people who sounded like characters from a crime syndicate—bully, wisecracker, whiner, undertaker, downer, deadwood, browbeater, saboteur, and grumbler. Needless to say, it was a lively discussion, but at the end, the group was able to compile a list of *the ten toughest people to work with* (no consensus was reached on rank order):

▲ **Jerk:** obnoxious, rude, annoying, irritating, offensive, inconsiderate, unpleasant, interrupts and disrupts others

▲ **Whiner:** frequent complainer, grumbler, griper, highlights problems, likes to raise worries and concerns, hard to satisfy

▲ **Bully:** mean, dominating, demanding, aggressive, controlling, threatening, condescending, enjoys browbeating and embarrassing others

▲ **Know-it-all:** outspoken, arrogant, egotistical, wisecracker, talks about everything and anything, grandstander, always right, never wrong

▲ **Cynic:** resistant to change, skeptical, suspicious of people's motives, "If it ain't broke, don't fix it," doom and gloom, distrustful, likes to say, "I told you so"

▲ **Slacker:** low work output, takes shortcuts, ducks responsibility and accountability, last one in but first one out, never volunteers for anything, deadwood, does just enough to stay out of trouble

▲ **Undertaker:** sad, negative, pessimist, fatalist, can put a pall on any subject, never seems happy, a downer to be around

▲ **Victim:** sympathy seeker, injustice collector, emotional, overly sensitive, worrier, blames others, self-pity, "woe is me," "I don't deserve to be treated this way"

▲ **Passive-aggressive:** nonconfrontational, risk averse, distrustful, revengeful, saboteur, deceptively agreeable, emotionally weak

▲ **Procrastinator:** disorganized, easily distracted, time-management challenged, idler, unfocused, slow starter, an expert on excuses, defers to others

What do all these people have in common? They are the most challenging employees to supervise and are commonly known as difficult people and underperformers. We use fun and amusing names to label these low performers, but there's nothing fun and amusing about them. They can significantly affect the morale, productivity, and reputation of a work team. The job of the project team leader is to recognize, address, and remedy any cases of low job performance and ensure the high morale and productivity of the team.

Characteristics of Difficult People and Underperformers

Difficult People

Difficult people are people who *impede the progress of others*. They are known to frustrate, distract, and disrupt others by complaining, criticizing, debating, antagonizing, controlling, or exhibiting other unwanted behaviors that adversely affect the progress of projects and work teams. Difficult people are one of the most demotivating human factors when it comes to working together as a team. They reduce the effectiveness of others in doing their work, solving problems, making decisions, collaborating, and enjoying work.

At times, everyone can be difficult, but what distinguishes a truly difficult person is the frequency and intensity of their negative behaviors. Difficult people make it a habit to disrupt, disturb, and discourage other people. Managing difficult people is one of the most challenging and time-consuming issues for today's team leaders.

There is no single profile of a difficult person. They come from all walks of life—young and old, rich and poor, introverted and extraverted, passive and aggressive, emotional and intellectual, and everything in between. Difficult people are unpredictable and can act up at any time and any place. They can act up in one circumstance today and not act up under the same circumstance tomorrow. To make matters worse, difficult people can be difficult in many different ways—including being excessively emotional, cynical, critical, controlling, and annoying. They are multitalented in their abilities to disrupt good projects and give headaches to project team leaders.

Underperformers

In contrast to difficult people, underperformers do not impede the progress of others; they *hamper their own performance* due to their inconsistent, inefficient, and/or unreliable work that can indirectly bring down the performance of their team. Typical underperformers are well meaning, cooperative, compliant, friendly, and supportive. They give a good effort and are capable of doing good work but their output is variable, low, or barely acceptable. They tend to get easily distracted, confused, and stuck.

A variety of human factors can be attributed to underperformance, including low confidence, personal conflicts, poor communication, stress, poor time management, and fear, and it results in low and/or inconsistent performance. Underperformers are as common as or perhaps more common than difficult people. Although being difficult may be considered more damaging because it negatively affects other people, underperformers can also become difficult when they lower the morale of the team due to their persistent low or inconsistent performance.

Under the right circumstances, anyone can be difficult or underperforming at times. Understanding and practicing this skill can help you reduce low-performing behaviors in your team.

How to Get Poor Performers Back on Track

In the workplace, project team leaders are neither trained nor expected to be therapists in dealing with poor performers and their personal problems. However, project leaders are expected to motivate, facilitate, and get the work done on time and with high quality. Since the primary effect of difficult people or underperformers is to impede the progress of others or struggle with their own progress, respectively, the basic strategy in correcting poor performers is to help them *move productively forward*, which means improving their attitude (see Skill Four) and getting the work done— get them to drop those negative, impeding behaviors and choose a more productive path. In other words, your

> "The basic strategy in correcting poor performers is to help them move productively forward."

role as a project leader is to help difficult people and other low performers get off their negative bent, get back on the ball, get into the game, and contribute to the team effort.

Running a successful team project is similar to *rolling a ball forward to a target*, where the "ball" represents your team's project, "rolling" refers to productive actions, "forward" means making continuous progress, and the "target" represents your project goals. To shorten the phrase, we will use "roll the ball forward" to mean executing the team's project with excellence by working together to efficiently implement the project's work plan, complete deliverables, achieve goals, and meet all stakeholder expectations. Execution is the essence of project management, and it requires overcoming problems and barriers. Difficult people and underperformers are key barriers to project success.

As a project leader, it's important to understand the effects of low performers on your project. Difficult people and other types of low performers undermine team projects by hindering their progress. Underperformers are also underachievers (not always on the ball) who struggle to stay on track and are often ineffective, inefficient, and in need of help. In fact, some underperformers are seen as minimalists —they're just along for the ride, doing only what they're told, giving minimal effort, and expecting to get the same recognition and rewards as others.

In contrast, difficult people are more impactful and seemingly want to give a high effort, but instead they expend their energy resisting, resenting, fighting, doubting, or acting in ways that undermine the team's effort. Fundamentally, difficult people are self-centered, controlling, insecure, and fearful and struggle to cooperate, collaborate, and trust the team. They are counterproductive due to their need for control, attention, acceptance, and/ or affirmation. Thus, *underperformers need help and guidance while difficult people need control and attention*. Difficult people create friction, tension, and antagonism, which prevent the ball (project) from rolling productively and efficiently forward. Not only do difficult people bog down the

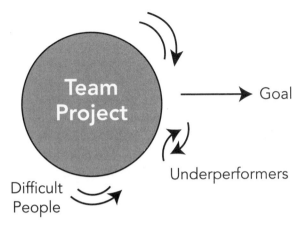

Figure 5.1 Project impeders: difficult people and underperformers

process, they are known to even reverse and roll back the project by causing re-work or extra work for the team (Figure 5.1).

As depicted in Figure 5.1, underperformers and difficult people have different effects on a project:

▲ Underperformers *struggle to keep pace* and tend to get stuck or spin their wheels because they are inconsistent in meeting deadlines, completing assignments, submitting error-free work, maintaining productivity, and staying focused on their work. They do some things well and some things not as well. They want to help the team move forward, contribute to the effort, and be good performers, but due to a variety of problems or conflicts, they can't seem to perform well on a regular basis.

▲ Difficult people impede and *undermine the progress of the team* and projects, resulting in drama, frustration, anger, conflicts, and discontent within the team. Left unchecked, their behaviors demotivate, discourage, and demoralize the team. They disrupt the function and progress of the team, *dragging both themselves and the team down.*

Good project leaders are aware of this dynamic and take prompt actions to ensure that underperformers and difficult people do not persist and drag down the performance of other team members. Using ERAM and the other models and processes described in Skill One, project leaders must properly diagnose, pinpoint, and correct these performance problems with good coaching, performance planning, feedback, and reinforcement,

Table 5.1 Time Perspectives and Effects of Difficult People, Underperformers, and High Performers

	Difficult People (Negative Effect)	Underperformers (Variable Effect)	High Performers (Positive Effect)
Past	Remember past injustices, inequities, and bad experiences; they always have excuses for their problems	Remember the comfort, stability, and security of the past; things were better and easier then	Remember good and bad experiences as positive growth experiences and learnings
Present	Worried and troubled about how things are today; they have an alternate or distorted view of reality	Things are now tougher, faster, and less forgiving; work seems confusing	Enjoy the challenge of solving today's problems; work is rewarding and enjoyable
Future	Fearful, cynical, and skeptical going forward; they see problems ahead	Resistant to changes; feel uncertain about the work, responsibilities, and accountability ahead	Excited to plan and work on new opportunities

including disciplinary actions if needed. As a team ground rule, there should be zero tolerance for poor performance.

The Different Time Perspectives of Difficult People, Underperformers, and High Performers

When you compare difficult people and underperformers with high performers, it becomes clear that each has a very different perspective on the past, present, and future (Table 5.1). To understand why difficult people and underperformers inhibit the progress of the project, it's important to understand their thinking and the motivations behind their behaviors.

▲ Difficult people like to dwell on the *past*, make excuses, believe things are unfavorable today (*present*), and are skeptical and cynical about the *future*. *Every timeframe has potential problems or downsides* in the minds of difficult people. They see barriers where there are no barriers. They can't seem to move productively forward due to perceived problems with the past, present, and/or future. This negative mind-set results in negative behaviors that slow or stop projects.

▲ Underperformers like how things were done in the *past*, dwell on how things are tougher today (*present*), and have concerns about the changes and challenges ahead (*future*). They feel most comfortable with the past, cautious about the present, and uncertain about the future, which leads to variable, unproductive performance.

▲ High performers prefer to learn from the *past*, apply those learnings and take actions to improve their performance today (*present*), and look forward to the opportunities in the *future*. They are humble and grateful for the past, energetic and excited about the present, and optimistic and enthusiastic about the future. High performers drive the ball forward (Figure 5.2).

Note that the dividing line in the table between underperformers and difficult people is thin, which indicates that their perspectives can overlap with each other; the perspective of high performers is more distinct and consistent, and it seldom overlaps with those of underperformers and difficult people, as symbolized by the solid, thick line in the table.

In short, *high performers* value past experiences and are opportunistic and **positive** about the present and future; *underperformers* prefer the pace, stability, and familiarity of the past and are more uncertain and **variable** about the present and future; and *difficult people* carry bad memories of the past and are more skeptical and **negative** about the present and future. *The secret is to help difficult people and persistent underperformers assume a more positive, factual, forward-looking perspective* that high performers possess. Exactly how to do this will be explained later in this skill. First, we need to understand what holds difficult people and underperformers back and the strategy for moving them forward.

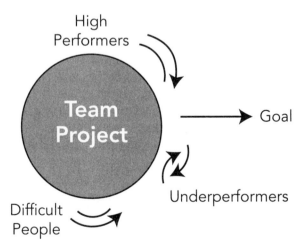

Figure 5.2 Difficult people impede, underperformers get stuck, and high performers drive the ball forward

What Holds Back Difficult People and Underperformers

Most difficult people and underperformers have a hard time overcoming their negative or down attitudes. It might be a bad case of fear or excessive mental baggage, which weighs them down, distorts reality, and prevents them from moving forward. It's an accumulation of bad feelings or worries that they can't seem to reconcile, and sometimes it's a fear of failure, criticism, uncertainty, or inferiority that keeps them from moving confidently forward. Regardless of the underlying causes, difficult people and underperformers struggle to roll forward productively.

Poor performers have a tendency to cover up their mistakes and inadequacies or blame them on past experiences *outside* their control—"I was never trained properly"; "I was unfairly treated"; "My supervisor doesn't like me"; "I wasn't given enough time to do my work." Assigning blame, covering up, and making excuses are telltale behaviors of a low performer. *High performers* don't rely on excuses to reconcile their mistakes but rather take the initiative, responsibility, and actions to promptly correct them (roll the ball forward); *underperformers* prefer to wait, defer, or take the safest route to make corrections; and *difficult people* spend their time defending and rationalizing their mistakes and taking countermeasures to fend off any criticism or blame.

Strategies for Correcting Difficult and Underperforming Behaviors

Difficult people and underperformers are not bad people; they just have unproductive attitudes and behaviors that were never properly corrected. Remember that most subpar performers do not have bad intentions—they do it out of *fear*, which means excessive worry, anxiety, or concern. Essentially all bad behaviors, such as poor communication, indecisiveness, resentment, jealousy, and passive-aggressiveness, are rooted in fear. *Adding more fear through punishment and threats will not frighten people back to good performance—you're just compounding the fear.* You may succeed in replacing one fear behavior for another, but it doesn't change the situation. Also, excessive fear motivates minimal, compliance behaviors with little improvement in productivity and accountability ("I just do what I'm told"). That's why managing difficult and persistently underperforming employees can be frustrating. Also, it's sad when team leaders are satisfied with having a compliant, low performer, declaring a small victory and living with the situation. This ignores the fact that the bar has been lowered and everyone else on the team knows it.

Oftentimes, excessive fear creates not only a different perspective of time but also a *distorted* reality or *alternate* understanding of expectations and circumstances. This alternate reality causes low performers to have a different perspective of their behavior and to provide false rationalizations for it, such as, "People are jealous of me," "I work harder than anyone else," "Following standard procedures is a waste of time," "No one believes in those values," "I know better," "Nobody cares what I think," and, "It's their problem if they don't like how I work." This behavior occurs more frequently and persistently in difficult people than in underperformers. In a sense, difficult people live in a different realm and, in that context, believe their behaviors are justified. Thus, *poor performers possess excessive fear that distorts their reality, which in turn leads to a poor attitude, bad behavior, and conflicts.*

> "Excessive fear creates not only a different perspective of time but also a distorted reality or alternate understanding of expectations and circumstances."

Given that *fear* and an *alternate reality* are key barriers in keeping difficult people and underperformers from moving in the right direction, you need a strategy that addresses these two key factors in order to raise performance. The secret is to address those fearful attitudes and correct misconceptions. In today's workplace, people don't like to be judged or told what to do, and you can't control the behavior of other people. Thus, your best strategy is to facilitate a behavioral change by compelling a *change in thinking.*

A change in thinking gets you closer to the root causes of the problem (fear and alternate reality) and increases the probability that the person will be accountable for the change. The basic performance improvement model is to facilitate change by *rolling the ball forward in the right direction.* For the difficult person, "rolling the ball forward" means mentally moving him or her from an impeding, fearful, backward, false orientation to an enabling, hopeful, forward, reality-based orientation. In the case of an underperformer, "rolling the ball forward" means helping the employee see and believe in a more positive and productive present and future.

Difficult people—who expend their energies in the wrong direction—and underperformers—who struggle to keep pace and make deadlines—are caught in a mental trap and struggle to move forward. Difficult people, and underperformers to a lesser degree, can't move forward until they feel safe, acknowledged, and in control. The strategy to *"roll the ball forward" creates hope and security in people, which are two human factors powerful enough to overcome the effects of fear in difficult and underperforming employees.*

Process Model for Turning Around Difficult People, Underperformers, and Other Problem Employees

Skill Five introduces my *Past-Present-Future Model* to improve and "roll forward" employee performance. This process model works for small and big issues, highly intellectual or emotionally charged problems, and employees who are difficult, underperforming, or just having a work problem. Having a well-defined process for correcting behavioral problems is critical because *process depersonalizes, de-emotionalizes, and de-antagonizes* the encounter between supervisor and employee. Your relationship with difficult people and underperformers should not be polarizing, antagonistic, "me vs. you" combat. Instead, *be an advocate and facilitator and let the process do the dirty work for you.* Your mind-set regarding your problem employee should be based on the following beliefs:

▲ Your work problem is important to me.

▲ I want to listen and understand your work problem and concern.

▲ I'm not against you.

▲ I want to help you resolve your problem.

▲ I'm on your side.

▲ I want to know the truth.

The Past-Present-Future Model works well for a wide variety of employee problems but like with any skill, it takes time, practice, and experience to master it. But you can do it! I will demonstrate how this model works by using two common workplace scenarios and drawing from the skills that you have previously learned. Scenario A demonstrates how to solve an impromptu problem that is brought to you by an employee who seems troubled and unhappy and is having a problem at work. Scenario B demonstrates how to conduct a planned performance review with a poor performer whose behavior is adversely affecting the team.

SCENARIO A: HOW TO SOLVE AN IMPROMPTU EMPLOYEE PROBLEM

A troubled, unhappy employee brings you a complaint or problem. He is struggling, conflicted, and feeling down about something that's affecting his work. He can't reconcile it and is looking to you for help. The Past-Present-Future Model was designed to help you solve this common problem.

Use of the Past-Present-Future Model is analogous to directing a three-scene movie consisting of three separate timeframes:

▲ Scene 1—Past: Inquire, listen, understand background of employee's problem and concern

▲ Scene 2—Present: Diagnose, do a reality check, address the root problem

▲ Scene 3—Future: Explore possible options, agree on next steps, roll the ball forward

The process is to talk the employee through each scene in sequence regarding their problem. *Once you shoot a scene, don't go back; keep moving forward.* Also, a "movie" is not just an intellectual exercise; it's an emotional and sometimes dramatic undertaking. As you move through the three scenes, please remember that rolling the ball forward requires both intellectual and emotional resolution. Even if you move forward intellectually, you can still fail if you don't move forward emotionally too, because *fear is the most common emotion that holds people back* from performing at a higher level. All too often, supervisors reach an agreement with an employee on actions but these actions never materialize because the employee still doesn't feel satisfied about the issue emotionally.

*   *   *

Scene 1—Past: Inquire, Listen, Understand Background of Employee's Problem and Concern

An employee approaches you and says he would like to talk to you regarding a problem. It's not urgent, but the employee is anxious to meet with you, so you set aside time that day to talk. Entering this meeting, your goal is to listen, acknowledge, understand, and empathize with the employee's problem. The key in this first scene is to create a safe zone, a place where he can speak openly and honestly and feel heard and understood. The strategy is to open the conversation broadly; allow the employee to say whatever is on his mind; start narrowing, clarifying, and pinpointing the problem as much as you can; and then close this part of the discussion. I call this the "open-narrow-close" sequence, which is explained further as follows.

Open

Start with the past and *open* the conversation by asking the employee, "Can you tell me what's happening?" or "What can I help you with?" Be an active listener and allow the employee to play out the scene and share what he has experienced. *Patience and active listening* are the keys in Scene 1. Go slow to go fast; resist jumping ahead and trying to solve the problem—this is the most common mistake that team leaders make. Be patient and allow the employee to tell his full story and how it's affecting him. This is an "opening scene," which

> **"Resist jumping ahead and trying to solve the problem—this is the most common mistake that team leaders make."**

means the employee is the main actor and he has your full attention. Try to listen without judgment or prejudice. Be aware that, left unchecked, the employee may start recycling his story. Mitigate this by taking written notes and giving friendly reminders when the employee starts to recycle (such as, "I think I've captured that already. What more can you tell me?"). Keep the scene moving forward by using the next technique.

Narrow

Ask questions to help *narrow* and clarify the problem. While the employee is telling his story, it's always a good practice to minimize interruption, but do ask questions as needed. For example, it's very important to *hold the employee accountable* for any vague stories, claims, or allegations. Ask questions such as, "Can you please provide a specific example?"; "What do you mean when you say . . . ?"; and "How does that affect your work?" The secret is to shift from generalities, innuendos, and ambiguity to a more specific, *pinpointed definition of the problem*. Additionally, make sure it stays work focused. Sometimes dubious claims are made or the story is embellished by emotion or non-work-related issues, so ask clarifying questions.

Case in Point An employee claims people are being mean to him and he feels put down all the time. It would be effective to ask, "What did they specifically say to you?"; "What were the words that they used?"; "Was anyone else present who may have heard this conversation?"; "Who are you referring to?"; "Who else was involved or may know more?"; "What did you say in response?"; and "How did this impact your work?" Be trusting, but hold the employee accountable for what he is saying. Refrain from asking, "What should you have said?" or "Why didn't you try to . . . ?"—these are problem-solving questions that are better asked later. Hone in on the problem first, not the solution.

Don't let the employee amplify the problem or allow it to become a bigger problem than it is. Keep things in the right perspective for the employee—*keep small things small*; it may be a tuna fish sandwich–type problem (a simple miscommunication, Skill Three). Don't be surprised to find that the real problem may be due to an unrelated issue or another encounter. The key is to remove the fluff and bluster and get to the real problem or "plot of the story." You'll find that your clarifying questions will help get to the *root* problem.

Close

Once the employee has clarified his story, summarize and confirm it by saying, "Did I get it right?" and then close Scene 1 with, "Is there anything else to the story?" or "Is there anything else you're concerned about?" to ensure that you heard the story accurately and the employee has gotten everything out so you can move to the next scene. Oftentimes employees feel a lot better just talking it out, and they get a great sense of relief knowing that they have been heard and understood. Once the employee feels heard, he is ready to listen to you and move to the next scene.

* * *

Scene 2—Present: Diagnose, Do a Reality Check, Address the Root Problem

This scene gives you the opportunity to work with the employee to help him get the accurate perspective. This is where you want to shift to a more objective, systematic mode of diagnosing, giving proper context, and addressing the root of the problem.

Diagnose

This is where you use the proper hat (Skill Two) to determine which part of the wedge (Skill One) applies to the problem. If it's a legal, regulatory, ethical, or health issue, it may belong to *management* and you will need to take it there; if not, it might be a *work team* issue.

Case in Point When diagnosing people problems, if it involves a specific policy, such as workplace harassment, you would wear your management hat or supervisor hat to advise the employee of the appropriate venue and process for resolving the issue. If the problem involves the person's individual work performance, it's likely an ERAM issue (Skill One)—a problem with expectations, resources, ability, or motivation. If it's an interpersonal conflict, you or a company representative may need to verify the employee's story by investigating and seeking other sources. If the employee is struggling with a team project, then you need to wear you supervisor's hat and determine whether it's a team issue with content, process, or behavior (CPB, Skill One).

Do a Reality Check

The goal of Scene 2 is to put the employee's problem into the right context. This means giving the employee your authoritative, objective perspective of the problem, which entails advising him of the applicable rules, policies, expectations, and other *reality-based* facts regarding the problem.

Case in Point If the employee's problem is regarding work absences, compensation, a promotion, a performance review, a complaint, or another administrative issue, wear your management hat and inform the employee of the policy or procedure and how it applies to the situation. If it regards work expectations, you may need to remind the employee of your expectations or the expectations of your customers, sponsors, and other stakeholders.

The secret to solving this problem is in the *reality check*, which entails going to the appropriate authoritative source to put the problem into the proper context. In other words, before you start solving the problem, make sure it is grounded in reality. Keep in mind that most employee problems are either misjudgments or misunderstandings of the issue. In some cases, the employee complaint or problem may require you to call a time-out to further investigate the issue, consult with experts, initiate mandatory company procedures, talk to witnesses, and perform other fact-finding actions. Scene 2 is not a subjective debate of who's right or wrong; it's about finding and informing the employee of the objective, authoritative facts. You are *not arguing* views with the employee; you are *enlightening*, *helping*, and *correcting* him by providing him with the facts of the matter.

> **"Before you start solving the problem, make sure it is grounded in reality."**

Examples of authoritative sources include the following:

▲ company rules, policies, and procedures

▲ company goals and strategies

▲ organizational and team values

▲ laws and regulations

▲ expert opinions

▲ historic precedents

▲ team ground rules

▲ management and customer expectations

▲ testimonies from other parties or witnesses

▲ notes and documentation

Address the Root Problem

As covered in Skill Three, when employees feel excluded, unhappy, or unfairly treated, it's human nature for them to assume negative intentions. As we learned in Skill Four, problem employees tend to reside in the bottom of their cones and let fear drive their thinking and behaviors. It's not uncommon for employees to need to vent, "cry wolf" to get attention, or seek reassurance that they're not being excluded. Your job is to respect the concerns of your employees and not dismiss them. Their perception is their reality unless you correct it. Be sure you're addressing and solving the *real* root problem. This helps facilitate the transition from a perceived world to an objective world.

*   *   *

Scene 3—Future: Explore Possible Options, Agree on Next Steps, Roll the Ball Forward

This scene is about moving the discussion forward to the problem-solving stage. After shooting the first two scenes and assuming it's an employee performance (ERAM) problem, shift back to an inquiring mode and ask the employee future-oriented questions such as, "What ideas do you have for solving this problem?"; "What can you do to make it better?"; "What would you like to see happen?"; "What do you think would be a positive next step?"; or "How would you like this discussion to end?" Hopefully, you will get some

"It's your role to help the employee, but don't let him leave you holding the problem."

constructive ideas that you can build on and provide additional guidance. Don't feel pressured to come up with the answer. Just keep your focus on moving the problem and ball forward and *keep the ball on the employee's side of the court*. In other words, don't roll the ball for him. Personal responsibility and accountability are important aspects of any future actions. It's your role to help the employee, but don't let him leave you holding the problem.

If the employee is struggling with a personal issue, such as health or family issues, and it's affecting his work, then make sure you wear your team member hat—show sincere care, concern, and empathy. Then wear your supervisor hat and explain the company resources that may be available to help the employee get through a difficult time.

SCENARIO B: HOW TO CONDUCT A PLANNED PERFORMANCE REVIEW WITH A PROBLEM EMPLOYEE

This is a situation in which you have a problem employee who is repeatedly underperforming and her inconsistent performance is starting to adversely affect the team. You have provided some impromptu guidance and encouragement but her performance has not improved. In this case, an effective option is to initiate a planned performance review to correct the problem.

The purpose of the planned performance review is to give the employee an opportunity to do the following:

▲ express what she likes most about her work and her performance to date

▲ voice any concerns and problems about her work

▲ state what improvements or changes she would like to make

▲ get your feedback and guidance on improvements needed

▲ get clarification on future expectations

To efficiently facilitate a discussion on these topics, I suggest using my *Six-Step Performance Review Process*.

Six-Step Performance Review Process

This process is an extension of the basic Past-Present-Future Model, which entails the following steps:

1. **Premeeting Assessment:** In advance, both parties write down what has gone well and not so well.

2. **Past:** Begin the meeting by listening to what has gone well and acknowledging the employee's positive behaviors.

3. The employee describes what has *not* gone well, where she can improve, and what concerns she may have about her work.

4. **Present:** Give your feedback on the employee's work and behavior, the impact on the project or work team, and provide a reality check for her.

5. Describe the desired behaviors and improvements—make the case for change.

6. **Future:** Reach agreement on needed changes and actions and confirm expectations.

The Six-Step Performance Review Process parallels the Past-Present-Future Model by getting the employee's *past* perspective, giving your *past* perspective, and moving to the *present*, and then stating your *future* expectations, exploring options, and agreeing on actions.

The following describes the six steps as well as the techniques and tips to help you succeed.

1. Premeeting Assessment—What Has Gone Well and Not So Well?

Start by making an appointment to speak to the employee in private to review her performance. In preparation for the meeting, ask the person to write down the top three to four things that she has been doing well and three to four things she hasn't been doing as well and would like to improve. Tell her that you will do the same from your perspective—as a project leader, your mental focus (Skill Two: supervisor hat) should be on *what behaviors you want to reinforce* and *what behaviors need improvement* (Skill Four: affirming positive behaviors). When the employee knows you will be doing the same assessment in advance, it motivates her to think about what you might say (take your perspective) and to self-report any problems rather than to hear them from you (people like to be in control).

In addition to the premeeting assessment, you may want to use the ERAM tool (expectations, resources, ability, and motivation) as described in Skill One to diagnose individual underperformance. The performance deficiency may not be entirely clear and may require more discussion with the employee; the performance review thus serves the purpose of verifying your initial ERAM assessment as well. Again, this is not an adversarial meeting—be an advocate and facilitator and let the process do the dirty work for you.

2. Past: What Has Gone Well?

Start by having the employee share what she's doing well and her accomplishments. Acknowledge her specific contributions and then share two or three positive contributions that you have observed, with particular emphasis on the *behaviors* that you have liked. Acknowledging the employee's positive contributions serves to reinforce the behaviors you desire (Skill Four: recognize positive behaviors) and also to signal to the employee that this is not a punitive or biased process. Since the employee is underperforming, don't send mixed signals by spending too much time glorifying her performance when you aren't pleased with it. Again, you are only reinforcing desired behaviors, not her overall performance. Don't spend too much time here.

3. Employee Describes What Has Not Gone Well and Her Concerns

It's always a good practice to *give the employee the first move*, which means that before you get into what *you* feel hasn't gone well, you should give the employee an opportunity to confess her performance problems. This is especially true for "difficult achievers" (employees who do excellent work but demotivate others—more on this later in this chapter) who are usually harder on themselves than you'll ever be. They take pride in owning their shortfalls.

Without judgment, try to quiet your mind and listen. Show active listening by writing down what you hear and periodically echoing back a few key words for emphasis. You're gathering data and context to assist you in the next steps. Once the employee has finished, thank the employee for her open and honest assessment and her self-awareness of what hasn't worked well.

"Your job is not to try to solve her fears but rather to enable her to verbalize and vent about what she is struggling with."

After determining what hasn't gone well, ask the follow-up question, "What concerns do you have about your work?" This is an open question that begins to reveal what fears may be affecting the employee. Your job is not to try to solve her fears but rather to enable her to verbalize and vent about what she is struggling with and any

misconceptions she may have about her work situation, relationships, mistreatments, or other issues that may be hindering
her performance. Remember, essentially all bad behaviors are
rooted in fear. As described in Scenario A, make sure you seek
clarification and accountability for any claims, allegations, am-
biguities, and innuendos.

4. Present: Give Feedback and Provide a Reality Check

This is where you can begin to *correct any misconceptions or
alternate realities* regarding the employee's work performance
and address her concerns.

a. Give specific feedback on the employee's description of
   what hasn't worked well by relating it to your list of what
   needs improvement (your premeeting work from Step 1). In
   this critical step, you want to connect and build on what the
   employee feels hasn't worked well. You are relating the employee's list of what hasn't worked to your list of needed
   behavioral improvements. It may not be a perfect match,
   but tie the two together somehow. This way, you are agreeing
   with the employee and building on what areas need improvement. Again, you are not operating against the employee;
   you are working on the same side.

b. Give a *reality check* on three fronts: (1) describe how the employee's behavior has affected the team, project, company,
   and/or other stakeholders (keep the description clear, specific,
   and observational)—go for quality, not quantity; (2) state
   how the employee's behavior and consequences are unacceptable at the management level—for example, behavior is
   inconsistent with company policies, procedures, standards,
   strategies, or management directives, or team level—for
   example, her behavior is contrary to team values, ground
   rules, and team leader expectations; and (3) make it clear
   that it's your job as her supervisor (Skill Two: know your
   three hats) to correct any behaviors that adversely affect the
   project or are inconsistent with company or team expectations. The key is to stay objective and observational; *judge
   the work and its impact, not the person.*

   At this time, ask confirming "I" questions such as, "Did I
   make myself clear on how these behaviors have impacted

the project?" and "My role as your supervisor is to correct and improve any performance deficiencies—did I make myself clear on what areas need improvement?"

c. When conveying your messages in (a) and (b), try to include the concerns that the employee expressed in Step 3. It's not unusual to find that an employee's personal worries, her perception of what hasn't worked well, and the effect they have had on others are related. This stepwise model enables you to see the bigger picture before making any decisions and seeking remedies.

*5. Describe the Desired Behaviors and Improvements—
Make the Case for Change*

Hopefully by this point you have described the employee's behaviors and her impact, provided a clear reality check, and clarified that a change of behavior is required. Avoid dwelling on bad behaviors—start transitioning to a discussion of the specific behaviors and performance level that you want and provide a clear and compelling case for change. This is best done by describing the *consequences* of the employee's past performance, how and why it is unacceptable to you and the organization going forward, and how a change in her behavior will benefit the team or project (Skill Two: wear your supervisor and management hats for more power).

It's essential to explain the *consequences of making the change versus not making the change.* Although nothing is guaranteed, more of the same behavior and performance is unacceptable, whereas a positive change in behavior and performance will likely yield a more favorable outcome for the employee and team. It's a matter of explaining the gain of change versus the pain of the status quo. You're not pleading with the employee; you're giving her a choice: either change or continue to perform in the present manner and suffer the consequences, which you, as the team leader, are prepared to administer. *The employee must want to change.*

> **"Explain the consequences of making the change versus not making the change."**

The key to moving to the present is to help the employee realize the following:

▲ We cannot do anything about the past.

▲ A change of behavior is necessary and beneficial.

▲ The employee can make a course correction *right now*.

▲ She has the ability to change, and you'll support her.

▲ It's her choice—she can suffer under the status quo or choose to make a change.

▲ You and the team are counting on her to perform—the employee's job is important and valued.

Continue the process of rolling the ball forward by asking, "I believe these problems can be solved—do you feel the same?"; "Are you up for the challenge?"; and "Can I count on you?" Remember, you're inviting the employee to make a choice—join us or exclude us (Skill Three: exclusionary behavior). If the employee chooses to self-exclude, then you must wear your supervisor or management hat and explain the expected consequences of her not changing her behavior.

6. Future: Reach Agreement on Needed Changes and Confirm Expectations

Based on your discussion, confirm expectations and the employee's commitment to change by requesting an improvement *action plan* from the employee, then express your hope for the future (for example, "I look forward to seeing what changes you make"). Don't accept cynicism or distracting remarks from the employee (for example, red herrings such as, "Like most goals, these goals are going to change anyway"). Don't fall for this trap of speculating about the future. It's another no-win situation. The secret is to get the employee to *focus on the behavior and process, not the outcome*—she should worry about what she can control (her behaviors and work tasks) and not what she can't control (outcome).

> *"The secret is to get the employee to focus on the behavior and process, not the outcome."*

The future scene is not about ignoring the past but rather about learning from it and being inclusive. Send a clear signal by saying, "I and the team need you," "You're an important part of this team," "People notice and are affected by what you say and do," and "You can have a real positive influence on the team." Then ask the employee to take some time to think about the discussion and focus on the specific behaviors and performance goals that she *wants to achieve going forward*. Set a clear deadline for those actions and suggest some interim reviews to help the person. Just as with Scenario A, it is important that the employee take personal responsibility for her future actions.

When the action plan is drafted, have the employee send you a copy for review and then set up a meeting to give her your feedback. Have her finalize the plan and send you a copy. Remember, *what gets measured gets done; what gets written gets understood*. With a plan in place, take the time to follow up often and give active reinforcement during the performance period. Again, the focus is on behavior and process, not the outcome.

The Best Tips and Techniques for Difficult Conversations

When having corrective discussions with employees, you may feel uncomfortable giving feedback, expressing what behaviors need improvement, and explaining the consequences of changing and not changing, and you may fear an employee backlash. The secret is to be inclusionary and avoid personalizing (Skill Three: make them feel needed, interdependent, and trusted). Here are some useful guidelines to help you succeed in these difficult conversations:

▲ **Make observations, not judgments.** Express what you have *observed* in the person's *behavior*—actions and interactions, what the person does and says—that needs improvement and how those behaviors *impact* the team's project. Negative behaviors are inconsequential unless they have a detrimental effect on the work. Expressing *observations* takes the subjectivity and judgment out of the discussion. You want to make observations, not judgments. Remember, no one likes to be judged.

▲ **Be specific and use examples.** The problem becomes much clearer and real to the employee when you are able to pinpoint the undesired behavior. Give one or two very clear examples of the context in which the difficult behavior was observed. A little bit goes a long way, so be concise. *Avoid using too many examples*, and, more importantly, *never use weak examples* that can be subject to different interpretations. Weak examples are too easy to contest, and they can make you appear as a nitpicker.

▲ **Judge the work, not the person.** As the project team leader, it's your job to *judge the work* (quality, organization, and content), *not the person* (for example, calling the employee lazy, undisciplined, uncaring, or apathetic) or the employee's *personality* (for example, shy, too sensitive, humorous, or self-centered). Too often, we're quick to judge the person instead of objectively assessing the work, and we let the person's personality influence our judgment. Your role as a supervisor is to assess the person's work quality, productivity, effectiveness, and impact. Set high work standards and hold your employees and yourself accountable to those standards. *Focus on the problem, not the person. Be tough on policies and standards, not people.*

▲ **Make "I" statements, not "you" statements.** By sharing your observations, you're making "I" statements, which is critical when giving constructive feedback. Avoid "you" remarks as much as possible unless you're making a positive remark or asking the employee a question. "You" statements are notoriously accusatory, judgmental, and condemning to the employee, who can *internalize, emotionalize, and personalize* them. People stop listening and get defensive when they feel judged, attacked,

> *"'You' statements are notoriously accusatory, judgmental, and condemning."*

or controlled. A difficult conversation is like a tennis match—if you want to make a volley (constructive feedback), stay on your side of the court by making "I" statements. Making observational, specific, work-focused, "I" statements results in a professional, nonjudgmental discussion.

▲ **Focus on behaviors, not intentions.** When people discuss behaviors, it can quickly turn into what they meant or did not mean to do—"What I was trying to do was . . ." In a highly inclusive team, everyone presumes good intentions (Skill Three: mutual trust), including difficult people and underperformers, but intent is not the issue.

   Your main focus should be on the *difficult behavior, not the person's intent.* Because you're not a mind reader, debating the intent of a difficult person is a no-win situation. When people make judgments about others (for example, "You don't seem to care," "You're not putting forth any effort," "You need to get your act together"), they are speculating, personalizing, and emotionalizing the discussion and making character judgments (via "you" statements). One can easily lose control of the discussion and get on a very slippery slope. Also, difficult people are apt to draw you in and use their good intentions to justify their behaviors (for example, "I didn't mean it" or "They took it the wrong way"). Don't fall for this trap.

▲ **Communication is not what you say but rather what the other party hears and feels.** In a difficult conversation, the employee (and you) may not be hearing or understanding everything that is being said. Make it a habit to summarize key points to verify mutual understanding. Ask questions frequently to check for understanding and capture all agreements in writing.

▲ **Be more *ask* assertive than *tell* assertive.** To ensure you are effectively communicating, listening, and facilitating, try to refrain from jumping to conclusions. Instead, ask questions to show your sincere interest in hearing the employee's side of the matter, get a better sense of how the employee feels (empathy), check to see whether the employee is hearing and understanding what you are saying, and ensure the employee is taking ownership of the problem. For example, instead of saying, "Next time you should come to me with that problem," it's usually more effective to ask, "What do you think would have been a better way of handling that problem?" And if the employee doesn't have an answer, then ask, "Do you think bringing the problem to my attention might have been a less confrontational option for you?"

▲ **Avoid "why" questions.** Use "who, what, when, and where" questions to pinpoint the observed problem, but avoid asking "why" questions. "Why" questions are attempts to understand a person's motives—as just described, you don't want to go there. However, asking "why" questions to understand the root causes of nonbehavioral problems such as process, technology, or goals is useful.

▲ **Stay focused on the present person.** When discussing behaviors, difficult employees may attribute their fault to others—for example, "John is much worse than I am. Why are you picking on me?" This is another common trap. Don't fall for the "Other people do it too" or "Why are you singling me out?" defense. Just respond, "We're not here to talk about John's or other people's behavior; we're here to talk about *your* behavior. Let's stay focused."

▲ **Identify the critical few.** It's best to limit your discussion to one or two critical deficiencies or behaviors that need improvement. Identifying much more than two behaviors tends to make the discussion too negative and can dilute the effect of the meeting. Take it one step at a time and start with the one or two critical behaviors that are most detrimental to your team or project. The objective is to get the ball rolling forward in the right direction—don't try to address every adverse behavior in a single meeting.

Be Aware of Difficult Overachievers

There is one other type of problem employee that is sometimes overlooked: the overachiever. Although difficult people and underperformers can be problematic to a team, overachievers can also have an adverse effect, even though most project team leaders would love to have more overachievers. For overachievers, the problem is their tendency to move too quickly in their drive for success. It's not a bad problem for a team leader, but overachievers can demotivate and exclude others or overwork and burn themselves (and others) out. Although their dedication is admirable, overachievers can exhibit impatience, intolerance of less skilled team members, and an excessive fear of failure. This fear can result in overly demanding, domineering, and insensitive behaviors. Concerns include excessive stress, work-life imbalance, and other personal health issues.

Overachievers work well with high performers in *leading, pulling, and racing the team forward* (Figure 5.3), although sometimes they may work too hard, move too fast, and leave team members feeling run over. When this happens, *overachievers can become difficult* since they are impeding the progress of others. Their impatience to achieve is only exceeded by their overly high expectations of themselves.

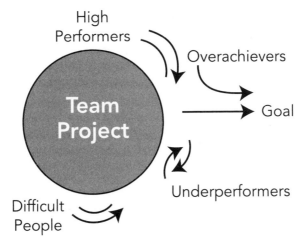

Figure 5.3 Opposing effects of low and high performers

Coaching and mentoring are excellent tools to prevent overachievers from pushing themselves and others too hard. Overall, the net effect of an overachiever is usually much more positive than negative, whereas the opposite is true for difficult people and underperformers. *Toning down a high-performing engine is much easier than trying to rev up a malfunctioning one.*

Skill Five Summary

Skill Five looks at the characteristics and behaviors of difficult people and underperformers in the workplace. Difficult employees frustrate, distract, and obstruct others by complaining, criticizing, discouraging, annoying, or otherwise inhibiting the progress of others. Whereas difficult people may impede the progress of *others*, underperformers hamper their *own* progress due to their inconsistent, inefficient, and unreliable work output.

The basic model for correcting difficult behaviors and underperformers is to help the employee move forward in a more productive and purposeful direction.

Leading a team project is similar to rolling a ball forward to a target, where the ball represents your team's project, "rolling" refers to productive actions, "forward" means making continuous progress, and the "target" represents the team's goal. "Rolling the ball forward" means effectively and efficiently making deadlines, achieving milestones, and meeting stakeholder expectations all the way to your team's project goal.

Difficult people and underperformers are key barriers to project success, and they can't seem to move forward and work productively due to various problems, conflicts, fears and misconceptions. The performance improvement strategies offered in this skill are designed to get low performers back on track, improve their behaviors, and get the ball rolling again by using the Past-Present-Future Model and the Six-Step Performance Review Process. These two processes are effective ways to help difficult people, underperformers, and other problem employees get over past problems, conflicts, and worries and get back on the ball.

To illustrate the Past-Present-Future Model and Six-Step Performance Review Process, two specific workplace scenarios are presented: Scenario A, an unplanned, real-time problem with a troubled, unhappy employee; and Scenario B, a planned performance review with a poor performer who is adversely affecting the team. Each scenario requires a multistep process that entails actively listening, acknowledging employee concerns, correcting misconceptions, keeping the problem in the proper context, and facilitating a solution that the employee owns. Also, twenty of the best ideas and techniques are provided to help you have successful discussions with low performers. It takes practice and repetition to master these strategies, processes, and techniques, but you'll find that your efforts will be highly rewarded by your increased confidence and success in helping others.

Skill Five Memory Card

Tools, Tips, and Techniques for Turning Around Difficult People and Underperformers
Roll the Ball Forward

For Improving Performance	For Difficult Conversations
1. Use the *Past-Present-Future Model* for impromptu employee problems	1. Make observations, not judgments
2. Use the *Six-Step Performance Review Process* for improving underperformance	2. Be specific and use examples
	3. Judge the work, not the person
3. Don't rush to judgment—get the whole story	4. Make "I" statements, not "you" statements, when giving constructive feedback
4. Change thinking to change behaviors	
5. Let the process do the dirty work	5. Focus on the behavior, not the intent
6. Keep things in perspective—keep small things small	6. Communication is not what you say but what others hear and feel
7. Do reality checks to correct misconceptions	7. Be more *ask* assertive than *tell* assertive
8. Make clear the gain of change versus the pain of status quo	8. Avoid "why" questions
9. Focus on the behavior and process, not the outcome	9. Stay focused on the present person
10. What gets measured gets done; what gets written gets understood	10. Identify the one or two behaviors critical for improvement

SKILL SIX

How to Motivate the Right Team Behaviors
The ABC Boxes

Skill Six is probably the quintessential skill for project leaders because it addresses the one factor that can make or break projects: team behavior. If you don't have a plan for managing team behavior, you're leaving the fate of your project to luck or hope. You're hoping that people will get along, show the right behaviors, and not have any bad people problems. This is known as wishful thinking or ad hoc people management, and it's not the strategy you want to use.

You can't leave behavior to chance and assume everyone will work together well. What is your strategy for identifying, deploying, and ensuring that your team will demonstrate the right behaviors? Most project leaders don't have one or rely on project management processes to take care of it. Skill Six offers an effective model in behavioral management for project leaders to define, shape, and facilitate the right behaviors for team success.

CASE 6.1: THE AMBITIOUS PROJECT MANAGER—DOES THE END JUSTIFY THE MEANS?

Marty was a young, entrepreneurial marketing manager for a rapidly growing, domestic telecommunications company that was looking to expand operations to a new region. This expansion required a bright, fast-moving, creative project manager who was willing to break new ground and compete with many well-established companies in the market. Although Marty was relatively young and new to the business, his entrepreneurial spirit and proven track record of increasing sales in many previous jobs made him the best choice for the job. Excitedly, he accepted the new position and looked forward to recruiting a team and launching this major project.

After several months of planning and deliberations, the company management approved the expansion strategy, business plan, goals, budget, workforce numbers, and timeline. It was not going to be a feeble effort, as the project was well resourced and had an aggressive schedule and clear business and marketing goals. Marty felt fortunate to have such great support and was given a free hand in selecting his sales team.

In forming his team, he wanted people who had the ambition, initiative, and drive to not only dedicate themselves to this project but also be willing to work hard, make sacrifices when needed, and go above and beyond to make this expansion a success. He handpicked people internally who were energetic go-getters with business savvy, and he also hired some new, outside employees to give the team a fresh perspective and greater diversity. Marty and his team were given new office space in a high-profile part of the facility, which made the entire team feel special. With all this attention and visibility, it was now a matter of executing their plans and meeting the high expectations of the company.

It was clear from the start that their competitors were not going to roll over and let this new company into their territory. They redoubled their marketing efforts and introduced new promotions to counter the expansion efforts of Marty and his team. As a result, the team struggled in the first year of operation and was clearly discouraged when they missed their initial marketing goals. Management was concerned about the new business, but Marty assured them that the slow start was normal and things would pick up soon.

As they entered their second year, Marty was frustrated by the slow start and knew he had to send a clear message to reignite his team. He wondered whether some of his experienced associates were moving too conventionally. The prevailing conservatism appeared to have dampened the enthusiasm of the younger associates. So he transferred two of his veteran employees, along with one low-performing associate, to another division and held a team meeting to express his disappointment and admonish the team for not meeting company expectations.

However, Marty was astute enough to know that he needed more than admonishment to create a more productive sales force. As a way of reinvigorating his team, he introduced a special incentive program that would award large cash bonuses based on the number and size of contracts each person was able to deliver. Marty knew that incentives, as well as some healthy internal competition, were effective in motivating higher performance. Marty had a couple of his office assistants devise an online dashboard to track new contracts and also made sure that all major achievements were recognized with team celebrations each quarter.

The incentive program proved to be the jolt that the team needed. In nine months, sales doubled, and then they quadrupled in the ensuing two quarters and were projected to double again in the next quarter. Not only did the team increase revenue, but they also landed many large contracts with major businesses in the region. By the end of the second fiscal year, Marty's team had exceeded expectations. Management was pleased and rewarded Marty with a special presentation to the board of directors. It was an amazing story. It proved that with the right incentives, talent, resources, and leadership, teams can accomplish extraordinary goals and achieve breakthroughs in performance.

The next year, the team continued to do well, consistently landing new contracts. Due to their successful project, Marty and many of his team members were promoted and given better opportunities. He kept his team together just long enough for the company to establish a more permanent organizational structure. The future looked bright for Marty and the company.

As the new organization was established in the region, the new operations and finance managers conducted a review of the lucrative contracts that Marty's team had put in place. While reviewing the contracts, they noticed that the contracts contained substantial credits and future discounts to their customers that appeared extraordinarily generous.

Upon further review, it was discovered that the sales staff had the freedom to write very flexible, generous, long-term contracts with credits and other incentives that made it very economical for their business clients to not only sign up for their services but also continue those services at lower net rates. Going forward, these contracts essentially "gave away the store," which meant the company would be operating at a substantial loss. Also, these large credits and other customer incentives were treated as part of the start-up investment and were capitalized, kept off the books, and hidden from the cash flows. This meant that profits from the region were inflated and not accurately reflected in the company's books. Upon further investigation, it was determined that the employees had been operating contrary to company standards and acting in what could be construed as unethical business practices.

As a result, the company had to disclose these discrepancies to its board and the authorities, and it eventually declared insolvency for the regional business. The company never recovered from this disaster, and the assets were sold in an auction a few years later.

Lessons from the Story

The lessons from this story are not so much about the repercussions of writing bad contracts as about how easily a company can lose its way when people's behaviors are poorly managed. Indeed, the end does not always justify the means, and behavior matters. Marty was highly driven to meet company expectations but unfortunately ignored the underlying human factor that determines the success or failure of any project: team behavior.

"A company can lose its way when people's behaviors are poorly managed."

To manage team projects successfully, no factor is more important than managing people's behavior, which means managing the actions and interactions of others. Effective behavioral management has three main parts, and unfortunately, Marty fell short on all three:

1. **Establish the right basis for people's behaviors.** Behaviors don't just happen. They require a compelling reason or behavioral basis for taking action, which has two components: internal and external. Marty did a good job on setting the external basis—land new contracts or we fail. But he failed to find his internal basis, which resides in your heart and soul—your values and desire to do the right thing. Your values drive behavior, and the right behavior starts with the right set of values, which is your basis for determining right from wrong, good from bad, and true from false. Marty did not have the right team values in place. *You must have the right basis and values to drive the right behaviors.*

2. **Identify the right way to do things.** Marty wanted his employees to secure new contracts aggressively but didn't define the *right way* to write those contracts—which is in an ethical, economical, and legal manner. Marty failed to define the right behaviors for success. Although the types of workplace behaviors are endless, some behaviors are more important than others depending on the type of business or project. To be successful in managing behavior, you need to determine the behaviors that are critical for your organization's success. *Define the right behaviors to drive the right results.*

3. **Recognize the right behavior, not the right outcome.** Marty made the mistake of motivating his employees to get more client contracts and did not specify the *values* and *behaviors* his employees should demonstrate in obtaining those contracts. Bottom-line results are undoubtedly essential, but human values and behaviors are the underlying enablers for long-term success and are far more important in determining the sustainability of an organization. Marty made a key mistake that is common among team leaders today—being too outcome focused and basing incentives, rewards, and recognition solely on end

results. That's why it's critical to *focus on the behavior, not the outcome.*

Summary

Marty's three learnings indicate that the model for managing behavior and getting people to do what you want them to do is to establish the *right basis* for the behavior, demonstrate the behavior in the *right way*, and *recognize the right behavior*, not the outcome. Together, these three components constitute Skill Six, which I call the *ABC Box Model* for behavioral management. This model is rooted in applied behavioral analysis (15), which I have adapted in Skill Six for project management.

The Best Model for Facilitating Team Behaviors

ABC is an abbreviation for *antecedent, behavior,* and *consequence* (Figure 6.1). *Antecedents* are the *right bases* or things that *precede* a behavior; *behaviors* are the *right way* to do things and they are the actions and interactions of people, and *consequences* are the *right recognitions* and reinforcements that *happen after* the behavior. Desired behaviors are evoked when the right bases or antecedents are present; and whether that particular behavior gets repeated depends on the consequences following the employee's behavior. ABC represents not only the components for motivating the right behaviors but also the sequence in which it is done. The ABC components can be visualized as three separate boxes filled with different contents. In the following sections, we will examine these three boxes and I will explain what's in each of them and how they are used in motivating team behaviors.

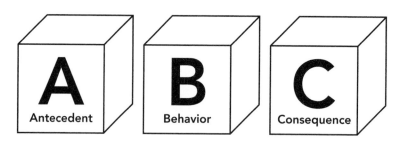

Figure 6.1 The ABC Box Model

Triggering the Right Team Behaviors: Box A

Antecedents are things that precede, prompt, or stimulate a given behavior. Examples of tools that are commonly used to evoke desired behaviors include rules, policies, standards, and procedures. They are a collection of tools that can be used when specific, consistent behaviors are required, such as safety, maintenance, regulatory compliance, and teamwork (Figure 6.2). It's a toolbox because antecedents are used to "build" and maintain desired team behaviors.

In most organizations, project leaders are provided with a preloaded box of organizational antecedents, such as the following:

▲ company mission, vision, values, objectives, and strategies

▲ company standards and policies

▲ organizational goals and metrics

▲ organizational procedures

▲ company compliance manuals

▲ professional standards

▲ management expectations

▲ laws and regulations

These types of administrative antecedents are company-wide directives, but unfortunately, most of them are too lofty to apply directly to project teams. Also, when it comes to managing team behavior, there are no standard rules, procedures, or manuals. That's because every team has different types of people, with different backgrounds, skills, knowledge,

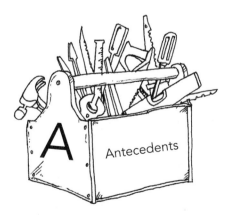

Figure 6.2 Use antecedents to prompt desired behaviors

experiences, and ways they like to work. Each team must discover its *own basis* and determine its *own way* of working together.

Antecedents are things that we do every day, but we don't consciously identify them as "antecedents" or utilize them fully to improve our ability to manage behaviors. *Antecedent* is a technical term used in behavioral sciences to refer to things that trigger specific behaviors. In practice, team leaders prompt the behaviors they want by either telling employees *how* the work is to be done or explaining *what* needs to be done and letting employees determine how best to accomplish it. Most times, the former approach works well for standard, routine behaviors, whereas the latter strategy works well when you want individuality or creativity, such as in giving a presentation or developing options for a problem. But neither approach is effective for most work situations, especially when they involve any of the following:

▲ attempting to change well-established work behaviors

▲ adopting new behaviors

▲ requiring certain behaviors in high risk situations (health and safety, environment, ethics, government regulations, and legal)

▲ needing a significant or rapid improvement in performance

▲ managing poor performers

▲ forming new teams

To be effective in these situations, you need strong antecedents to drive the right behaviors. As a project leader, you can't monitor all your employees all the time, and employees don't want to be micromanaged either. The secret is to have effective tools and processes in place that will trigger the right behaviors.

Examples of antecedents that are commonly used to drive desired behaviors in teams include these:

▲ team work plan

▲ team values

▲ team ground rules

▲ critical success behaviors

▲ team processes

▲ team communications plan

▲ team risk management plan

▲ employee training

▲ team performance metrics

Case in Point One common complaint from teams is that meetings do not start or end on time. What antecedents would you implement to help your team solve this problem? Here are some ideas:

▲ Establish a team ground rule stating that the team agrees to arrive on time for every team meeting.

▲ Establish a team feedback process in which, at the end of every meeting, you ask the team, "What worked well and what needs improvement?" and include whether the meeting started and ended on time.

▲ Give out recognitions at the start of each meeting.

▲ Put repeat latecomers first on the agenda—and establish a ground rule that specifies that if they're late, their topics don't get covered or they get pushed to the end of the agenda.

▲ Make starting and ending meetings on time a team performance metric that will be measured regularly and reviewed by the project's management—*what gets measured gets done.*

Not starting and ending meetings on time is a team behavior that everyone wishes they could change. You can change behaviors by developing effective antecedents that fit the situation and drive the right behaviors. It takes considerable effort to build a high-performing team, and setting up the right antecedents is essential. But it's a choice—either devise a set of antecedents upfront to motivate desired behaviors or assume nothing bad will happen and correct employees as you go. You'll find that the latter will cost you much more in headaches and unhappiness in the long run. Before you start the project, it's worth investing in the right antecedents to motivate the right team behaviors.

Organizational Values

As we learned from Marty's story, the most critical antecedents and the best basis for shaping the right behaviors are your organizational and team *values.* Values are the organization's strongest beliefs and principles, reflecting the cultural norms and history of the organization. They define how you conduct your business, maximize value for the organization, and how employees treat each other. In essence, values drive the behaviors that the organization wants to see in all its employees.

Values represent the "right" way to do things and the criteria for making the "right" decisions and judgments, such as on employee selections, employee performance, disciplinary actions, recognition, rewards, and promotions. As a team leader, you are expected to make decisions at work

> *"As a team leader, you are expected to make decisions at work that are consistent with the values of the organization, not your personal values."*

that are consistent with the values of the organization, not your personal values. The lens through which you see and judge the actions and interactions in the workplace must be that of the values of your team and organization. This doesn't mean you ignore your own personal values; rather, *align your values* to those of the organization. Just as you adapt your values to a given personal situation, you are doing the same for the workplace. The key is to use the right *priority* of values when making decisions and judgments. For example, safety carries a higher priority than production, ethics trumps economics, and team success is valued over personal success.

As a team leader, it is your role to communicate, clarify, coach, and reinforce organizational and team values, but, more importantly, it's your responsibility to translate these values into daily behaviors, which brings us to our second box, demonstrating the right behaviors.

Defining Your Team's Critical Success Behaviors: Box B

Box B contains *behaviors*, and you want to fill it with behaviors that are essential for the success of your project. I call these behaviors: *critical success behaviors* (CSB). *CSBs are specific behaviors that, if not effectively practiced, will likely cause the project to fail.* As project team leader, it's incumbent on you and your team to clearly pinpoint the most important behaviors and incorporate them into your project work plan. Unfortunately, CSBs are often neglected in project management. Most projects lack explicit strategies and attention to behavioral management. Conventional project management is focused on meeting *project expectations*—purpose, objectives, goals, schedules, tasks, resources, deliverables, and deadlines. People are considered resources, providing labor, knowledge, skills, and experience to get the work done on time, on spec, and on budget. Project leaders tend to be more concerned about the *content and process* of their projects than the *behavior* of the team. This is one of the great missed opportunities in project management.

But what does it take to determine a team's CSBs? Deriving your team's CSBs should be an iterative process, taking input from *top-down* and *bottom-up* sources within the wedge (Skill One)—that is, management and individual team members.

Top Down: CSBs from Management Level

Your management sector provides and maintains your organization's MVVOS. As stated earlier, all these components are designed at a high level to motivate the right thinking and behavior in the organization. Also, we have learned that *values* are your biggest lever for driving organizational behavior and performance (Skill One). As a project leader, one of your most important roles is to translate the values of your organization into specific, pinpointed behaviors that your employees can understand and practice in the workplace. Remember, *define the right behaviors to get the right results*. Also, you want to ensure consistency in how each person expresses those values, especially under pressure. As illustrated in Marty's story, the values of an organization are vigorously tested at times, and they can't be dismissed for profit or expediency. Your CSBs must be clearly defined and constantly demonstrated in order to become engrained in your team's thinking and culture.

Case in Point How do you translate values into specific desired behaviors? Let's use three common organizational values to show how they are translated into specific team CSBs. Start by agreeing on the organizational values that are most relevant to your team's project. For example, let's assume your team adopts the following organizational values for your project:

▲ **Protection of the environment and human health:** Everything we do relies on the safety of our workforce and the communities around us; we care about the preservation and protection of our environment.

▲ **Teamwork:** We believe in the value of collaboration and respect each other and our diversity.

▲ **Honesty and integrity:** We adhere to the highest standards and ethics of business and personal conduct.

After selecting these values, you may want to make sure that the values and their descriptions have meaning and motivation for everyone on your team. The next step is to pinpoint the specific behaviors that would directly support those values. Table 6.1 shows examples of behaviors for each of these three values. Depending on the experience and maturity of your team in managing behaviors, the number and specificity of your CSBs may vary. Remember, the clearer and more pinpointed the better.

Values start from the top. Employees will take them seriously when they see their leaders take them seriously and exhibit those desired behaviors. As a project leader, your challenge is to demonstrate these organizational

Table 6.1 Values and Critical Success Behaviors

VALUES		
Protection of Environment and Human Health	Teamwork	Honesty and Integrity
BEHAVIORS	BEHAVIORS	BEHAVIORS
• Never walk by or look past a safety infraction • Perform safely or not at all • Act promptly to eliminate health, safety, and environmental hazards • Positively reinforce good safety behaviors on the spot • Make health, safety, and environment a part of decision-making and employee performance assessments • Focus on learning and preventing incidents, not assigning blame • Promptly conduct safety reviews of all incidents • Attend and participate in all safety trainings	• Encourage new approaches and ideas • Respect and value diversity in communications and actions • Foster participation, inclusion, and collaboration • Share information and invite input from others • Ensure clear roles, tasks, responsibilities, and authority • Work together to resolve disagreements constructively • Always act in the best interest of the team • Gladly fill in and support each other	• Ensure behaviors are consistent with team values—"walk the talk" • Be open and transparent with others • Confront inappropriate behaviors when observed • Readily admit mistakes and work to correct them • Provide open and honest feedback to others • Maintain ethical behaviors for both internal and external business activities • Value different perspectives and friendly debate • Be responsible and mutually accountable

values in everything you do. A good practice is to highlight team values in your team successes and failures. Also, in order to sustain desired behaviors, it's important to show how specific CSBs add value to the daily operations of your team. Otherwise, your values and CSBs will look dubious to your employees.

Bottom Up: CSBs from Your Individual Team Members

CSBs from your organizational values must be integrated and consistent with the personal expectations of your team members. Successful project leadership is about meeting people's expectations, not just project expectations. Some of the key questions for developing your team's CSBs include:

"The key to project leadership is to . . . fit the plan to people, not to fit people to the plan."

What do team members want from this project? What team values are most relevant? What *team behaviors* would the team like to see exhibited during the project? What types of work do team members like and dislike? How would team members like to be treated? The key to project leadership is to know people's expectations and then use that information to *fit the plan to people, not to fit people to the plan.* To increase project success, make sure your team behaviors are consistent with both organizational values (top down) and people's expectations (bottom up).

Behavior is the key determinant in the success or failure of a project. It's hard to imagine how a project can succeed if its CSBs are not defined and practiced. Hopefully, your CSBs will include one or more of the six critical team behaviors: mutual trust, interdependence, accountability, transparency, learning, and valuing individuality (Skill Three). You'll find that taking the time and effort upfront to fully define and detail your project's CSBs is one of the best investments you can make to ensure project success.

The Most Important Skill for Sustaining Desired Team Behaviors: Box C

Although antecedents are effective in initiating desired behaviors, just prompting people to do things doesn't guarantee results. In fact, more often than not, antecedents fail in compelling people to sustain new behaviors. They may last for a few hours or weeks, but most antecedents do not have staying power with people and their effectiveness in motivating the right behavior usually decays over time. For greater sustainability, behavior (Box B) needs more support—it needs *consequence*. Because consequence is the most effective tool for affecting employee behaviors, the skills in this section will be provided in more depth. First, some definitions of key terms used in this discussion:

▲ **Consequence:** A result or effect that occurs *after* the behavior—all behaviors have consequences; even "nothing happened" is a consequence

▲ **Feedback:** An *evaluative* appraisal of an employee's action—but not all behaviors result in feedback

▲ **Reinforcement:** An effect that makes the behavior more or less frequent or intense

As a team leader, you are constantly coaching, communicating, and giving *feedback* to your employees to encourage and *reinforce* certain work behaviors (Figure 6.3). Your positive or negative *feedback* after an employee's action has a *consequence* or effect on the employee, but not all consequences are feedback. For example, a fine or a reward can be a consequence for violating or following a rule, respectively, but these do not constitute feedback, which is an *evaluative* response.

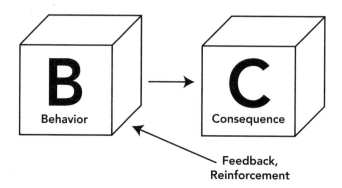

Figure 6.3 Future behavior depends on consequence, feedback, and reinforcement

The Four Consequences

The four possible consequences that can occur as a result of a behavior are *good, not good, don't know,* and *bad.* In this model, consequences are the effects that the person feels after the behavior. Let's express these four consequential emotions as inner "voices" in Box C: *"Yay!"* (good), *"Nay"* (not good), *"Nothing"* (don't know), and *"Ouch!"* (bad) (Figure 6.4).

Yay! (Yes! I'm good! I'm right!): Positive consequences are the things that employees *want, seek, and work for*—praise, recognition, encouragement, reward, and acknowledgment. Receiving a "Yay!" is *positive reinforcement,* and it motivates an employee to increase the frequency or intensity of the desired behavior.

Nay (No, not good, I'm wrong): Negative consequences are *negative reinforcements* for unwanted behaviors. "Nays" are responses that are *disliked* by the recipient. Negative consequences are administered to cause one to discontinue one behavior in favor of another. Thus, a "Yay!" stimulates a repeat of the same behavior, whereas a "Nay" elicits avoidance behaviors, but *they both increase a desired behavior* (reinforcement).

> *"'Nothing' is the most common consequence in the workplace—no consequence, no feedback, nothing happens."*

Nothing (I don't know, no feedback, nothing happens): Of the four consequences, "Nothing" is the most common consequence in the workplace—no consequence, no feedback, nothing happens; employees are left guessing, asking themselves, "Did I do it right?" or "Did you like it?" Some common examples of "Nothing" consequences at work include when you complete a task and get no feedback, suggest an idea and get no reaction, or ask for comment and get no replies.

Figure 6.4 The four consequences

Ouch! (I feel bad, terrible, unpleasant): Punishment is the worst and most feared consequence. Punishment is a punitive, mentally hurtful type of consequence that is intended to *stop an undesirable behavior immediately*. In the workplace, punishments may include harsh criticism, ridicule, embarrassment, rejection, citations, reprimands, and disciplinary actions.

How to Use the Four Consequences

Consequence is the most powerful tool in shaping people's behavior, yet most team leaders are not cognizant of its significance in motivating people. This is one leadership behavior that you don't want to ignore and leave to chance—it's a difference maker for both you and your employees. *Consequence is what makes or breaks behaviors.*

Project leaders can make the biggest improvement in managing behaviors by knowing how to give the right consequences in the right way for the right effect and resulting in the right outcome. It sounds like a lot to get right, but it's easy to learn when you break it down into these three basic skills:

▲ Use the right consequence for the right *effect*

▲ Give consequences with the right *frequency* and in the right *proportion*

▲ Administer the right *process* to consequent desired behaviors

Use the Right Consequence for the Right *Effect* Each consequence evokes a different feeling and effect on behavior (Table 6.2). Using the right consequence for a given situation is fundamental for motivating the right behaviors. You can quickly turn people on or off by using the right or wrong consequence.

Here are some good guidelines for giving consequences:

Positive ("Yay!"). It's best to use "Yays!" to recognize and increase the frequency or intensity of a desired behavior whenever a *discretionary*

Table 6.2 Consequences, Feelings, and Effects on Behavior

Consequence	Feeling	Effect on Behavior
Yay!	Good, triumph, happiness	Positive reinforcement (repeat desired behavior)
Nay	Not good, dissatisfaction, disappointment	Negative reinforcement (decrease unwanted behavior, increase desired behavior)
Nothing	Empty, dismay, wonder	Nothing (no reinforcement, status quo)
Ouch!	Bad, failed, hurtful	Punishment (stop unwanted behavior)

("want to") effort is needed. For example, use "Yays!" to recognize an employee for great customer service, for completing an important report, or for going above and beyond to help a coworker. Also, "Yay!" is the most effective way to *motivate and shape* a new behavior. *What gets recognized gets repeated*—without frequent encouragement, new behaviors usually don't last long. Refrain from giving "Yays!" for routine behaviors; save them for more critical behaviors to maximize effectiveness.

Negative ("Nay"). Use "Nays" to discourage unwanted behaviors and increase the frequency or intensity of a preferred behavior whenever a *compliance ("have to") effort* is needed. For example, give a "Nay" to an employee who shows up late for a meeting (for example, email a friendly reminder to the employee, stressing the importance of arriving to meetings on time); this will hopefully discourage the employee from future tardiness (to avoid an unwanted email reminder) and motivate him or her to be on time (preferred behavior). "Nays" are demotivators and can consist of a disapproving look, a negative remark, or the rejection of an idea.

No consequence ("Nothing"). Giving a "Nothing" response is acceptable when reinforcement is not necessary or you wish to stay neutral. If the behavior is within cultural norms or you feel indifferent about a behavior, then there is no need for reinforcement.

If you don't mind individual variability for a given behavior (such as dress code), the "Nothing" response is appropriate, as it sends a message that you are indifferent about the behavior. However, frequently giving empty consequences to high quality work or output can cause employee discouragement. Also, if you're trying to shape an important new behavior in employees, giving no consequences is deadly—the new behavior will quickly die off.

"Nothings" can sometimes feel like "Nays" (negative reinforcement). In the absence of feedback, people interpret a silent response as, "No one cares," "My work doesn't matter," "I guess no one liked it," or, "I'm not a priority." What's even worse, it leaves employees uncertain, twisting in the wind, and questioning their status—"Do I do the same thing again or not?"; "I guess no news is good news?"; or "What should I do next?" Many team leaders consider "Nothings" to be silent "Okays," which may be acceptable for certain tasks. But unfortunately, when silence is used too often, it can reduce performance.

Punishment ("Ouch!"). Punishment is the most effective consequence for *immediately stopping* an undesired behavior. "Ouchs!" are different from "Nays" in that "Ouchs!" are intended to halt an unwanted behavior, whereas "Nays" are meant to reduce one behavior in favor of another.

People who manage by fear are known to use punishment as a way of gaining rapid obedience and behavioral compliance. However, when used properly, punishment is an effective tool for unique situations such as disciplinary actions for poor performance; health, safety, and environmental violations; workplace bullying, harassment, and other egregious behaviors; or repeat violations of organizational policies.

Depending on the situation and the employee, there can be a fine line between a "Nay" and an "Ouch!" For example, if the employee receives "Yays!" for most work and then suddenly receives a "Nay," that "Nay" can feel more like an "Ouch!" for that employee. Conversely, after a long stretch of "Nothings" and "Nays," a "Yay!" may be received with great skepticism if not given correctly. Also, there's nothing more disappointing than to have received continuous positive feedback ("Yays!") from your previous supervisor and then get the silent treatment ("Nothing") from your new supervisor even though your level of performance has remained high.

One of the biggest mistakes team leaders make in managing behavior is the failure to use negative reinforcement and punishment to indict bad behaviors. They allow unwanted behaviors to continue through their avoidance, inaction, and silence ("Nothings"). Remember, inaction has consequences—silence can enable bad behavior.

CASE 6.2: SHARING BEST PRACTICES—HOW TO SHAPE A NEW TEAM BEHAVIOR

Let's use a graphic case example to illustrate how different consequences affect results. If you want your team to adopt a new behavior, you should start with the basis for the change, the *antecedent* (Figure 6.5). Describe *what* behavior you want and *why* it's important to change. This graph is a hypothetical timeline of how each of the four consequences affects a team's adoption of a new behavior ("% of Team Exhibiting New Behavior"). The goal is to get everyone to go from the old behavior (0 percent) to the new behavior at a high frequency (greater than 50 percent of the team is considered *good* and 100 percent is *great*). One hundred percent means everyone on the team is exhibiting the new behavior.

Let's say you want a specific behavior demonstrated once per month for each employee, such as sharing a best practice or valuable personal learning on the team's website. The old behavior is not sharing. Each month, you track the percentage of your work team that is showing the new behavior. Fifty percent means half the team exhibited the behavior, and 100 percent

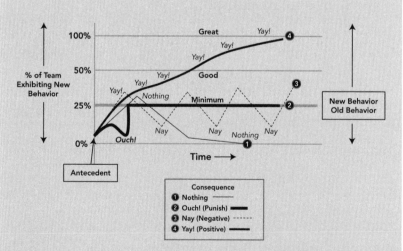

Figure 6.5 The effects of the four consequences in shaping a new behavior

means everyone shared a best practice or personal learning in that month. Twenty-five percent participation is considered the *minimum* acceptable performance level. Each "Nay" or "Yay!" on the chart represents a reinforcement by you, the team leader. A "Yay!" can be verbal praise, an email acknowledgment, or congratulatory shout-outs to people who posted a best practice. A "Nay" can consist of a verbal reminder expressing disappointment to team members or an emailed list of people who failed to submit a best practice or good learning for the month. However, the latter example, naming nonperformers, might be received as an "Ouch" by some.

The relative success of the new behavior is influenced by which consequence you use: ❶ using a "Nothing" response (inaction) yields the *least desirable outcome*—the team is mostly showing the old behavior, ❷ using an "Ouch!" results in *minimum success*—the team is showing the new behavior at a minimally acceptable rate (25 percent frequency), ❸ using a "Nay" strategy creates a "hot and cold" response—*behaviors alternate between new and old*, and ❹ using a "Yay!" reinforcement produces the *most favorable outcome*—rising to 100 percent participation.

Let's further examine the effects of each consequence in the graph:

1. **Nothing—gradual decline.** Soon after introducing the new behavior, no consequences ("Nothing") are given, team members start reverting to their old behavior, and, with continued "Nothings," the frequency of the new behavior gradually diminishes until no one on the team is sharing best practices.

2. **Ouch!—fall in line.** Team members start slowly toward the new behavior but begin slipping to their old behavior. When they receive punishment ("Ouch!"), they immediately correct themselves and shift to the new behavior but only at a minimum compliance level (25 percent of the time), just frequent enough to avoid further punishment. Behavior remains defiantly flat, just above the compliance level due to fear.

3. **Nay—mixed results.** The new behavior is successfully launched, but there's no positive reinforcement, so the team steadily reverts to its old behavior. When negative consequences ("Nays") are applied to correct their behavior, the team temporarily complies to avoid the negative consequence but declines again when there are no incentives. Their new behavior is only partially adopted.

4. **Yay!—success!** The team receives positive reinforcement ("Yay!") early and frequently in the learning phase, resulting in the active practice of the new behavior. The employees enjoy the positive consequences and are motivated to continue posting best practices and learnings. The positive reinforcement, coupled with peer pressure and the recognition that the new behavior is worth the effort, causes the team to adopt the behavior readily. In short order, the entire team is on board (100 percent).

Lessons from the Story

In early development, frequent "Yays!" are essential to encourage and reinforce the new behavior. But the "Yay!" consequence is additionally reinforced by the team's belief that the new behavior has value and it's worth the time and effort to make the change. And it'll continue as long as the employees believe that the change provides a net benefit. The ABC Model is not simply a "carrot and stick" approach—you can give out ice cream, but if the change doesn't make sense, the behavior will likely die off. Success is never guaranteed and it's not always a straight line up, but for a new behavior, the probability of success is much higher if you frequently reward good behavior with a "Yay!" and the benefit of changing is apparent to the employees.

"Below-the-Line" versus "Above-the-Line" Team Leaders

Team leaders who manage by *catching people doing things wrong* and applying punishment ("Ouchs!") and "Nays" as consequences are what I call below-the-line leaders, and they raise employee performance through fear and intimidation. In comparison, "above-the-line" leaders *catch people doing things right*, believe people want to do a good job, and use predominantly "Yay!" consequences to motivate employee performance. It's not a matter of incentivizing performance but rather one of motivating performance through positive encouragement, a compelling purpose, and positive recognition.

"Below-the-line leaders . . . raise employee performance through fear and intimidation. . . . 'Above-the-line' leaders . . . use predominantly 'Yay!' consequences to motivate employee performance."

Summary

Actively giving "Yays!" is essential for shaping a new behavior. But employees are human, and they will have missteps and setbacks in learning a new behavior. So it is quite healthy to use *some* below-the-line consequences to get back on the right track. At times, "Nays" may be the most effective in making course corrections. In severe circumstances, an "Ouch!" may be part of the consequence as well. But the key is to use "Yays!" predominately to raise performance through discretionary ("want to") efforts.

Give Consequences with the Right *Frequency* and in the Right *Proportion*

***Project leaders often fail to give consequences with the right* frequency.** Giving consequences is the most effective process for managing behaviors; however, when they are given with the wrong frequency and in the wrong proportion, the behavioral effect can be disappointing. Of the four possible consequences that follow a behavior, three are unwanted—"Nay," "Nothing," and "Ouch!"—and only one—"Yay!"—is wanted. So, if the four consequences were given randomly, employees would have a three-in-four chance (75 percent) of getting what they *don't want* ("Nay," "Nothing," or "Ouch!") and only a one-in-four chance (25 percent) of getting what they *do want* ("Yay!")—these are not good odds. Even worse, if we look at the frequency of positive reinforcements *actually given* in the workplace, most employees will tell you that they receive a "Yay!" (praise, ap-

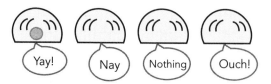

Figure 6.6 Seeking a "Yay!" is like playing a shell game

preciation, or recognition) at work much less than 25 percent of the time and probably closer to 10 percent or less!

"Yay!" is a shell game. A shell game is a trick in which a small ball or pea is shown to a player and then hidden underneath one of four shells (Figure 6.6). Then the shells are quickly and cleverly shuffled by the game operator and the player bets on the location of the pea. Due to the operator's sleight of hand, the player usually guesses wrong. It's sometimes called a "con game" because the game operator gains your *confidence* and then entices you to play a rigged game. Chasing "Yays!" at work is similar to playing a shell game in which you're seeking one consequence out of four ("Yay!"), but you're not sure when, where, and how you'll get the recognition (analogous to finding the pea). Like a pea under a shell, the location of the recognition is not apparent to you, and your supervisor is the game operator. Of course, your supervisor is not trying to trick you, but it's still a *game of consequences* that is controlled by your boss and "confidently" played by everyone. (See Skill Eight for more on managing your boss.)

Similar to a shell game, the success rate for recognition on the job is low (less than 10 percent) and the process for garnering a "Yay!" becomes a guessing game for the employee because the game is controlled by the supervisor. It's supposed to be a fair game, but many employees will tell you that the probability and predictability of getting a "Yay!" are disappointingly low.

As an employee or supervisor, it's an eye opener to realize that the game we play at work—competing for "Yays!"—is successful less than 10 percent of the time, which is much lower than random chance (one-in-four, or 25 percent) and also lower than the gambling games in Las Vegas! Furthermore, you have no control over your boss's behavior, and the feedback is not always explicit. At least with craps (a dice game) and blackjack (a card game), you are directly participating in the process and the *result is explicit.* Can you imagine playing a game of blackjack, making a bet, and, even though you predominantly get nothing or something worse in return, you keep on betting? It sounds ridiculous, but it's a common routine at work— do your job (game), work hard (make a bet), and your boss gives you no feedback ("Nothing") or finds fault with your work ("Nay"). Indeed, you get paid for your work but a "Yay!" is about motivation and feelings, not compensation. Your pay is in hard currency; your recognitions are in soft "Yays!" People need both to feel satisfied with their jobs.

You would get more positive recognition at work if the system were merely a game of chance where every time you completed an assignment, you would have a 25 percent chance of getting praised and rewarded. That sounds silly, but isn't it also silly to play a game each day in which you only have a 10 percent chance of receiving recognition? Maybe that's part of the reason employee satisfaction in the United States remains below 50 percent (16). Why do we continue to play a 10 percent game? Perhaps team leaders believe that employees are happy getting a paycheck as their "Yay!" and they have accepted the fact that praise and recognition are going to be infrequent. In this scenario and in the long run, you would likely get mediocre to occasionally above average performance at best.

The good news is that as a team leader and "game operator," you can change the game today by *increasing the frequency of "Yays!"* and giving more encouragement and happiness to your deserving employees. Yay!

***Project leaders often fail to give consequences in the right* proportion.** We know "Yays!" are infrequent, but the proportion of the other three consequences can also be better managed to improve employee performance. In the eyes of an employee, the typical supervisor in an organization usually gives mostly "Nothings," sometimes a "Nay," less frequently a "Yay!," and now and then an "Ouch!" The typical employee response is, "I usually don't get much feedback from my supervisor on my work, but when I do, it's usually because I did something wrong"—ouch!

When managers rule by absence ("Nothing"), negative feedback ("Nay"), or intimidation ("Ouch!"), the proportion of the four consequences is skewed to unwanted consequences (Figure 6.7, proportions reflected in size of word bubbles). To employees who fear their managers, "Nothings" are viewed as minor victories, and employees are resigned to accepting a "Nothing" as a pseudo "Yay!"—"No news is good news." This is *not* how you want

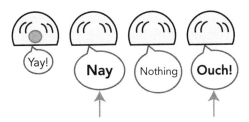

Figure 6.7 Consequences that motivate "have to" behaviors

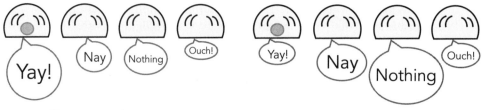

Team Leader's View   Employee's View

Figure 6.8 Different perceptions of team leaders and employees

to treat your employees. When employees see heavy doses of "Nays" and "Ouches!", it's a formula for compliance ("have to") behaviors. People are reluctant to speak up or take a risk because they're afraid of the consequences. Instead, they may choose to play a different game altogether, such as, "I play not to lose" (low initiative and aversion to risk), or, "I just do what I'm told" (low accountability), which are both passive avoidance behaviors.

How team leaders see themselves. In contrast to how employees see consequences, team leaders usually have a more upbeat view of their behaviors. They see their behaviors as positive, motivating, and active in giving praise, recognition, and encouragement to their deserving employees. They believe "Nays" are infrequently given and "Ouches!" are very rare (Figure 6.8, proportions reflected in size of word bubbles). Some supervisors believe, "As a leader, I go out of my way to make sure my employees feel respected, valued, and motivated at work. I routinely express my appreciation every day. As for myself, I'm self-motivated—I don't need a pat on my back."

How employees see their team leaders. It is not uncommon for employees to see their team leaders as giving mostly "Nothings," "Nays," and some "Ouches!," whereas team leaders commonly see themselves as giving mostly "Yays!" Why the discrepancy in the perceptions of employees and team leaders? It's clear that the positive consequences from their team leaders are not being received as such, and "Nothings," "Nays," and "Ouches!" are perceived by employees to occur at a much greater frequency. Remember, for a "Yay!" to be effective, it needs to be *sincere, consistent, on time, on values,* and *personalized* (Skill Four: SCOOP). Too often, a thank-you fails to be specific and personalized. Also, generic pats on the back or trinkets are frequently regarded as disingenuous, impersonal, and sometimes insulting. A "Yay!" needs to be meaningful to the recipient for it to be felt as a positive consequence. Also, project leaders need to be aware that negative feedback is often amplified and remembered much longer by employees than positive feedback.

Make it your goal to close the gap between your perception and your employees' perception of "Yay!" consequences, and be aware that "Nothings"

Table 6.3 Different Behaviors Call for Different Proportions of "Yay!" and "Nay"

Type of Behavior	Yay–to–Nay Proportion
Maintain/Modify a Key Behavior	4:1
Learn a New Behavior	6:1
Learn a Critical New Behavior or Break an Old Habit	8:1

can feel like "Nays" and "Nays" can feel like "Ouches!" Transparency and empathy can go a long way in reducing unintended consequences.

Getting the right mix of consequences is essential for sustaining high team performance. The right proportion for the four consequences depends on the type of work, behavior, and circumstances. Here are some general guidelines on behavioral reinforcement, using a simple yay-to-nay ratio (Table 6.3). Please keep in mind that these ratios may need to be adjusted depending on circumstances, type of work, composition of the workforce, risks, and other workplace variables. High-performing organizations are known to routinely deliver between four to one and six to one yay-to-nay ratios. To shape new behaviors or change old habits, "Yay!" and "Nay" reinforcements must be given often and effectively. In project leadership, actively role modeling and rewarding desired behaviors are effective antecedents and consequences, respectively, for motivating a new behavior. Once employees are fluent with the new behavior, self- and peer reinforcement should take over and lessen the need for you to provide frequent consequences.

Administer the Right *Process* to Consequent Desired Behaviors In most cases, positive and negative reinforcements are best given on the spot when the employee exhibits the desired behavior. Giving latent consequences greatly reduces the effectiveness of shaping and reinforcing new behaviors. Here is an effective, real-time coaching tool for project leaders to administer "Yays!" and "Nays" to employees.

When you observe a *desired* behavior, meet with the employee as soon as you can and do the following:

1. Describe the situation and the specific desired *behavior* that the employee demonstrated.

2. Describe the *favorable* result or effect.

3. Give *positive feedback*—an evaluative appraisal of how the behavior or consequence impacted you, the team, and/or the organization— and express sincere appreciation, which *reinforces* the desired behavior.

When you observe an *unwanted* behavior, meet with the employee as soon as you can and do the following:

1. Describe the situation and the specific unwanted *behavior* that the employee demonstrated.

2. Describe the *unfavorable or inappropriate* result or effect.

3. Give *corrective feedback*—an evaluative appraisal of how it adversely impacted you, the team, and/or the organization—and ask the employee what *behavior* would have been more effective. Praise the employee for a good response; if the response is not good, then advise the employee of the desired behavior in specific detail and explain why it's preferred (*reinforcement*); then ask the employee if you can count on him or her to show that behavior going forward. Thank the employee for his or her commitment to change.

In closing, the ABC Box Model offers an effective, easy-to-remember strategy for shaping and managing people's behaviors. The secret is to know the CSBs that you want, set up the right antecedents (A) to prompt those critical behaviors (B), and then shape and sustain the behaviors through effective use of consequences (C). This skill can be a game-changer for you, enabling you to feel more knowledgeable, confident, and equipped to be a more positive force in helping others to perform at their best. Please remember that the ABC Box Model is a tool for motivation, not manipulation, as long as you use it with the intent and sincerity of helping others to succeed.

Skill Six Summary

There's no dispute that people are your greatest asset in any organization, and *people's behaviors* are what determine the success or failure of a team. This skill provides a simple, practical model for defining and managing employee behaviors that are critical to an organization's success. As a team leader, no role is more important than that of managing and facilitating the right behaviors, actions, and interactions among your employees.

What motivates employee behaviors are values, and having clear and compelling values is key to your success as a project team leader. In any organization, you must have the right values to drive the right behaviors and the right behaviors to drive the right results. In short, if people are doing the right things in the right way, you'll get the right results. For values to be useful, they need to be operationalized by translating them into specific, pinpointed behaviors that employees can understand, practice, and reinforce in the workplace.

Once you have defined the right values and behaviors, motivating employees to demonstrate those key behaviors is the essence of project team management. The ABC (antecedent-behavior-consequence) Box Model gives you an easy-to-remember system for motivating desired team behaviors. You need the right basis or antecedents (Box A) to evoke the right behaviors (Box B), and you need to give the right consequences (Box C) to reinforce those desired behaviors. Antecedents are intellectual tools that *start* the behavior, and consequences are the emotional motivators that *sustain* the behavior. The four main consequences that affect behaviors are positive reinforcement ("Yay!"), negative reinforcement ("Nay"), no reinforcement ("Nothing"), and punishment ("Ouch!").

Effective management of consequences is a key differentiator between good and bad leaders. Every team leader has a choice when it comes to managing behaviors—you can operate in a positive and encouraging manner ("Yay!") or manage in a negative and punishing way ("Nay" and "Ouch!"). It basically comes down to *whether you want to catch people doing things right or catch people doing things wrong.* The latter drives compliance behaviors and mediocre performance, whereas the former results in greater discretionary efforts and higher performance.

Successful management of work behaviors depends on your ability to administer consequences with the right balance, frequency, and timing; in the right situation; and for the right effect and outcome. However, your intended consequences may not be perceived the same way by your employees. To shape the right behaviors, it is important to administer both positive and negative reinforcements to improve employee performance. The ABC Box Model is a powerful facilitation tool to motivate the behaviors you want in your team.

Skill Six Memory Card

Motivating the Right Behaviors

Use the ABCs to Get Desired Behaviors

Antecedent: *Starts the Behavior*

1. Establish the right *basis* for people's behaviors, such as policies, standards, goals, and values
2. Values are the most effective antecedent for motivating the *right* behaviors

Behavior: *How You Want People to Act and Interact*

1. Define the right behaviors to drive the right results
2. Identify your team's critical success behaviors (CSBs) that meet organizational and team expectations and incorporate them into your work plan

Consequence: *Occurs After the Behavior*

1. Use the four consequences with the right frequency and in the right proportion to get the right effect on behavior: positive reinforcement (Yay!), negative reinforcement (Nay), no consequence (Nothing), and punishment (Ouch!)
2. What gets reinforced gets repeated
3. Yay! is the most effective consequence for *sustaining* desired behaviors
4. Be an "above-the-line" leader who catches people doing things *right* rather than a "below-the-line" leader who catches people doing things *wrong*

SKILL SEVEN

How to Succeed When Faced with Change, Problems, and New Challenges
The Black Box Effect

What do change, problems, and new challenges have in common? They all involve managing *uncertainty*. In project management, uncertainties are normal, expected, unavoidable, and inherent in the work. You have to contend with uncertainties in project execution, schedules, budgeting, procurement, contracting, and technology, as well as in leading people. Nothing in project management is predictable or guaranteed, so you'd better be good at managing uncertainty.

How is managing uncertainty a people problem? Uncertainty causes *fear* in people—often manifested as worry, concern, and anxiety—and excessive fear is the root cause for bad behaviors, conflicts, and poor performance. One of the most adverse behaviors that fear creates is risk aversion, and one critical behavior for overcoming the effects of fear from uncertainty is *risk taking*.

To run a successful team project, avoiding risk is not an option—you have to take risks. You're taking a risk just by managing a project and leading your team through changes, conflicts, problems, and new challenges. You're expected to help your team take risks in seeking better and faster ways to get things done, trying new approaches to solve problems, and improving work processes.

You can't be a good risk taker without overcoming the negative effects of fear. Fear is inherent in all people—you can't get rid of it or suppress it. To be an effective project leader, you must be effective in managing fear and risk taking. Unfortunately, this is a tall order because everyone struggles to some degree with the fear of taking risks. What holds people back from acting on new opportunities, applying themselves, and seeking higher achievement? Why is it so difficult to get teams to make significant changes and try new things? It's clear that uncertainties and risks make people feel uneasy, unstable, and insecure. It's hard to move a team forward when people prefer to play things safe. So how do you countervail the excessive fear and risk aversion that are prevalent in many project leaders and teams today? Skill Seven addresses the root drivers of risk aversion and how to manage uncertainty and fear to your advantage.

CASE 7.1: THE CROSS-COUNTRY CHAMPIONSHIP— THE RISK TAKER

Cross-country running is not the most glamorous sport in high school, but it is one of the most challenging. The participants are a small group of highly dedicated individuals who run long, grueling distances in all types of weather and on all kinds of race courses. At a local high school in Northern California, one of the cross-country runners was a young girl named Sarah, a sophomore with a genuine joy for running. She liked the coaching, training, team camaraderie, and opportunity to compete against other runners in the area. She was not the fastest runner, but she had performed well enough to make the varsity team. In the races, she would always give a good effort and finish in the middle of the pack.

After an average season, the team disappointingly finished third in their local division but ran well enough to qualify for the year-end sectional championship finals. In preparation for the finals, the team trained extra hard for two weeks to increase their strength and endurance for the championship. Unfortunately, the increased training wore out Sarah, who, between studying for final exams and running practices, became ill and missed several of the final practices. It was questionable whether she would be healthy enough and have sufficient energy to run in the finals. The team assumed that she would miss the race, but she remained hopeful that she would be able to run; if not, she was content to at least make the trip and support the team.

On the morning of the championship, Sarah ate a hearty break-fast and felt good enough to suit up for the trip to the finals. She would decide at the time of the race whether she would run. Upon arriving at the championship, it was clear that the event was going to be special—over forty high school teams in the state from three different divisional levels were compet-ing. The cross-country course was a four-mile trek that started at one end of a large, open grass field one hundred yards wide and gradually narrowed down to a paved gateway that led to a hilly pathway for another two miles. Sarah's team was running in the highest division and scheduled to go last as the premier race. They were expected to finish in the lower tier among the competing high schools, with the top state runners slated to dominate.

As the team was setting up on the starting line, they were sur-prised to see Sarah there. This gave the team a bit of a lift, but what really surprised them was what she said: "Look guys, this race is a one-time opportunity, and we can make this our best race of the year—let's make it a race that we can all remember." The team appeared encouraged by her message, and she fur-ther remarked, "To finish high, we have to run hard and stay with the best teams in this race."

Sarah knew that the key to the race was to get to the narrowed section of the course called the gateway as quickly as possible along with the best teams. She urged the team to "go for it," stay with the leaders, and "run to win," instead of running with the pack and ending up in the bottom third. Many of her team members suddenly grew concerned, expressing to Sarah that this was not only a last-minute change in strategy but also an impossible task, given the caliber of runners there. As one team member said, "We will die if we try to run with the leaders." Sarah responded by saying, "Just follow me." At that moment, the runners were called to the starting line. A long band of runners from fifteen schools, stretching across a hundred yards, readied themselves as the official fired the starting gun.

It was like a prison break, with runners scattering and jockey-ing for position and finally coalescing into a large, spear-like formation that raced up the gentle, dewy slope toward the gateway. It was a broad, straight course for the first mile and a half, and it seemed to take forever to run up the long, grassy slope. Everyone knew that getting to the gateway was the key to finishing well. Sarah knew that, too, and sprinted with all her might toward that gateway with over one hundred runners. The dominating teams were leading as expected, but midway up the slope, a small runner dressed in yellow and green and wearing bib number 1160 sprinted decisively ahead of the pack and became the tip of the spear—the runner was Sarah (Figure 7.1).

Not far behind were two of her teammates, hanging with her and pushing hard up the slope. With several top competitors dressed in black jerseys on her heels, Sarah led the entire mass to the top of the slope, and just as her competitors were bearing down to pass Sarah at the throat of the gateway, Sarah picked up her pace and beat all the girls through the gateway. The coaches were speechless and in disbelief as Sarah passed the gawking spectators at the gateway.

If this were a fairy tale, we could make believe that Sarah and the team went on to win that race. Actually, after another few hundred yards, Sarah and her teammates faded back into the pack, but to the delight of everyone, they hung tough for the rest of the race and finished third out of fifteen teams; it was a great race and the team finished much higher than they had ever hoped, but it certainly didn't feel that way when they labored through the finish line. Sarah finished first on her team,

Figure 7.1 Sarah, bib 1160, running for the gateway in the cross-country championship

but it was probably the hardest race for her and the pain she endured in the race must have been extraordinary. All in all, the girls gave a tremendous effort and Sarah certainly gave everything she had. But was Sarah's effort to win the race *too risky and foolish*? Did she walk away feeling, "I'll never do that again—that was stupid," or, "Geez, I feel like a fool for pushing the team so hard"?

After the race, one spectator wondered why she took such a big risk, asking, "Didn't you realize that your crazy start could have ruined the entire race for you and your team?" Sarah smiled and said, "Of course! But I didn't care. I wasn't going to just sit back and watch. I believed we could do it. It was the best chance we had, so why not go for it? It was hard, but I'll get over it." Sarah had absolutely no regrets or disappointments. In fact, in the following year, her experience enabled her to be one of the best runners in the area—she made it to the state finals, and one year later she ran cross-country for a top-rated university.

Lessons from the Story

▲ **You can't do great things without taking some risks.** It's clear that high achievement and success require acts of courage and risk taking. Sarah was very courageous in light of her compromised physical condition and the magnitude of the challenge, and her spirit and boldness inspired her teammates. As a project leader, you are expected to challenge and encourage your employees to try new things, improve processes, suggest new ideas, create new products, and not be afraid to take some risks.

▲ **Being a leader means overcoming many fears.** People naturally look to their team leaders for guidance and direction, but when faced with change, problems, and new challenges, people will not blindly go along with taking risks. Sarah's teammates pushed back hard when she urged the team to run faster. These are times when your will and inner strength are tested. As a leader, not only do you have to deal with the uncertainty of the circumstances but you also have to contend with your team's fears, which can lead to team disagreements, conflicts, rejection, and criticism. Such discontent would make any team leader hesitate, back off, and lose confidence. Yet, to perform at a high level, project leaders are expected to overcome these concerns, trust their abilities, and be willing to "go for it" as Sarah did in her race.

▲ **Risk taking is a behavior.** Sarah's story illustrates that risk taking is an action and a behavior and not a process. In this skill, *risk* is defined as the probability of losing, failing, or getting an undesirable consequence. Skill Seven is not about risk assessment and risk management, which are both processes. This skill is about looking at risk taking as a *behavior*, examining the thinking and behaviors of risk takers versus non–risk takers, understanding the mental barriers that make people risk averse, and improving the risk behaviors in yourself and your team. You can find tons of literature on risk management, but much less is written about the behavior of risk taking, which is an important skill for team leaders and project teams. As we discuss the behavior of risk taking in this skill, more lessons will be drawn from Sarah's story.

> *"Skill Seven is not about risk assessment and risk management, which are both processes. This skill is about looking at risk taking as a behavior."*

Summary

This story is about fear, uncertainty, and risk taking; Sarah's decisions and actions in the championship race illustrate the unique thinking and behaviors that are essential in project management when faced with change, problems, and new challenges.

How Uncertainty, Fear, and Risks Affect People: The Black Box Effect

If you're like most people, you want to take more risks but can't seem to pull the trigger when the time comes. Instead, you think about it, collect more information, analyze it, debate it, weigh your options, see what others do, wait for approval, wait for the right time, or wait for something better. Why do people *wait*? Why not go for it and take a chance? What holds people back? People want to break free and take more risks, but the mental bonds tend to be too strong.

Risk taking is an action characterized by uncertainty, similar to opening a black box. There is a fear of the unknown—you're not sure whether it's going to be a trick, trap, or treat. Not knowing what may be lurking in the box, you and others hold back from going in too fast and too deep. You're *uncertain* what may happen and you don't feel in *control*. Thus, in this skill, the concept of *a black box is used as a metaphor for a high degree of risk, fear, and uncertainty.*

The anxiety that you feel when facing any unknown element is natural and common to most people, and your feelings of apprehension don't reflect negatively on the strength of your character. When facing a risk from a new change, problem, or challenge, the cautiousness that you feel probably stems from your survival instincts and past negative consequences. No matter how many positive experiences you may have had in your career, the ones that weigh most on your mind are the painful ones, which can hurt your risk-taking ability.

In project management, three main uncertainties (potential "black boxes") arise when facing changes, problems, and new challenges. I call them the *"three uncertainties in risk taking,"* and they each correspond to one of the boxes in the ABC Box Model from Skill Six (Figure 7.2). These three uncertainties represent the key mental barriers that you and your team need to overcome in order to be successful in managing change, solving problems, and meeting new challenges.

A. **The uncertainty of the *circumstance*** (antecedent, Box A): Not knowing the meaning, difficulty, and scope of the change, problem, or new challenge

B. **The uncertainty of your *ability* to perform** (behavior, Box B): Unsure of your skills and ability to successfully execute the actions required in response to the change, problem, or new challenge

C. **The uncertainty of a *bad outcome*** (consequence, Box C): The chances of potential failure and other negative outcomes from the change, problem, or new challenge

Case in Point In the cross-country race, Sarah was highly focused and motivated and likely felt a moderate level of fear and uncertainty about (A) the *circumstance*—she was familiar with the course and its length, but she'd never raced in the championship or with these top runners; (B) her *ability to perform*: she was unsure how she and her team would endure the rapid initial pace and the competition; and (C) the

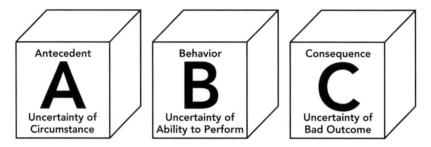

Figure 7.2 The three uncertainties in risk taking: circumstance, ability to perform, and bad outcome

prospects of a *bad outcome*—she didn't know how the race would unfold and where her team would finish.

Risk taking is about taking action in the face of the three uncertainties: circumstance, ability to perform, and a bad outcome. Since these three uncertainties exactly parallel the three boxes in the ABC Box Model (Skill Six), we will use this model to understand the differences between risk takers and non–risk takers and their unique views of Boxes A (antecedent or circumstance), B (behavior or ability), and C (consequence or outcome). Sarah's running story is a good case for illustrating these three uncertainties, how the ABC Box Model applies to risk taking, and the characteristics of risk takers and non–risk takers. In this skill, the terms *risk taker* and *non–risk taker* refer to both individuals and teams. Now let's break down the secrets to risk taking and how to overcome the uncertainties of the *circumstance, ability to perform, and a bad outcome.*

The Secrets to Overcoming the Uncertainty of the Circumstance

As we learned in Skill Six, people's actions and inactions are regulated by three boxes: antecedent (A), behavior (B), and consequence (C). Basically, antecedents are prompts, stimuli, and directives that can be viewed as opportunities or threats. Box A represents your view of the *circumstance*—such as when you are confronted by a *change, problem, or challenge.* Whether you perceive the circumstance (antecedent) as an *opportunity or a threat* dictates your response. People are compelled by opportunities and repelled by threats.

In the cross-country championship, Sarah saw the event and the strategy to start fast (antecedent) as an *opportunity* to win the race, whereas others saw it as a *threat* to lose the race. *Where successful teams and risk takers see opportunities, non–risk takers see potential danger.* Box A can be either an opportunity or a threat, and the uncertainty and fear of the antecedent can be viewed as acceptable or unacceptable. Unacceptable risks are treated as black boxes—that is, they either pose too much risk to proceed or too much uncertainty to trust.

Although the antecedent appears exactly the same to both risk takers and non–risk takers, the perceptions of risk takers and non–risk takers are different. *Risk takers don't see antecedents as black boxes—they see them as opportunities.* They are especially curious, challenged, and excited by what may happen, whereas non–risk takers see the same antecedent as a possible trick or trap and it's better to be safe than sorry. Basically, risk takers willingly accept the uncertainty and fear associated with new circumstances as *gifts*, whereas non–risk takers view them as potential threats or *black boxes*. In other words, Sarah and other risk takers are not afraid to run toward opportunities (gift antecedents) to experience a change, solve a problem, or conquer a new challenge, whereas non–risk takers find the uncertainty and fear to be unacceptable and therefore tend to pass on those same opportunities (Figure 7.3).

Whether the circumstance is perceived as an opportunity or threat depends on your values, beliefs, emotions, conscience, experiences, and temperament. This blend of human factors, more often than not, can cause you to hesitate, wait, hold back, and avoid rather than engaging the opportunity. The first box is the most important in risk taking because once you choose to pass on an opportunity, the other boxes don't matter. Also, your experiences (memory) from new circumstances (Box A) will likely affect your future outlook and behaviors regarding the other two uncertainties (Boxes B and C), which we will discuss later in this chapter.

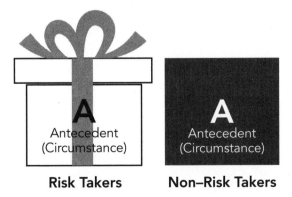

Figure 7.3 New circumstances are gifts to risk takers but black boxes to non–risk takers

Case in Point Police, firefighters, and other first responders have a special courage and gift for facing new challenges and emergencies on a regular basis. They are compelled to take action in life-and-death situations and see them as *opportunities* to do good, help others, and save lives. This motivation comes from their values, beliefs, conscience, emotions, experiences, and temperament. That's what motivates them to take the risk. It's dangerous work, but to them, it's the right thing to do and they wouldn't be in the business if they didn't believe they could save lives and property. They are true risk takers, putting their own lives on the line to help save and protect others. But you also can find courageous risk takers in many other occupations in public service, nonprofits, and industry, such as the military, energy, education, engineering, finance, and medicine, as well as project management. Furthermore, people take risks in buying a home, running a small business, investing in their own education, having children, and other circumstances. You can find courageous risk takers and heroes throughout our society. Risk taking is not a special, narrow skill but rather a common behavior that we can all value and demonstrate in many different ways and under many different circumstances.

Is Fear Good or Bad?

When a team lacks certainty and predictability in something, both risk takers and non–risk takers are apt to feel fearful, cautious, and insecure. As uncertainty rises, fear rises. Both risk takers and non–risk takers experience symptoms of fear, such as worry, concern, and anxiety. Although it is often said that risk takers are fearless, that is a myth. It is likely that Sarah felt the same level of anxiety about running as her teammates, or perhaps even more so as she hadn't practiced much before the championship, but it's what Sarah did with that fear and anxiety that made a difference. Fear is a primitive, instinctive human emotion that everyone experiences, and it is not only inborn but also necessary for survival. This means that risk taking is a conscious, mental behavior that can be learned and managed. When managed well, fear can serve as an ally and motivate you to perform at a higher level. *It is the management of fear that differentiates risk takers from non–risk takers.*

Taking a risk is not about eliminating fear— it's about embracing it and using it to your advantage. Fear has advantages and disadvantages—an extremely low level of fear tends to make you and your team complacent, content, and passive, whereas a moderate level of fear helps you to focus, take action, and perform, but excessive fear can cause you and your team to avoid, stop, and underperform. The effect of fear on a person's ability to perform when facing an uncertainty has a bell-shaped curve (Figure 7.4) (17). Theoretically, a moderate level of uncertainty and fear is the most favorable for achieving optimal performance. Your optimal performance is also your risk threshold—any risk less than your optimum (to the left of your risk threshold) is considered an *acceptable* risk, and anything beyond your optimum (to the right of your risk threshold) is seen as an increasingly *unacceptable* risk (black box), indicating that you will pass on or withdraw from the challenge. The secret is to *avoid becoming excessively fearful and uncertain* when you encounter change, problems, and challenges. Excessive fear and uncertainty drives you into the "black box" zone and this effect applies to all three uncertainties in risk taking.

> *"A moderate level of uncertainty and fear is the most favorable for achieving optimal performance."*

Reducing the Fear of the Uncertainty of the Circumstance

In the cross-country race, Sarah confronted her fear of the circumstance by taking control of it and not letting it drive her into the "black box" and diminish her performance (Figure 7.4). She welcomed fear and used it to her advantage to *take control of the race and not let fear take control of her.* Her actions helped her team run faster. Sarah was able to overcome her fear of the race's uncertainties by using it as motivation and directing that energy to action rather than standing by and doing nothing. Sarah took

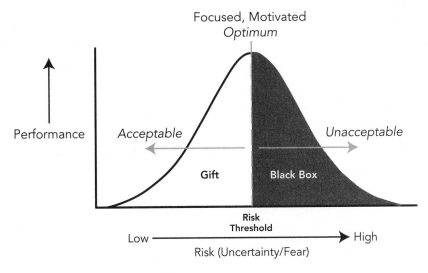

Figure 7.4 Bell-shaped effect of fear on performance

control of her fears and reduced the uncertainty of the new circumstance (antecedent) by initiating a new strategy.

People Respond Differently to New Challenges and Risks

Fear is an internal human factor that affects everyone. Each time you win or lose, or make a judgment on whether a change, problem, or new challenge is an opportunity or threat, you're leaving what I call a *trace memory* inside of you. When you repeatedly perceive and judge changes, problems, and challenge as negatives, you are conditioning yourself to avoid taking a risk; conversely, when you regularly perceive and judge things as positives, you are conditioning yourself to seek wins. Ask yourself, are your first thoughts usually negative or positive? Are you more pessimistic or optimistic? I have found that most people's first thoughts tend to be negative, skeptical, and critical, which likely stem from their consequent history of getting frequent unwanted consequences ("Nays," "Ouches!" and "Nothings," Skill Six). As a result, these negative trace memories of risk taking can gradually accumulate and diminish your acceptance of risk, causing you to become more risk averse, not only for Box A but also subsequently for Boxes B and C. Similarly, when positive trace memories of risk taking are repeated over time, your ability to take risks increases almost imperceptibly to the point that you learn to become more risk seeking and this affects your mind-set toward Boxes B and C as well.

This mental aggregation of trace memories dictates your general risk tolerance. It's common to find that people and teams have different levels of risk tolerance for different situations, such as starting an unfamiliar project, reorganizing a team, or adopting a new technology. Each person possesses a different level of risk tolerance depending on his or her values, beliefs, feelings, experience, knowledge, skills, and familiarity with the given circumstance (Figure 7.5). If we compare the general risk profile of risk takers with that of non–risk takers, we can see that risk takers have a higher threshold or tolerance for risk than non–risk takers. *A higher risk tolerance means the bell curve is farther to the right than average*, indicating that the individual *accepts* a greater and wider range of risks (from 0 to 3). In contrast, non–risk takers have a much lower optimal level of fear than risk takers and possess a lower and narrower range for risk taking (from 0 to 1), which shifts their bell curve to the left (lower risk level). The base case in the figure represents the majority of the population, which has a risk range of 0 to 2. The ranges of 0 to 1 and 0 to 3 are the "comfort zones" for non–risk takers and risk takers, respectively.

Risk takers and non–risk takers operate on different curves—the optimal level of fear and uncertainty for a risk taker, 3, is considered excessive for a

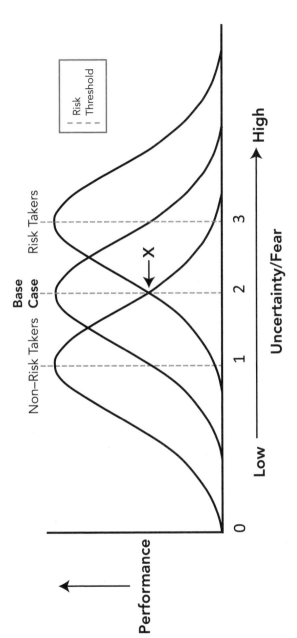

Figure 7.5 Risk tolerance profiles of risk takers and non-risk takers

non–risk taker. A risk-averse individual would have a lower optimal level of 1. Thus, in a given opportunity (base case) with the same level of risk (the X in Figure 7.5), risk takers such as Sarah are quite comfortable taking on the challenge (acceptable risk; the X is on the left side of her bell curve and within her acceptable range [less than 3]), whereas non–risk takers are uncomfortable and would pass on the same opportunity (excessive risk; the X is on the right side of their bell curve and beyond their comfort zone of 1 or less).

Building Risk Tolerance

Risk taking is a learned behavior, but risk tolerance is something that you *build* from experience and hard work. Experiences and effort help you to improve your ability to take more risks. It makes sense that the more skilled and knowledgeable you are, the more *motivated* you are to initiate action. Unbeknownst to her team members, Sarah was accustomed to such risks because she had taken similar risks before. It's the same with a project team—you take on new opportunities as your team builds more experience working together and going through both good and difficult times. What you and your team learn from taking new risks is that *you can do it*; what you learn from taking a risk and failing is that *you will survive*; and what you learn from each experience adds to your risk-taking ability.

You and your team can widen your comfort zone and increase your risk tolerance by knowing your team's values, beliefs, and assumptions and increasing your knowledge, experience, and opportunities. Every risk-seeking and risk-taking experience should be seen as a positive trace memory that adds to your skills and abilities—you learn and become skilled by taking risks more often. You learn not only about taking risks but also about taking better, smarter risks. The process of learning is a benefit that is often overlooked and undervalued by people who are risk averse. By learning to take negative fear and emotions and redirecting that energy into positive, productive actions, you are steadily increasing your risk tolerance (Figure 7.5, shifting your bell curve to the right). Start by taking small steps and building a continuous stream of positive trace memories for you and your team. This doesn't mean you should start doing things recklessly. As a first step, practice taking control of your fears and treating new challenges as a positive opportunity, not a negative threat—redirect your energy into realizing the benefits, not the risks, of the circumstance. The secret is to train yourself and your team to take that first step—*taking control to reduce the uncertainty of the circumstance*. Sarah was successful in taking control of the race with

> *"Redirect your energy into realizing the benefits, not the risks, of the circumstance."*

a new strategy and lessening the negative effects of a new challenge. Another case example, Case 7.2, is provided in the next section.

Summary: Best Tips for Overcoming the Uncertainty of the Circumstance (Antecedent, Box A)

▲ Look at change, problems, and challenges (antecedents) as *gift opportunities*, not "black box" threats.

▲ A *moderate level of uncertainty* and fear is good—it increases your focus, motivation, and performance.

▲ *Take control* of your fears; otherwise, fear will take control of you and drive you into a black box.

▲ Non–risk-taking individuals and teams have relatively low risk tolerances, which decreases their ability to act on new opportunities. Avoid settling into a low-risk comfort zone.

▲ Increase your risk tolerance by redirecting negative fears and energy into positive, opportunistic thinking and action.

▲ Successful risk taking is a *learned behavior*. As you and your team gain more experience and positive trace memories in risk taking, your risk tolerance will improve (shift to the right in Figure 7.5) and your *risk range and comfort level will expand* for all three uncertainties.

The Secrets to Overcoming the Uncertainty of Your Ability to Perform

Risk takers treat new circumstances and challenges (antecedents) as gift opportunities and cannot wait to open them, whereas non–risk takers see the same circumstances as black boxes with unacceptable uncertainty and will wait and avoid the risk. Your fears and risk tolerance affect not only your attitude toward antecedents (new challenges, opportunities, changes, and problems) but also your behaviors. As we have discovered with antecedents (Box A), risk takers and non–risk takers also *behave* (Box B) differently in response to new circumstances.

Uncertainty creates a mental void (void of uncertainty) inside of you, like the inside of a black box, that gets naturally filled by fear unless you have a countereffect. Your ability to respond successfully to uncertainty lies in your balance of self-confidence and self-doubt. Like with fear, some self-doubt is healthy and can enhance performance. However, non–risk takers who have a low risk tolerance are apt to fill their Box B with excessive self-doubt and pessimism and feel uncertain about themselves and their abilities to perform. In other words, they fill their voids of uncertainty with more uncertainties, which is similar to adding fuel to a fire. Their "behavior" box becomes a black box—darkened by fear, worry, and negative thinking. Their behaviors are controlled by their fears, which cause them to refrain and retreat. They relinquish control of their emotions to fear. This leads to inaction, resistance, and avoidance. In contrast, risk takers fill their voids of uncertainty with self-confidence, optimism, and certainty about their knowledge, skills, and abilities (Figure 7.6).

Your self-confidence is highly influenced by other people, resources, relationships, and support. That's why teams and teamwork are so important in project management and risk taking. You are more effective in seeking and taking risks when you have people behind you who encourage, support, and root for you. Gain greater confidence in facing changes, problems, and challenges by believing in yourself and having others believe in you too.

Good project leaders and teams take action to *reduce the uncertainty of their abilities to perform through good teamwork, practice, knowledge, competency, preparation, support, and resources.*

In essence, *Box B represents your level of self-confidence*, and your behavior reflects the confidence that you have in yourself and your team. As we learned in Skill Two, nothing is more certain than your authentic self, so to believe in yourself, *just be yourself*—this requires you to trust your judgment and abilities.

If you believe in yourself, have good support, and feel certain about your skills, knowledge, and abilities, then your behavior (Box B) becomes more confident, assertive, and risk seeking; but if you and your team doubt

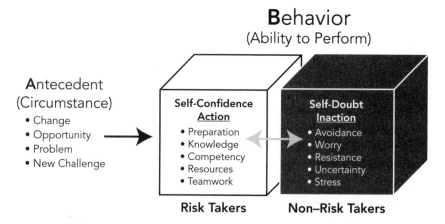

Figure 7.6 Risk takers take action, non–risk takers go inactive

yourselves and your abilities, then your Box B becomes a black box—filled with uncertainty and fear. In short, *risk takers* fill their boxes with *confidence and self-trust*, whereas *non–risk takers* fill their boxes with excessive *self-doubt and uncertainty* about their own abilities, which creates a black box effect.

When facing the uncertainty of a new circumstance or antecedent (Box A), the secret lies in your inner motivation to *initiate* action. For managing the uncertainty of one's ability to perform (Box B), the secret is to have *self-confidence*, a belief in your ability to *take action with great purpose and resolve* (behavior). When you are confronted with the uncertainty of your abilities, fear naturally creeps in and automatically fills that uncertain void inside of you. How you counter that fear is what determines whether you are a risk taker or a non–risk taker and whether you are a successful or an unsuccessful project leader. When fear calls, how do you answer that call— with self-doubt or self-confidence (Figure 7.6)? Do you shift your bell curve

> **"When fear calls, risk takers get busy."**

left (Figure 7.5) and go into a defensive position of self-doubt, or do you shift to the right, refusing to let fear win and taking confident action? Not only do successful risk takers shift their bell curves to the right and lessen the effects of fear, but they are also able to counter their fears with self-confidence, action, optimism, and a forward-looking mind-set. In other words, fear becomes a wake-up call for focused, urgent, decisive action. When fear calls, risk takers get busy. *They use fear to their advantage by treating it as a call to action.*

Most non–risk takers prefer to play things safe and choose inaction over action, thinking that they can avoid a bad consequence by avoiding the risk; however, *inaction only avoids action, not bad consequences.* Inaction has its own set of rationalizations and consequences, such as the following:

▲ **Lost opportunities:** Opportunities that you pass up may not show up again.

▲ **Regrets:** People do not regret the things they *do*; they regret the things they *don't* do.

▲ **Excuses:** You can always find good reasons *not* to do something.

▲ **Fear:** Inaction merely reinforces the same fear that has been holding you back.

▲ **Time:** Not having time to pursue an opportunity is a common rationalization for inaction; rationalizations are excuses.

▲ **Reduced confidence:** Inaction is a behavior that diminishes your belief in yourself and increases self-doubt.

▲ **Settling:** Many people don't take risks because it's uncomfortable; they prefer to settle into their comfort zone, which can become a mental trap.

▲ **Spectator effect:** Observing is safer than playing, but you can't win if you don't play.

In summary, for Box A, risk takers redirect their fears to *take control and reduce the uncertainty of the circumstance*, and for Box B, they use fear to *take action to increase the certainty of their ability*. Both these concepts are illustrated in our next case.

CASE 7.2, PART 1: OVERCOMING THE RISK AND FEAR OF GIVING A PRESENTATION—THE FIRST TWO STEPS

After several months of planning, research, and analysis, the corporate benefits team was ready to roll out the new 401(k) retirement plan for their employees. Mike, a highly trained and experienced benefits and investment counselor, was given the task of presenting the new plan at one of the company office locations. He disliked giving talks and pushed to do the roll-out online, but the leadership team favored in-person sessions at their major locations. To Mike, this challenge was not a gift opportunity but a black box. He had given talks before, and they were all nerve-racking and difficult. He confided to his boss that he was worried about it and confessed that he wasn't good at giving talks and was certain he would not perform well. He wanted to know what he should do to better cope with this new challenge. His boss recommended that he talk to Judy, an experienced management coach in the company.

Mike immediately made an appointment to see Judy, and when they met in her office, Mike shared his fears about giving talks. The following is their conversation:

Judy [with a sympathetic tone]: Mike, you're not alone in your concerns about giving a presentation. Public speaking is one of the top fears for people, but I think I can help you. I find that many people like you feel uncomfortable giving talks [they see it as a black box]. They typically hope for the best, brace for the worst, and pray they survive. They feel they're not good at it and will probably fail. I find that many people are so frightened about giving talks that they have already resigned themselves to defeat. Fear has taken control and adversely affected their thinking [they have filled their Box B (behavior) with self-doubt and pessimism]. That's why public speaking is such a nightmare to many.

Mike [nodding]: I agree with what you just said, but how does that help me with my problem?

Judy: Well, overcoming your fear of public speaking takes *three mental steps*. First, I know you're afraid to give this talk, but that's good because fear will give you motivation, focus, and energy. The secret is to use that energy as a *positive motivator, not a negative motivator.*

Mike: How do I use fear as a positive motivator?

Judy: Make it work for you by redirecting that negative fear and emotion into positive motivation and acting to *reduce the uncertainty of the circumstance.* Use fear to your advantage and control it; otherwise, it will control you [antecedent, Box A].

Mike: How do I do that?

Judy: First, take control of the process. Develop an agenda, have a clear schedule, and define the process for the meeting. Visit the venue to get familiar with the room and how the equipment works. Set up the room in a way that makes you feel comfortable. Also, develop strategies for handling the elements of the event that cause you the most anxiety. For example, if you're worried about taking questions face to face, have the attendees write down their questions on cards so that you can pick and choose the ones you want to answer. You can also solicit questions in advance instead of taking them all at the session. I'm sure you can think of other strategies, but the key is to reduce fear by taking control of the process and thereby reduce the uncertainty of the circumstances of your talk.

Mike: Those are good ideas, and I can certainly do that. What is the second step?

Judy: The second step addresses the thing that causes your fear.

Mike: What would that be?

Judy: Being unsure about your ability to give an effective talk [behavior, Box B].

Mike: I'm unsure of my ability because I know I'm not good at it. How do I deal with that?

Judy: It's similar to the first step, but instead of taking control to *reduce* the uncertainty of the circumstances, you want to take positive actions to *increase* the certainty of your ability to perform.

Mike: What does that mean? Can you please give me some examples?

Judy: Take actions to build your self-confidence and skills in giving a presentation, such as preparing, practicing, learning, and doing some research. Schedule a rehearsal with your friends and co-workers to run through your talk in the actual room. You build greater confidence when you take productive actions, seek help from others, and feel more certain and optimistic about your ability to perform. Do productive things to reduce your stress and worry.

Mike: I'm also meeting with a graphics expert to show me how to make better visuals.

Judy: That's right, you've got it. Build your self-confidence by being highly prepared and build your ability by being more skilled. It takes hard work, support, and practice to gain greater certainty and confidence.

Mike: I like these suggestions, but I'm still worried about how I'm going to do in front of a live audience.

Judy: Oh, that's an easy one.

Mike: Really?

Judy: The most powerful thing you can do to boost your self-confidence and ability in facing a live audience is simply to *be yourself* during your talk. Be yourself, be honest, speak from your own mind and heart and not from a script, and if you don't know the answer to a question, say, "I don't know, but I'll find out for you." Audiences like presenters who are genuine and honest. When you read from a script, people see you as an actor or a messenger, not a real person. Let go of your fears by trusting yourself and who you are. *Being yourself is the best way to give a good talk!* And it's easier because being yourself doesn't require any extra preparation or rehearsal.

Mike: Wow, that's powerful. Being yourself, taking control, working with others, and taking action . . . I like it all. Thanks, Judy. But I'm still worried about one thing—what if I do all this and I still fail? I know that's negative thinking, but I can't help it.

Judy: That's where the *third step* comes into play. But before we talk about that, how about we take a quick break?

The third step will be disclosed in the next section.

Summary
Best Tips for Overcoming the Uncertainty of Your Ability to Perform (Behavior, Box B)

▲ For successful risk taking, Box A is about *taking control* and *reducing the uncertainty* of the circumstances, and Box B is about *taking action* to *increase the certainty* of your ability.

▲ When confronted with changes, problems, and challenges, *self-confidence* leads to action, whereas excessive self-doubt leads to more fear, uncertainty, and inaction.

▲ The behavior box becomes a black box only when you feel *uncertain* about your own abilities and motivation.

▲ Believe in yourself by trusting and increasing your abilities, skills, motivation, and resolve.

▲ Fill any voids of uncertainty with self-confidence and optimism, not self-doubt and pessimism.

▲ You gain confidence and optimism when you have people who encourage, support, and root for you. Draw confidence from the people who support you.

▲ Use fear as a *call to action*—redirect any negative fears and energy into positive, productive actions.

▲ When the challenge exceeds your risk tolerance and you are compelled to play it safe, remember that inaction has consequences—*inaction avoids action, not bad consequences.*

The Secrets to Overcoming the Uncertainty of a Bad Outcome

In the ABC Box Model, risk takers and non–risk takers have different perspectives on Boxes A and B. Risk takers see more opportunities than threats (Box A), and their behaviors (Box B) are self-confident and action oriented, whereas the behaviors of non–risk takers are characterized by self-doubt and inaction. But the most important difference between risk takers and non–risk takers is in how they manage the uncertainty of a bad outcome, Box C.

Non–Risk Takers Are Content to Play the Game of Consequences

As discussed in Skill Six, every behavior is followed by a consequence. One of four types of possible consequences occurs after an action: positive ("Yay!"), negative ("Nay"), no consequences ("Nothing"), and punishment ("Ouch!"). Especially in project management, consequences are difficult to control and predict.

Non–risk takers are content in playing the Box C "con game" (shell game, Skill Six)—working hard and hoping for a "Yay!" instead of a "Nay," "Nothing," or "Ouch!". But the chances of getting a "Yay!" are uncertain, and your consequences are usually in the hands of your boss, customer, or others. For non–risk takers, *Box C is a black box*—you are uncertain and not in control of your consequences. Getting a "Yay!" is analogous to trying to find a pea in a shell game because it's infrequent, unpredictable, and in control of the game operator. As discussed in Skill Six, employees get mostly "Nothings" and "Nays," with some "Yays!" and "Ouches!" in between. It's amazing how many people are resigned to play this con game when the chances of winning are so low. What's the alternative? You have another choice: *don't play the con game—think outside the box.*

Successful Risk Takers Don't Play the Con Game

Successful risk takers not only treat antecedents differently, which leads to different behaviors, but also choose not to play the four consequences game. It's way too confining. Box C contains only four consequences; the outcome is unknown, and you're not in control. So *risk takers don't play the con game and aren't fazed by what negative consequences may or may not happen.* They do not act to avoid negative consequences; they act to achieve positive outcomes.

> **"[Risk takers] do not act to avoid negative consequences; they act to achieve positive outcomes."**

Figure 7.7 Risk takers play outside the black box

To successful teams and risk takers, Box C is not a scary black box of unwanted consequences but rather a belief that the outcome will be a win ("Yay!") (Figure 7.7). They are not delusional and recognize that a bad outcome could result from their actions, but if it does, as Sarah put it in her story, they'll "deal with it." They believe in themselves not only to take action on an opportunity but also *to correct, mitigate, or simply learn from any unwanted results*—it's an attitude of, "Whatever happens, we can figure it out and deal with it." So they demonstrate not only self-confidence but also a confidence in their *resourcefulness, resilience, and ability to fix and recover from an undesirable outcome.* That's all part of the risk-taking process. Risk takers don't fear Box C as a black box—they're not as concerned about unwanted consequences as non–risk takers are. Receiving "Nays," "Nothings," and "Ouches!" are all part of being successful.

As we learned in Skill Six, employees typically receive mostly "Nothings," "Nays," and an occasional "Ouch!" as consequences. When the game is rigged in favor of no appreciation, no reinforcement, and unwanted consequences, employees exhibit more risk-avoidance behaviors than risk-taking behaviors. No wonder risk aversion prevails in so many people and teams! They prefer to comply with the rules, play it safe, and avoid unwanted consequences.

In contrast, accomplished risk takers choose not to play a rigged game and prefer to play their own game—*risk takers play outside the box.* They are willing to take their chances and defiantly refuse to play the shell game. They have the ability to move forward (Skill Five, roll the ball forward). In contrast, non–risk takers are content to play the con game (Box C). They are conditioned to the process and satisfied with giving up control and playing the game. This enables them to avoid owning the results and therefore feel safe if things go wrong.

In summary, risk takers are not afraid to own the results and take full responsibility. This enables them to continue to control and expedite the process of recovering or fixing whatever is broken. Risk takers want to be free, operating outside the box and not dependent on the con game. They are not confined to the four consequences—*they control and define their own consequences*. You can't be a risk taker by playing the con game. Break the bonds that hold you to the con game and liberate yourself and your team by playing outside the box more often.

CASE 7.2, PART 2: OVERCOMING THE RISK AND FEAR OF GIVING A PRESENTATION—THE THIRD STEP

Let's return to the story of Mike and Judy and his quest to overcome his fears of giving presentations.

Mike: Judy, I'm going to use those first two steps that you described to control my fears and redirect them into productive actions, but I'm still feeling uncomfortable about speaking to an audience. What if I blow the presentation? What if I forget my points? What if the audience gets nasty? What if I run over my time? What if . . .

Judy: Let me interrupt by saying that your concerns are very valid and reasonable, but "what if'" questions are just another sign of fearful thinking. Indulging too many "what ifs" is not healthy; it just reinforces your fears. All those "what ifs" that you mention are bad outcomes ["Nays" and "Ouches!"]. Instead of allowing fear to control your thinking, take control and feel certain that the outcome is going to be favorable.

Mike: Do you mean I should use positive thinking?

Judy: Not exactly. As I said before, uncertainty about your own skills creates fear, which we can channel into productive actions to give you more certainty and confidence in your ability to speak. But your "what ifs" are worries about the *uncertainty of the outcome* and your fear of possible failure and looking bad.

Mike: Isn't that what everyone's worried about? That you're going to mess up?

Judy: How would you feel if I could guarantee you, one hundred percent, that your talk is going turn out fine?

Mike: I would feel wonderful, but how can you be so *certain*?

Judy: Before I answer that, how would you specifically feel, both going into the talk and giving the talk, if you knew it was going to turn out fine?

Mike: I would feel relaxed, relieved, and happy. But tell me, how is that possible?

Judy: The secret is to feel certain, not uncertain, about the outcome of your talk. You can do this by not only working hard to gain confidence in your ability but also knowing in advance that there are only three possible outcomes for your talk: one, your talk turns out *good*, with no problems; two, the talk is *great* and everything goes really well; or three, it's a *fantastic learning experience*! That's it! There are no other outcomes—you have *three certain outcomes*, I guarantee it: it'll be good, great, or a fantastic learning experience. You can't lose; you're going to come out ahead no matter what—it's an absolute certainty. And what's even better, the outcome is in your control—you make the call. So if you want to feel relaxed, relieved, and happy about your talk, just remember the *three certain outcomes*! Instead of fearing the uncertainty of a bad outcome, you are now certain of a good outcome ["Yay!" and thinking outside the box, Box C]. Also, being in a relaxed, relieved, and happy frame of mind will enable you to give a more genuine and confident talk. Now you know the secrets for overcoming your fear of giving talks!

Lessons from the Story

If you're wondering how Mike did in his talk, you probably know—it's one of the *three certain outcomes*. Mike's story illustrates that overcoming the risk and fear of giving a presentation takes *three mental steps*, which parallel the three uncertainties in risk taking: the uncertainty of the circumstance (antecedent), the uncertainty of your ability to perform (behavior), and the uncertainty of a bad outcome (consequence). This new three-step model and the three certain outcomes not only are the keys to giving good talks but are also instrumental in overcoming uncertainty and fear when faced with change, problems, and challenges in project management.

Summary

Best Tips for Overcoming the Uncertainity of a Bad Outcome (Consequences, Box C)

▲ Don't let unwanted consequences scare you away—do not act to avoid negative consequences; *act to achieve positive outcomes.*

▲ Don't be conditioned by and dependent on the four consequences in the black box; you can control and *define your own consequences.*

▲ Even when things don't turn out in your favor, have confidence in yourself and your team to correct, mitigate, or simply learn from any unwanted results—trust your abilities and resourcefulness.

▲ Break free from the con game and the four consequences, think outside the box, and bet on the *three certain outcomes*: good, great, and a fantastic learning experience.

How Risk Taking Has Enabled Your Success

Sarah's cross-country team never forgot their run to the gateway, led by Sarah's unexpected courage. Mike was able to muster up the courage to face his fears by taking control, taking action, and knowing the three certain outcomes. Mike's newfound confidence and Sarah's courageous run exemplify what risk taking is all about—new circumstances are opportunities, ability takes hard work and self-confidence, and bad outcomes occur when you choose to stay inside the black box. When you embrace these key concepts, you are ready to *make changes, solve tough problems,* and *conquer new challenges.*

Use the following facts to help motivate and inspire your team to be better risk takers and succeed when faced with change, problems, and new challenges:

▲ High achievement requires taking risks.

▲ When you look back, you'll likely see that wonderful things happened when you took risks—your best moments were likely a result of your initiative and personal actions.

▲ Even successful risk takers recognize that past failures enabled many later successes—losing is part of winning.

▲ It's common to find that your proudest achievements appeared too difficult and beyond your reach at first, but once you committed to it, you rose to the occasion.

▲ It's likely that taking risks and having the courage to change, speak up, step up, do new things, and challenge yourself have strengthened your character and ability.

▲ Recognize your past achievements and successes—your past experiences with risk taking are likely more positive than you realize.

▲ Your trace memories of successes and failures have enabled you to be a better, smarter risk taker.

▲ Being a good risk taker gives others courage and inspiration to follow.

Skill Seven Summary

As a project leader, risk taking is part of your job description. In project management, there are uncertainties and risks in everything you do, so you must be good at it. Risk aversion is one of the biggest barriers to high performance, and you can't achieve ambitious goals if you wait, hold back, or avoid tough challenges. Risk taking is an essential skill for project team leaders.

Skill Seven provides an effective model for understanding the differences between risk takers and non–risk takers and how you can improve your ability to take risks. This skill is not about risk assessment or risk management, which are processes—it's about managing risk taking, which is a *learned behavior.*

Your risk-taking behavior is a by-product of your past experiences, trace memories, and consequences. Managing risk taking is about understanding your fears, uncertainties, and risk tolerance. In project management, there are *three uncertainties in risk taking,* and they each correspond to one of the boxes in the ABC Box Model: (1) the uncertainty of the circumstance (antecedent, Box A), (2) the uncertainty of your ability to perform (behavior, Box B), and (3) the uncertainty of a bad outcome (consequence, Box C). Risk takers and non–risk takers treat antecedents, behaviors, and consequences differently. Non–risk takers and risk-averse individuals are prone to view new changes, problems, and challenges (antecedent) as potential threats; they allow fear and uncertainty to create self-doubt (behavior); and they are conditioned to play the unfavorable "con game" (consequence).

Risk taking is an action that has uncertainties, similar to opening a black box. You feel *uncertain* and not in *control*. The black box is a metaphor for a high degree of uncertainty and fear. Threat, self-doubt, and fear create a black box effect in people in which uncertainty and loss of control prevail. In contrast, risk takers see new circumstances as opportunities, not threats; their behaviors are self-confident and action oriented, not self-doubting and inactive; and they prefer to define and control their own consequences and not let consequences control and scare them.

Anytime you are challenged with fear and uncertainty, you have two ways to go: (1) you can rise to the challenge and combat fear with optimism, self-confidence, control, and the support from others; or (2) you can step away, go inactive, and let fear fill your mind with self-doubt, worry, and passivity. Taking a risk is not about eliminating fear—it's about confronting fear and using it to your advantage. Fear has advantages and disadvantages—an extremely low level of fear tends to make you complacent and passive, whereas a moderate level of fear helps you to take action and perform, but excessive fear causes you to avoid and underperform.

This skill presents new and unique principles, strategies, and processes for improving your risk taking: the *black box effect*, the *three uncertainties in risk taking*, the *three mental steps*, and the *three certain outcomes*. These tools will enable you and your team to take more risks and overcome the fear and uncertainties of change, problems, and challenges in project management.

Skill Seven Memory Card

Overcome Change, Problems, and Challenges
Avoid the Black Box Effect

Overcome the Uncertainty of the Circumstance
1. High achievement requires taking risks—embrace new challenges as gift opportunities, not black box threats
2. Redirect negative fears and energy into actions to reduce the uncertainty of the circumstance—control your fear or fear will control you
3. Risk taking and risk tolerance are improved through practice, experience and even failure

Overcome the Uncertainty of Your Ability to Perform
4. When facing uncertain change or problems, gain self-confidence by increasing certainty in yourself through hard work, practice, training and support from others
5. To believe in yourself, be yourself—trust your judgment and ability to take action
6. Inaction only avoids action, not bad consequences

Overcome the Uncertainty of a Bad Outcome
7. Don't let unwanted consequences scare you away—do not act to avoid negative consequences; act to achieve positive outcomes
8. When bad outcomes happen, have confidence in your resourcefulness to fix it
9. Think outside the black box and you'll be certain to do good, great, or fantastic

SKILL EIGHT

How to Gain Favor and Influence with Your Boss
Be More Visible

Skill Eight is one of the toughest and most important people skills that you'll ever need—working with your boss. It's not because your boss controls your compensation, job responsibilities, work goals, and performance expectations but because the relationship with your boss affects your health and happiness. The level of help, support, and recognition that you get from your supervisor greatly influences your well-being and motivation. There's nothing better or worse than having a good or bad boss, respectively, and this skill provides you with strategies, tools, and tips for strengthening your relationship and influence with your boss and working with a difficult boss.

Working Well with Your Boss: Your Happiness Depends on It

A Harvard Business School survey of almost twenty thousand employees showed that people who felt respected by their managers have better health, better psychological well-being, and greater satisfaction with their jobs (18). Also, numerous other studies have shown that your level of happiness, engagement, stress, frustration, and commitment is highly related to your relationship with your immediate supervisor. One such study was a Gallup survey of 7,272 U.S. adults that revealed that one in two had left a job at some point in their careers to escape from their managers and improve their overall life (19). Also, employees who are supervised by highly "engaged managers" are more likely to be engaged as well.

Having a good relationship with your boss is important for your happiness and well-being. Also, your boss affects the productivity, efficiency, and leadership of your team. Your boss can be either an enabler or a disabler of your work, and it hinges on your ability to "manage up."

Mutual Dependence

In this skill, *boss* is defined as your supervisor, manager, or person who directs, evaluates, and formally oversees your daily work performance. The boss-employee relationship is based on mutual dependence—the boss relies on your knowledge, skills, and experiences to complete projects, and you depend on your boss for resources, work direction, prioritization, timing, quality, and content. If you have an effective boss, hopefully he or she provides wisdom, vision, insights, and inspiration for your work, serving as your leader, coach, mentor, and champion. Your role is not to serve with blind obedience but rather to understand and translate the expectations of your boss into a set of actions that makes sense to you and fits your ability to accomplish them.

"The imbalance in position, power, and information between supervisor and employee shouldn't develop into an imbalance in respect, trust, honesty, integrity, and dignity."

The mutual dependence of bosses and employees creates a partnership, but it's also a subordinate relationship in which your boss typically has more organizational knowledge, power, authority, and ego than you do. Also, there may be customs in your organization that treat bosses and employees differently, such as titles, office accommodations, privileges, resources, and access to information. But *the imbalance in position, power, and information between supervisor and employee shouldn't develop into an imbalance in respect, trust, honesty, integrity, and dignity.*

Unfortunately, more often than not, employees do not feel comfortable speaking freely, sharing their interests, debating different viewpoints, or getting familiar with their bosses due to an undercurrent of fear, positional power, and potential rebuff from the boss. They find that the better path is to go along to get along—don't make waves and keep your nose to the grindstone. As discussed in Skill Seven, for many people, the boss is a *black box*—fearful, unpredictable, constraining, and uncertain.

As in any relationship, the more you know about the other party, the better you understand, communicate, and get along with each other. In the workplace, some of the most important human factors in a relationship include understanding what motivates and demotivates each party, the person's communication and work preferences, and how each party likes to be treated—in short, understanding what brings out the best in each of you. This might sound straightforward, but you would be amazed by how little bosses and employees know about each other.

Case in Point When bosses and employees are asked how they could improve their work relationship, the answer from each party is predictably, "Get to know each other better." That's the right answer, but other than having an occasional chat, most bosses and employees seldom make the effort. For example, one of the best questions that bosses and employees can ask each other is, "What motivates and demotivates you at work?" The most common reasons that *bosses* give for not asking include the following:

▲ "I don't need to know people's motivations; people should be self-motivated."

▲ "When I came through the ranks, nobody wanted to know my motivations."

▲ "I don't have time to worry about whether my employees are motivated."

▲ "I know people pretty well, and I provide motivation when it's needed."

▲ "If people aren't self-motivated, they don't belong here."

▲ "I avoid asking any personal questions of my employees. It can be taken as an invasion of privacy."

When *employees* are asked why they don't tell their bosses what motivates and demotivates them, their responses include the following:

▲ "I really don't think my boss is interested in hearing my personal motivations and feelings."

▲ "I can tell my boss what motivates me, but nothing's going to change."

▲ "My boss may think I am somehow criticizing him and saying that he needs to be a better motivator."

▲ "My boss hates touchy-feely things like that."

▲ "I'm not comfortable talking about my personal preferences with my boss."

▲ "My boss expects me to be self-motivated."

▲ "My boss knows what work I like to do, and that's good enough for me."

You can tell from these responses that employees are not comfortable talking openly and honestly with their bosses because they fear that their bosses would take it the wrong way or it would not be well received. In essence, bosses and employees would like to know more about each other, but due to workplace paradigms, a lack of process, and personal insecurities, their preferences remain a mystery.

What Are the Consequences of Not Knowing?

In the absence of not knowing each other's work preferences, bosses and employees operate in a trial-and-error mode and make assumptions about each other's behaviors. In other words, it becomes a guessing game. Unfortunately, it's a game that usually doesn't work in your favor. You can't gain favor and influence if you don't know your boss.

Also, when people lack mutual understanding of each other, the chances of having conflicts greatly increase. It only takes one bad conflict or misunderstanding to ruin your relationship with your boss. And the most important understanding centers around your boss's expectations of your performance.

Weak Performance Expectations In most organizations, the boss defines the work, strategies, and priorities, which includes establishing work expectations, setting goals for the year, monitoring progress, and conducting periodic employee performance reviews. Truth be told, most bosses consider performance planning and reviews a real burden on their time. They seem to go through the motions without having their hearts in it and often struggle to say the right things, not wanting to be too harsh or too lenient. As a result, performance planning becomes a "wiggle" game.

The term *wiggle* refers to the fact that neither the boss nor the employee wants to be pinned down on anything and both want wiggle room in case things change. Certainly, change is constant and flexibility is important; however, ambiguous expectations do not work in your favor. Not taking the time and effort to develop a clear and compelling performance plan with your boss is a missed opportunity. It's a

"Discover and act on the things that your boss favors and you will gain favor with your boss."

chance to express your goals, propose new ideas, explore new opportunities, and get your boss's feedback, priorities, preferences, and opinions regarding your work. In other words, you need to find out what's going to gain you favor and influence with your boss going forward. You have two choices: have a quick and painless planning session and leave with vague, wiggly expectations, or find out what your boss truly favors. *Discover and act on the things that your boss favors and you will gain favor with your boss.*

Knowing your boss better and building a good relationship will yield greater opportunities, recognition, trust, and support for you, especially when problems, conflicts, and failures occur. Earning your boss's trust and confidence gives you more freedom and control of your job. However, when you have low mutual understanding, influence, and trust, you become vulnerable to your boss's bad behaviors, including the behavior that all employees fear—being *micromanaged*.

Averting the One Thing That Everyone Fears from the Boss

Micromanagement occurs when your boss applies excessive control, scrutiny, and oversight to your work. It's probably one of the top reasons for employee dissatisfaction with a boss. When bosses feel a need to micromanage or when employees feel overly scrutinized, it's a telltale sign of a poor employee-boss relationship.

Micromanagement often stems from bosses' need for control, their desire for reassurance that the work is being done in a timely and correct manner, or their belief that their scrutiny is helping your work. Deep down inside, your boss may have good intentions for closely overseeing your work, but when your mutual trust and relationship are not strong, your boss is left feeling uncertain, which can lead to the following:

- ▲ a fear of failure that drives your boss to control, check, and approve your work
- ▲ a concern that you won't deliver it exactly as expected
- ▲ feelings of insecurity and a fear of getting surprised by a problem, which in turn lead your boss to monitor your work more closely
- ▲ a belief that close supervision prevents problems and increases productivity and quality
- ▲ a belief that you may not report or recognize a problem until it's too late
- ▲ a belief that scrutinizing your work will motivate you to perform at a higher level

With so many reasons for micromanaging, it's no wonder supervisors are prone to this unwanted behavior. Being micromanaged is not fun, and although you can whine, complain, and blame your boss, the behavior is actually a painful consequence of not effectively managing and earning your boss's trust. A lack of trust is deadly in any relationship, and it requires an effort on

"The less you manage your boss, the more your boss will micromanage you."

both sides. But when such a breakdown occurs, it's *you* who pays the price, so it's worth making the extra effort to build trust. Remember, the less you manage your boss, the more your boss will micromanage you.

The Key to Managing Up

Managing up means taking action to establish a positive, sustainable work relationship with your boss and management that creates mutual value for you, your boss, and the organization. When you effectively manage up, your boss treats you better, you get what you want, and you gain greater favor, influence, trust, respect, recognition, and enjoyment of your job.

As much as you would like to be more comfortable working with your boss, you can't control your boss's behaviors. However, you can take steps to improve *your* behaviors and interactions with your boss, which in turn can improve your influence and work relationship. The key to managing your boss and closing gaps on problems related to trust, misunderstandings, and performance expectations is to *be more visible*, which means being more proactive, engaged, competent, productive, creative, impactful, and supportive of your boss, team, and organization.

As Figure 8.1 illustrates, when you're not getting what you want from your boss, you have a fundamental choice: you can either stay quiet, keep plugging along, and wait for your boss to notice your work (low part of the curve), believing that your boss will somehow learn what a good job you're doing, or choose to be more visible, manage up, and strengthen your favor and influence with your boss. If you do not show yourself, your boss will likely not only form misconceptions about you and your work but also assume a negative or indifferent view of you (Skills Two and Three).

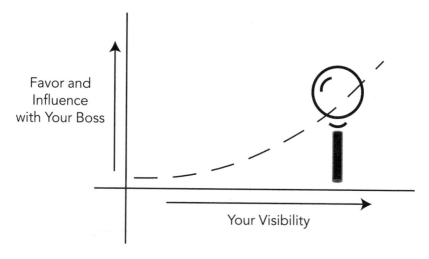

Figure 8.1 Increase visibility to increase influence

Managing up is similar to raising a magnifying glass between you and your boss, thus increasing your visibility to your boss in the following ways:

▲ broader understanding of who you are—your diversity, character, knowledge, skills, experiences, and abilities—which enables your boss to better see your values and work preferences, and improve his or her communication, confidence, and interaction with you

▲ stronger awareness of the skills and abilities that you offer to the team—so your boss can better utilize your strengths and interests in team projects, tasks, and responsibilities

▲ greater appreciation of your actions and efforts in contributing to the progress and success of the team

▲ clearer knowledge of what you want and what things are important to you so your boss has a better understanding of your goals, ambitions, and expectations

Magnifying yourself means expressing who you are and what you want and demonstrating your strengths, abilities, experiences, knowledge, talents, and value. You're showing your high commitment, energy, enthusiasm, and teamwork, such as doing superior work, engaging in team meetings, volunteering for special assignments, and actively helping others on your team. Magnification means your work quality, productivity, and unselfish teamwork exceed expectations and your work has such a big impact that your boss can't help but notice it. Increasing your visibility is not about grandstanding, bragging, pandering, or exaggerating your work performance—it's about enlarging your work impact, value, and presence.

Strategies for Gaining Favor and Influence with Your Boss

Being visible has tremendous benefits for you, and it enables you to work in a manner that causes your boss to trust you, have confidence in you, and appreciate your value. Based on my personal surveys with managers, supervisors, and team leaders in project management, the top seven strategies that you can practice to improve your visibility, favor, and influence with your boss are the following: increase personal engagement, possess a can-do attitude, continue to build your competency, communicate and keep your boss in the loop, seek a win-win relationship, be a go-to resource, and know what behaviors your boss favors.

Increase Personal Engagement

Engagement is the demonstration of your commitment to the work and the success of your team and organization. You care about the quality and value of your work, and you're motivated to do your very best in delivering on your promises, satisfying your customers, and meeting your team's expectations. Engagement is manifested in your attitude, communications, productivity, actions, and interactions.

Case in Point You show visible engagement when you make noticeable efforts to do the following:

▲ Actively participate, collaborate, and contribute to team projects, meetings, and activities.

▲ Demonstrate confidence and belief in yourself and others.

▲ Express hope and optimism when fear and pessimism reign.

▲ Speak up when others are silent.

▲ Help those who are struggling the most.

▲ Listen actively.

▲ Contribute solutions to problems and improvements to processes.

▲ Always arrive on time or early for meetings.

▲ Volunteer for important tasks that others are reluctant to do (such as emergency preparedness, event organization, team representation, charity volunteering, hosting of outside visitors, meeting facilitation, or open house events).

▲ Regularly attend optional work events, such as potlucks, lunch events, seminars, work celebrations, after-work gatherings, town hall meetings, and charity events.

▲ Help welcome and train new employees.

Some of these behaviors may seem trivial, but when you participate, collaborate, express yourself, contribute, show up on time, volunteer, and support others, your boss sees you as an unselfish, caring, reliable, responsible, loyal, and dedicated team player. These behaviors make you more impactful and valuable to your boss and organization. It doesn't mean you start acting like a busybody or socializer. In fact, it's the opposite—it's your ability to *send silent messages* of support, respect, empathy, teamwork, and commitment that builds your reputation and increases your influence. Remember, half the battle is just showing up. So step up and engage, and don't get trapped into the mentality that you're "too busy" or "have more important work to do."

Possess a Can-Do Attitude

You are more visible when you make things happen—when you are an initiator, self-starter, go-getter, implementer, achiever, and hard worker. Nothing beats good old-fashioned hard work to catch attention and praise from your boss. *Bosses like employees who reliably do the right things, in the right way, and exhibit a positive, upbeat attitude.* Let's face it: no one likes to work with people who are down, negative, cynical, and unable to do things. People who are achievers readily rise to the top and gain favor with their bosses. Can-do people have a halo effect—they earn more challenging assignments, extra privileges, better salaries, faster promotions, and greater rewards and recognition. Managing up pays off when you can show that you can get things done and have a can-do attitude. Without a doubt, can-do people are highly prized by bosses.

> *"Without a doubt, can-do people are highly prized by bosses."*

Case in Point Showing that *you can get things done* is one of the most impactful behaviors that you can exhibit to gain significant influence with your boss. Some ways to demonstrate a can-do attitude include the following:

- ▲ Get your work done *ahead* of the deadline.
- ▲ Show that you're an "and" player ("*I can* deliver multiple work products"), not an "or" player ("If I do this task, then *I can't* do my other assignments—you need to take something off my plate").
- ▲ Demonstrate that you can change your work priorities for your boss and not complain about it—*you're a doer, not a whiner.*
- ▲ You *gladly volunteer* for tasks that others won't do.
- ▲ You readily admit your mistakes and promptly *work hard to correct* them.

Continue to Build Your Competency

You may have the greatest can-do attitude in the world, but if you can't perform the work competently, you will likely reveal weaknesses, not strengths, in your abilities. Build greater competency by continuing to increase your skills, knowledge, and experience. Most organizations have an employee training and development program that may include in-house training, internships, rotational assignments, tuition reimbursements, special projects, and external training. To make this behavior more visible, work with your boss to get agreement on what knowledge or training would add the greatest value to you, your boss, and your team.

Go for quality over quantity and learn skills that your organization will need in the next three to five years. Improving your skills in writing, business, computing, and communications is always valuable, but try to obtain skills and experiences that will make you stand out when you're competing for future positions. Strengthening your knowledge and skills strengthens your confidence. *Make sure you have the skills to support your can-do attitude.*

Communicate and Keep Your Boss in the Loop

Don't make your boss guess on what's happening. Take the initiative to communicate frequently with your boss, including in-person contact, meetings, phone calls, emails, texts, and instant messages. When you make the effort to keep your boss informed on the status of your work and share information that *your boss values*, it conveys loyalty, trust, collaboration, and honesty. It'll keep your boss from micromanaging you as well. Like everyone else, bosses like to be *in the loop* (Skill Three) and hate to be surprised. The secret is to keep it concise, timely, and observational and leave any speculation and judgment to your boss.

It's hard to overcommunicate, but you don't want to be a nuisance, so check in with your boss periodically to ensure that the frequency and types of communication are useful and determine what kind of information your boss likes. That way you can continue to improve your communications and keep delivering good, useful information to your boss.

Seek a Win-Win Relationship

Your visibility increases when you frequently develop new ideas, improvements, and solutions *with* your supervisor. You are more effectively managing up when you plant seeds and facilitate change with your supervisor rather than debating and fighting for your ideas. *Never compete with your boss.* When you compete with your boss, you are creating a win-lose relationship in which, one way or another, you will end up losing. Your probability of success increases when you seek a win-win outcome with your boss. You gain more favor and influence when you "bet with the house"—that way, when your boss wins, you win also.

> *"Never compete with your boss. . . . One way or another, you will end up losing."*

Case in Point No matter how great the relationship is with your boss, the boss still likes to be in charge. You win when your boss feels he or she has won also. Here are some examples of win-win behaviors that you can practice to convey your trust and loyalty:

▲ **Share ideas, improvements, and credit:** Work in partnership with your boss in developing new ideas and proposals. Although you could do it alone and take all the credit, you'll find that collaborating with your boss will increase your chances for success and it builds mutual trust.

▲ **Be an ally for change:** Be seen as a facilitator of change, not a resister. Actively help your boss implement new policies and support change with your boss.

▲ **Accept leadership chores:** Although you don't want to give your boss the impression that you're underworked, offer to cover a chore or responsibility that your boss would gladly delegate to you, such as attending a meeting that your boss dislikes, drafting meeting agendas, or tracking action items. You win by learning and playing a leadership role for your boss, which could lead to more important assignments for you.

▲ **Be a fixer:** Fix a problem that bothers your boss. Solve one of your boss's problems that you also would enjoy doing (win-win), such as introducing your boss to a new time-saving computer application or improving an administrative process that your boss dislikes.

Be a Go-To Resource

You want to be seen as a go-to person for your boss—a valuable source of information on current events in the field, a source of valuable opinions, and a sounding board for new ideas. Be a living kiosk of reliable news, data, and issues. Possess a strong network of contacts including internal and external experts, internal and external opinion leaders, industry and professional organizational contacts, management contacts, researchers, consultants, subscriptions, and other information sources that build up your knowledge and credibility.

Don't give your boss more information and analyses than he or she needs, especially in front of others—you don't want to show up your boss. Be a can-do, go-to confidant whom your boss can trust for information and opinions. Keep it professional and respectful; don't be a team tattler or gossiper. You build greater influence with your boss when you have insights and access to knowledge that your boss doesn't have.

Know What Behaviors Your Boss Favors

Do you know what "managing up" behaviors your boss favors and disfavors? Even if your boss is not as forthcoming as you would like and he or she is still a mystery to you, don't despair. As described in Skill Three, knowing

Table 8.1 Favored and Unfavored Behaviors by Personality Type

Boss's Personality Type	Favored "Managing Up" Behaviors	Disfavored "Managing Up" Behaviors
Rational "Thinker"	Objective, intelligent, strategic, analytical, competitive, clever, outspoken, problem solving, unemotional, competent, cuts to the chase, goal oriented	Complaining, whining, weak, passive, excessively apologetic, emotional, nonconfrontational, slow thinking, slow acting, small talk, incompetent, low enthusiasm
Guardian "Supporter"	Loyalty, passion for work, a doer and hard worker, disciplined, compliant, responsible, focused, accountable, reliable, practical, organized, modest, no nonsense, process oriented	Lazy, delinquent, rebellious, disruptive, grandstanding, disorganized, bragging, embellishing, all talk and no action, unstable, low accountability, unfocused
Idealist "Empathizer"	Thoughtful, respectful, caring, ethical, sincere, genuine, polite, courteous, gracious, compassionate, personable, listener, people oriented	Untrustworthy, political, troublemaker, deceptive, manipulative, bullying, aggressive, dominating, condescending, betrayal, unethical, impatient, rude, unfeeling
Artisan "Risk Taker"	Engaging, opinionated, idea generator, opportunistic, generous, creative, causal, bold, imaginative, resourceful, nonconforming, action oriented	Boring, sedentary, strict, uptight, inflexible, overly cautious, dull, unjust, risk averse, inactive, highly critical and judgmental, unresponsive

your boss's personality type will give you insights into his or her basic motivations and demotivations, strengths and weaknesses, and interpersonal behavioral preferences. If you know your boss's likes and dislikes, you'll be much more skilled in managing up (Table 8.1).

Managing up and increasing your visibility involves actively engaging, having a can-do attitude, increasing your competency, maintaining good communication, developing a win-win relationship, being a go-to resource, and knowing your boss's preferences. You are projecting a powerful image of yourself that sets you apart for better opportunities and greater favor and influence with your boss, including a future promotion.

How to Get That Promotion You Want

One successful outcome of managing up is earning a job promotion that recognizes your hard work, increased skills, greater knowledge, and higher value to the organization. The decision to grant a promotion depends on your performance, experience, and abilities, as well as your organization's needs, advancement opportunities, employee development goals, and compensation system. Your boss is the key decision maker who determines your readiness for a promotion.

The first step in seeking a promotion is learning the organizational process and decision criteria for advancement. Although they are related, promotions are usually treated differently from salary actions. A promotion is defined as an increase in rank and status within an organization. It can result from a selection process for a new job, job posting, job transfer, or advancement within a defined career ladder. You must either meet the promotion criteria or be selected as the strongest candidate among others competing for the job. Regardless, your candidacy relies heavily on the support of your boss.

Once you understand the system for job promotions within your organization, have a career development discussion with your boss to share your personal and career goals. The purpose of this discussion is to share your ambitions and also to get your boss's feedback on how best to achieve your goals and earn a promotion. It's important to hear your boss's view on the promotion process, confirm your understanding of the promotion criteria, and ask your supervisor what he or she sees as your best pathway for advancement. You don't want to appear pushy, but you do want to be open and transparent. You want to learn two things in this meeting: what is required for a promotion and the timeframe for earning that promotion.

Once you have laid the groundwork and are excited to advance your career, the next step is to strengthen your résumé for a promotion. The strategy for getting a promotion is the same strategy for managing up—make yourself visible through superior work performance, meeting your supervisor's expectations, and improving your value in the eyes of your boss and your key customers. Nothing beats having your customers behind you when bidding for a promotion.

It's important to work hard, smart, and in partnership with your boss. Working smart means working on the right things, which usually are the things that your boss, customers, and organization value the most. Your best chances for a promotion occur when you meet and exceed the expectations of your boss, customers, and the promotion criteria for your organization. If you do the right work; gain the right knowledge, experience, and skills; and perform your job at the right level, then you will make it easier for your boss to recommend a promotion. In short, *promote your performance to promote yourself.*

Don't wait until your résumé is completely full to discuss your promotion prospects with your boss. Maintain high visibility and keep your boss advised of your progress, accomplishments, and high performance during the performance cycle. Communicate early and often and steadily grow your case for a promotion over time. Promotions usually do not materialize after one achievement or at your year-end performance review with your boss. Promotions often require a long lead time during which your boss needs to manage up and build a promotion case with your company's management.

"The best thing you can do to build your case for a promotion is to demonstrate sustained high performance."

The best thing you can do to build your case for a promotion is to demonstrate *sustained* high performance. When you operate from a position of consistently high performance, it becomes difficult to deny you a promotion. You need to build a critical mass of accomplishments to strengthen your bid. Speak to your boss about the prospects of a promotion when you are continuously achieving at a high level and visibly contributing to the success of your team and customers.

It is your responsibility to feed your boss data and documentation to help him or her make your case to management—*help your boss help you.* Concrete examples of your high performance and valuable contributions will support your case for advancement. Also, it is important to do it in a way that doesn't threaten your boss or make your boss feel insecure about his or her position. The process of managing your boss for a promotion is a partnership that is built over time. Be patient, smart, humble, respectful, and highly visible.

Managing a Bad Boss

Two of the toughest situations that you may encounter with a bad boss are working with one who demonstrates a lack of integrity and working with one who is difficult and demotivating. Both will challenge your people skills and require many of the eight skills that you have learned—that's why this is the last section of this book.

CASE 8.1: CONFLICT WITH YOUR BOSS—DOING THE RIGHT THING

Amy was a project manager at Willow Park Systems, a large educational software company that produced standard and customized online learning programs. Before working at Willow Park for six years, she had successfully taught for three years at a local grammar school. Her current project at Willow Park was to design software for young, early school ESL (English as second language) students who would use it to get additional instruction at school or home. This eighteen-month software project was being sponsored by a nonprofit company called First Class, one of Willow Park's top clients.

After a few months of work on the new software program, Amy and her team were meeting most project deadlines but were running a bit over budget and slipping behind on graphics development. The slippage on graphics was going to delay the project by two to three months. Also, it was clear after a few months that one key technical function of the program would need to be modified for it to operate properly. Amy was hoping to solve some of the problems with additional help, which she was planning to request at a meeting with her manager, Russell. The purpose of the meeting was to prepare for the upcoming quarterly client meeting.

Russell was a kind, positive, upbeat person who exuded a can-do spirit that was very infectious and motivating. At their meeting, Amy went over the status of her project and indicated that the deadlines were being met except for graphics development. She estimated that this would add at least two months to the project schedule and would require more funding from the client. After further discussion, Russell came up with a

Figure 8.2 Amy, the project manager for Willow Park's ESL program

couple of ideas and some work reprioritizations that helped alleviate some of Amy's resource needs, but they both agreed that schedule and budget overruns were inevitable.

For the upcoming First Class client meeting, Russell suggested that she give a high-level briefing of the status of the project, emphasizing the accomplishments to date, and then give a quick demonstration of the program's capabilities. He would then step in and give the client a briefing of the next steps and what adjustments were required going forward. This was the third of six client project meetings, and he assured Amy that it would go fine.

On the day of the client meeting, Amy and Russell met with three senior representatives from First Class, and after some pleasantries, the meeting started with a quick overview of the project objectives, milestones, work plan, and timeline. Amy highlighted the project's progress and demonstrated some of the completed functionalities, graphics, and key features. After answering some technical questions and discussing some user interface concerns, Amy got some useful feedback and nice recognition from her client. But she knew the kudos would be short lived, as she had not disclosed that a key functionality needed modification in addition to the graphics problems, which would result in additional scheduling and budget adjustments. She was so glad her boss, Russell, was going to cover that for her.

Russell began by kindly thanking Amy for the technical progress report and congratulated her for the good work that she and her team had been doing. Russell promptly advised their client that one of the key functionalities of the program needed revisions but that an alternative approach had been identified that should still meet their needs. After some questions, the clients expressed concern but accepted the situation. He then went on to share that the graphics development was going well but remained the most challenging part of the project. This caught the attention of the clients, who asked, "Is this going to delay the project?" Russell answered, "No, but we'll let you know if it does."

At this point, the allotted time was almost up, and the clients closed by asking whether the budget was still on track and whether there were any other issues. Amy looked anxiously at her boss, anticipating a remark from him about the project budget, but he replied, "No, I am pleased to say that everything is on track." Then he turned toward Amy and asked, "Did you have any other items?" Amy hesitantly replied, "No, I'm okay." With that said, the meeting was adjourned.

Amy returned to her office and, after some reflection, went to see Russell to ask why he didn't tell the client about the budget and expected delays. As she entered his office, Russell complimented Amy on her briefing and remarked that the client told him that they were very pleased with her work. Amy thanked him for the compliments but quickly said, "I appreciate your help at the meeting today, but I was concerned that we didn't tell them about the budget problem and the need to adjust the project schedule." Russell responded, "Well, I didn't think it was necessary, and I thought maybe we could put the cost onto another project or charge First Class some other way. I wouldn't worry about it—I have confidence that you and your team will find a way to recover a lot of that time and cost as you go. I would love to talk more, but I'm running late for another appointment. Thanks again for your good work!"

Later that day, a couple of Amy's team members came by her office to see how the client meeting had gone. Amy said it went fine and that the clients left pleased with the progress that was reported. They asked Amy if they were okay on the schedule and budget issues. Amy replied that Russell was handling those issues and was strongly behind them in their work on the project. The team felt relieved and returned to their workstations. Amy quietly closed her door and got back to planning next month's work. But something didn't feel right to her.

Lessons from the Story

Amy's predicament with her boss illustrates a problem that occasionally occurs in the workplace—integrity. *Integrity* is the state of being truthful and honest with yourself and others, which means *behaving in accordance with one's values and beliefs and doing the right thing.*

> **"Integrity is the state of being truthful and honest with yourself and others."**

This story generates a number of questions regarding the integrity of Russell and Amy:

▲ Looking back on Amy's story, who do you think demonstrated integrity and who did not?

▲ Was Amy's boss, Russell, truthful and honest when he said that everything was on track even though he knew that the budget and schedule were about to slip and more money would be needed? Apparently, Russell didn't want to deliver bad news and upset their clients. He thought saying nothing was the *right thing to do*. Did Russell's proposal to possibly "put the cost onto another project or charge First Class some another way" seem acceptable to you?

▲ Was Amy demonstrating integrity by staying silent in the meeting or by telling her team that Russell was handling the budget and delay issues, thus leaving them thinking that everything was fine? She thought avoiding conflict was the *right thing to do*.

▲ Do you believe it was dishonest for Russell and Amy to choose not to tell the whole truth to their clients? Is it *right* not to give people the whole story in order to protect their feelings or protect the greater good of the organization? Does the end justify the means when the means are just minor nondisclosures or budget maneuvers and not really a big deal?

What Motivates Amy's Behaviors?

If you were in a similar situation and your boss stood up and proudly declared that your project budget was right on track when you knew it wasn't, would you correct your boss's declaration? Like Amy, you may choose not to reply for several reasons:

▲ "I'm not going to tell my boss that he's wrong in front of others."

▲ "He's just trying to be positive—nothing wrong with that."

▲ "It's only a little indiscretion—not a big deal."

▲ "He probably knows something that I don't know."

▲ "It's not the right time or place to say anything."

▲ "He just doesn't want to upset anyone."

These replies are simply rationalizations for not speaking up and correcting a misstatement. Because it's your boss, do you feel *obligated* to go along? Whether it's due to your fear of your boss or your desire to avoid conflict, you are still excusing yourself. When you choose not to speak or get involved to address something that is wrong, dishonest, or deceptive, are you acting with integrity? Does your inaction and silence make you complicit in the infraction? Would you feel differently if the transgression continued or if the consequences were more severe? Should your integrity or the integrity of the organization depend on what's at stake, such as economics, keeping a customer happy, or company reputation? And what is your basis for deciding whether a behavior is of high or low integrity? Should you adjust your integrity based on the situation? As you can see, integrity is one of those tough people problems that have more questions than answers.

What's the Answer?

Amy's story is a classic case of a *conflict in values* between herself and her boss and also between Amy, Russell, and the organization. *Personal integrity* stems from your personal values and morals, whereas *organizational integrity* is defined by the values, ethics, policies, and practices of your employer, profession, or institution. Personal and organizational values form your primary basis for determining right from wrong, true from false, and good from bad. Integrity is about *doing the right thing for yourself and your organization—both* parties need to feel right about your actions.

Doing What's Right for You

Integrity is a tough issue, but it's doubly tough when the issue involves your boss. When your personal values aren't compatible with your boss's or your organization's values, an internal conflict results that will surface in your behaviors. When you choose to let the values of your boss override your personal values, you are compromising your personal integrity. Does it matter whether the infraction is minor or major? Once lost, integrity is very difficult to regain. When Amy let her boss's omissions stand, she was lowering and jeopardizing her own integrity. Integrity can be a slippery slope—once you go down the path of rationalizing dishonesty and deception, you can become prone to other compromises as well.

> **"Once you go down the path of rationalizing dishonesty and deception, you can become prone to other compromises as well."**

Having a good working relationship with your boss is critical when such conflicts arise. If Amy had established a positive, visible relationship with her boss, she would be more apt to address the issue more openly and assertively than she did.

What Can You Do?

How would you handle Amy's dilemma with her boss? As we learned in many of the previous skills, Amy should *not seek blame but rather take responsible action* (Skills Three and Four) and move the issue (ball) forward with her boss (Skill Five). Amy needs to be transparent (visible) and speak honestly and openly with her boss about the discomfort she feels over the situation and her desire to make things right. The aim is not to seek blame and accuse her boss of unethical behavior but rather to focus on the fact that their clients did not get the full story. To do this, Amy could say to Russell, "Personally, I would feel better if the clients knew the full story; I believe full disclosure would be the *right* way to go."

After such a remark, what would be some possible responses from Russell?

▲ **Scenario 1:** Russell listens, acknowledges her concerns, and takes personal or joint action with Amy to correct the picture with their client, in a manner that satisfies both Amy and Russell.

▲ **Scenario 2:** Russell sticks to his story but offers a compromise: "If things don't get better in one month, then I agree we need to inform our clients."

▲ **Scenario 3:** Russell sticks to the story, refuses to take corrective action with their client, and tells Amy, "We don't need to do anything; it's not a big deal."

Doing What's Right for the Organization

Which of these scenarios is acceptable to you? Do all of them appear acceptable? Which ones demonstrate high integrity? There is no right or wrong answer because integrity is not absolute but simply about doing the right thing. Let's examine each scenario.

Scenario 1 would be a positive, win-win outcome in which the boss *acknowledges, respects* (Skill Four: gives ice cream to Amy), and *reinforces* Amy's behavior and concerns (Skill Six) and takes *inclusionary* action to the satisfaction of both parties (Skill Three).

Scenario 2 would appear to be a reasonable concession on the part of Amy's boss, but it could also be a delay tactic or a deception. To ensure *transparency* and *accountability* (Skill Three), it would behoove Amy to confirm their decision in a follow-up email or similar documentation right after their meeting (Skill Six: antecedent), outlining the agreement to meet in one month and advise First Class if things haven't improved. Remember, it is important to operate with trust, but *what gets written gets understood* (Skill Five).

Scenario 3 would be the toughest scenario. In this case, Russell is being difficult by acting as a barrier to resolving the issue. In this scenario, Amy can say, "I understand your position, Russell, and I appreciate your support on this, but this problem really bothers me. May I offer a suggestion? I understand the company has resources for these types of situations, and I think getting clarification from the company would make me feel better. I just want to make sure we're doing the *right thing* for everyone, don't you? They could possibly offer some good options for us. Would you like me to look into this for us?"

At first glance, this response may seem a little risky, but as a team leader, it's important to think *process* and taking the problem to the right level in the organization (Skill One: use the Wedge). This is an example of an issue that requires you to do the right thing in the right way to get the right results (Skill Six)—first by trying to work with your boss to get resolution (Skill Three: be inclusive; Skill Five: give him the first move), and second, if that fails, by using your leverage and wear your management hat (Skill Two) to ensure compliance with company policy and ethics.

As with most communication, it's not what you say but *how* you say it (Skill Five: difficult conversations). Instead of disagreeing or debating the issue with Russell, Amy's remarks are respectful (Skill Five: making "I" statements in difficult conversations), transparent, collaborative (Skill Three: Amy's remarks are a "you-me-we" sandwich), open-minded, and future oriented (Skill Four: upper cone), and she took control of her fears by taking action (Skill Seven). Anytime you find yourself at an impasse with your boss, always think *process* to depersonalize and de-antagonize the situation and, most importantly, *always operate from a position of greatest strength and leverage* when solving people problems (Skill One). In this case, Amy's strength resides in her values and personal integrity and the leverage comes from doing what's right for the company (that is, following company policy and ethics).

> *"Anytime you find yourself at an impasse with your boss, always think process to depersonalize and de-antagonize the situation."*

As an experienced manager, Russell knows that Amy can take the matter to the company without him. Hopefully, Russell will realize that his reluctance to fully disclose the problems to their client wasn't right in many ways and that a good boss would appreciate Amy's honesty, concern, and respect. If Russell is smart, he'll promptly do the right thing as well.

Summary

Amy's case is the type of situation that will test your conscience as a leader. When these situations occur, you have two choices: do what's right for you and the organization, or live with the consequences and possible regrets and disappointments. Integrity is not about avoiding or rationalizing a possible wrong or having the courage to challenge your boss; it's about *doing the right thing for yourself and your organization*—both parties need to feel right about your actions.

Working with a Difficult Boss

As we have witnessed in Amy's story, having a difficult boss is an extremely challenging situation. A difficult boss is one who inhibits or impedes your progress and makes your job harder. Bad bosses are often selfish, controlling, mean, intimidating, unfair, indecisive, uncaring, ill tempered, and/or autocratic. Amy's story illustrates that dealing with a difficult boss requires you to manage up and to use the people skills that you have learned. The secrets in working with a difficult boss are: stay on top of your cone, maintain visibility and positive influence, roll your ball forward, and control your own fate.

Stay on Top of Your Cone

As covered in Skills Four and Five, difficult people reside in the lower part of their "cones" and are driven by two factors: fear and an alternate reality. Essentially all bad behaviors can be attributed to fear—and your boss is no exception. The key is *not to let your boss's fear scare you.* When your boss is mean, negative, or rude to you, it is an indictment of your boss, not you. Don't internalize the bad behavior and feelings from your boss. What you do afterward is what matters most (Skill Four), so take positive actions when negative things happen. Also, try to find gratitude and solace in the many positive motivators that you have at work, such as your friends, team, colleagues, customers, projects, travel, training, and professional activities. It's hard to stay positive with a difficult boss, but if you internalize the good things that are happening at work, it will be easier to prevent your boss's bad behavior from affecting your self-confidence and self-esteem. In other words, *your boss may control your work, but don't let your boss control your feelings—especially the feelings that you have about yourself.*

If you have a lousy boss, it's easy to lose sight of the big picture. Getting down, negative, and cynical and getting revenge on your boss doesn't make you a better person. *Work hard for your bad boss and you'll come out ahead.* That may sound crazy, but remember that any drop in your work performance will adversely affect your project, team, and organization. Also, other supervisors and managers beyond your boss will take notice of your positive attitude and performance and your reputation will increase in their eyes. *Don't operate out of spite*—it's an unhealthy state of mind.

Maintain Visibility and Positive Influence

Don't perceive your difficult boss as a black box (Skill Seven) filled with uncertainty, fear, and distrust. Understand your boss's personality type and you'll get a hint of his or her values, fears, and behaviors. If you are effective in managing up and being more visible, you will gain favor and influence with your boss and he or she will be less likely to exclude you (Skill Three) and more likely to trust you as a can-do, go-to person (Skill Two: partnership). The goal is for your boss to see you as a positive rather than a negative influence and treat you with respect, fairness, and dignity.

Roll Your Ball Forward

Your boss is only being difficult when he or she impedes or disables your progress. You can't control your boss's attitude or actions, so you have a choice: continue to get frustrated and be disheartened by your boss's difficult behaviors, or take control of your emotions and devote your energy to something more productive (Skill Seven). Roll your ball forward by continuing to grow and develop your knowledge and skills, look for new opportunities and projects, and even seek a mentor and other in-house advocates to support your work and career.

Your boss is difficult only if you allow him or her to inhibit your growth and progress. Don't let difficult bosses steal your enthusiasm, fun, hope, and personal growth in your work and career. Continue to put faith in yourself, do great work, and maintain a can-do reputation.

Control Your Own Fate

Your boss defines your work goals, not your personal goals, passions, and ambitions, which enable you to stay positive and focused on the long term and not on the small, annoying things that happen each day. Set clear, specific, challenging, fun, exciting personal goals and live your dreams. Your personal goals and passions in life are much more important than work goals. Be self-accountable, self-motivated, and self-determined and don't leave your fate in the hands of others. You have your own unique path and pace. *You are more autonomous than you think—be your own champion.*

Skill Eight Summary

Employees who have a good working relationship with their bosses have better physical health, psychological well-being, and job satisfaction. Skill Eight is about "managing up," which means taking specific actions to establish a favorable and influential relationship with your boss that creates mutual value for you, your boss, and the organization.

The boss-employee relationship is characterized by mutual dependence— the boss relies on your knowledge, skills, and experiences to get the necessary tasks and projects done, and you depend on your supervisor for resources, direction, and support. As in any relationship, the more you know about the other party, the better you will understand and get along with him or her.

Some of the most important human factors in the boss-employee relationship include understanding what motivates and demotivates each party, their personal work styles and preferences, their temperament and personality type, and how they like to be treated. When bosses and employees do not know each other's work preferences, the two parties operate in a trial-and-error mode and make assumptions based on their perceptions of each other's behaviors, which can lead to interpersonal conflicts and misunderstandings. You can improve your relationship with your boss and your chances for success by helping your boss understand and value your talents, skills, positive attitude, knowledge, resources, and ability to get the job done.

The key to gaining greater favor and influence with your boss is to be more *visible*, which means being more proactive, engaged, competent, productive, creative, impactful, and supportive of your boss, team, and organization. Seven key actions are offered in this skill to increase your visibility and magnify your performance: increase personal engagement, possess a can-do attitude, continue to build your competency, communicate and keep your boss in the loop, seek a win-win relationship, be a go-to resource, and know your boss's preferences.

This skill also addresses two of the toughest situations that you may encounter: working with a boss who demonstrates a lack of integrity and working with a difficult boss. Integrity issues involve resolving conflicts between personal values and organizational values and understanding that organizational values have more power, relevance, and priority in the workplace. Managing a difficult boss entails controlling what you can control and not letting your boss control your feelings, goals, and fate. You can't control your boss's behaviors, but you can help shape how your boss interacts with you by using several strategies and techniques revealed in this skill. Managing up has more benefits than pitfalls, and you can deploy these proven techniques to vastly improve your influence and relationship with your boss.

Skill Eight Memory Card

Gain Greater Favor and Influence with Your Boss
Be More Visible

Strategies for Increasing Favor and Influence	Managing a Bad Boss
1. Increase personal engagement—show your commitment	1. Always act with integrity—do what's right for you *and* the organization
2. Possess a can-do attitude—be a doer, not a complainer	2. Let the process do the dirty work
3. Build your competency—increased skills mean increased value	3. Always act from a position of strength and leverage
4. Keep your boss in-the-loop—communicate your progress	4. Stay on top of your cone—keep a high reputation
5. Seek a win-win relationship—you win when your boss wins	5. Maintain visibility and positive influence
6. Be a go-to resource—be a kiosk of information	6. Roll your ball forward—don't let a bad boss inhibit your growth and enthusiasm
7. Know your boss's personality type and behavioral preferences	7. Control your own fate—be your own champion

Epilogue

If you step back and look at all the things you've learned from the Eight Essential People Skills, don't be surprised if you still have more questions and problems. People problems will always be constant and remain highly unpredictable, time consuming, and intellectually and emotionally challenging. The role of the project team leader will likely continue to expand and demand more sophisticated skills. But look at it this way: if the job were easy, they wouldn't need you. I hope you will take these eight skills and continue to develop and personalize them for your benefit.

The following summarizes the best recommendations drawn from the discussions on the eight essential people skills for team leaders:

1. **Skill One:** In diagnosing and correcting people problems, use the *wedge* to quickly and effectively find the root cause, apply the right performance and leveraging factors (knobs and levers, respectively), and facilitate corrective action.

2. **Skill Two:** When trying to solve tough people problems, always be your true self and wear the *hat* that gives you the greatest strength, opportunity, and leverage to solve the problem and help your employees succeed.

3. **Skill Three:** To build a highly successful project team, create a *loop* with a compelling mission that is supported by the six inclusive, "we" behaviors—mutual trust, interdependence, accountability, transparency, learning, and valuing individuality.

4. **Skill Four:** To boost people's attitudes, happiness, and performance, we learned that recognizing people's good work with *ice cream* works much better than leaving people feeling underappreciated and "coned."

5. **Skill Five:** Help turn around difficult people and underperformers by *rolling the ball forward*, letting process do the dirty work, and

helping poor performers transition to a more positive, productive, and forward-looking mind-set and behavior.

6. **Skill Six:** Motivating the right behaviors requires using the *ABC Boxes* which are the prompts (antecedents), actions (behaviors), and reinforcements (consequences) for shaping a sustainable change in people's performance.

7. **Skill Seven:** When facing change, problems, and challenges, control your fear and take actions to reduce the uncertainties in the circumstance, your ability to perform, and a bad outcome; otherwise fear will put you mentally in a *black box* and control your actions, distort your thinking, create greater uncertainty, and cast doubt on yourself.

8. **Skill Eight:** When trying to gain favor and influence with your boss, you have a choice of either increasing your *visibility*, managing up, and magnifying your value through superior performance, integrity, and teamwork or staying invisible and letting your boss control your motivation, integrity, feelings, and well-being.

These eight people skills will help you facilitate and shape the right team behaviors and increase your success in managing projects. In your career, you will likely find that projects come and go, but your efforts to help, coach, mentor, and inspire others are the experiences that you will remember and cherish the most. What makes them memorable are not the victories in solving people problems but the joys in leading and succeeding as a team.

Great team leaders who work hard to *make people feel good about themselves and their work* are in short supply. And they are needed in every department, organization, industry, trade, and field. So please keep learning and honing your people skills. The world needs you.

References

1. Nayar, Vineet. *Employees First, Customers Second: Turning Conventional Management Upside Down.* Boston: Harvard Business Review Press, 2010, 89.
2. Wong, Zachary A. *Human Factors in Project Management: Concepts, Tools, and Techniques for Inspiring Teamwork and Motivation.* San Francisco: Jossey-Bass, 2007, 149–189.
3. Dill, Kathryn. "The Top Companies for Culture and Values." *Forbes,* August 22, 2014. https://www.forbes.com/sites/kathryndill/2014/08/22/the-top-companies -for-culture-and-values/#22e0c3d93b7c.
4. Fortune Editors. "World's Most Admired Companies Ranked by Key Attributes." *Fortune,* February 19, 2015. http://fortune.com/2015/02/19/wmac-ranked-by-key -attribute/.
5. Heineman, Ben. "Wells Fargo Lessons: Will Leaders Ever Learn?" Harvard Law School Forum on Corporate Governance and Financial Regulation, April 26, 2017. https://corpgov.law.harvard.edu/2017/04/26/wells-fargo-lessons-will -leaders-ever-learn/.
6. Isaac, Mike. "Inside Uber's Aggressive, Unrestrained Workplace Culture." *New York Times,* February 22, 2017. https://www.nytimes.com/2017/02/22/technology /uber-workplace-culture.html.
7. Brown, Kirk W., Richard M. Ryan, and J. David Creswell. "Mindfulness: Theoretical Foundations and Evidence for Its Salutary Effects." *Psychological Inquiry* 18, no. 4 (2007): 211–237.
8. Seligman, Martin E. P. *Authentic Happiness: Using the New Positive Psychology to Realize Your Potential for Lasting Fulfillment.* New York: Free Press, 2002.
9. Jung, C. G. *Psychological Types.* New York: Pantheon Books, 1923.
10. Briggs, K. C., and I. B. Myers. *Myers-Briggs Type Indicator.* Princeton, NJ: Educational Testing Service, 1957.
11. Keirsey, D. *Please Understand Me II.* Del Mar, CA: Prometheus Nemesis, 1984.
12. Wong, Zachary A. *Personal Effectiveness in Project Management: Tools, Tips and Strategies to Improve Your Decision-Making, Motivation, Confidence, Risk-Taking, Achievement and Sustainability.* Newport Square, PA: PMI, 2013.
13. Harris Interactive. "Stress in the Workplace: Survey Summary." American Psychological Association, March 2011. https://www.apa.org/news/press /releases/phwa-survey-summary.pdf.

14. Perkins, E. L. "Why the Ball Gets Dropped: Hindrances to Performance Conversations in North Carolina Local Governments." Master's thesis, University of North Carolina, Chapel Hill, 2013.
15. Miltenberger, R. G. *Behavior Modification: Principles and Procedure.* 4th ed. Belmont, CA: Thomson Wadsworth, 2008.
16. Franco, L., J. Gibbons, and L. Barrington. *I Can't Get No—Job Satisfaction, That Is: America's Unhappy Workers.* Research Report No. 1459-09-RR. New York: Conference Board, 2010.
17. Yerkes, R. M., and J. D. Dodson. "The Relationship of Strength of Stimulus to Rapidity of Habit Formation." *Journal of Comparative Neurology and Psychology* 18 (1908): 459–482.
18. Porath, Christine. "Half of Employees Don't Feel Respected by Their Boss." *Harvard Business Review,* November 19, 2014. https://hbr.org/2014/11/half-of-employees-dont-feel-respected-by-their-bosses.
19. Harter, Jim, and Amy Adkins. "Employees Want a Lot More from Their Managers." Gallup News, Business Journal, April 8, 2015. http://www.gallup.com/businessjournal/182321/employees-lot-managers.aspx.

Acknowledgments

This book would not have been possible without the love and support of my wife, Elaine, who gave me the time and inspiration to write these skills. Thank you for all your precious gifts.

My deepest gratitude to Richard Clark, who has been an incredible friend, colleague, and supporter throughout my career—thanks for making a difference in my life; and to Judith MacGregor, who was the most fun, engaging, and kindest boss, mentor, and champion for me at Chevron—I am grateful to you.

In addition, this book was inspired by many other wonderful people and leaders whom I have met in my career: Helen Argyres, Kathy Baldwin, Jim Bus, Kathy Dougherty, Mike Hagler, Carol Henry, Mark Keller, Jiro Kodama, Chuck McGinnis, Manfred Michlmayr, Pete Stonebraker, Norm Szydlowski, Patricia Woertz, and Diana Wu.

Many thanks to the people who provided me the stage to perform and practice what I love to do: Debra Dobin, Marcus Emmons, Ray Ju, Rob Judd, Tom Kendrick, Sylvia Lee, Maria Marques, Carol Nishita, Clara Piloto, Cynthia Shafer, Ella Wong, Sam Woo, and Diana Wu.

This endeavor would not have been possible without the support of my family: Elaine, Sarah, Amy, Tony, Reynold, Pamela, Tom, Marguerite, Marilyn, Angie, Gary, Wendy, Courtney, Madeleine, Cassandra, Christie, Christopher, Kevin, Ashley, Lindsay, and Nicole.

In memory of Robert Almond, Michael Aufrere, June Carver, James Embree, Joseph Heisler, Jiro Kodama, Michael Lakin, Quan Loo (Po Po), K. C. Matthews, Eric Stine, Carmella Tellone, and Margaret and Wilfred Wong.

A big "ice cream cone" goes to my good colleagues, Richard Clark and Helen Argyres, who so generously and courageously reviewed my draft manuscript.

Thanks to the highly professional team at Berrett-Koehler for their belief in the book, especially Neal Maillet, Charlotte Ashlock, and Lesley Lura, as well as Jeevan Sivasubramaniam for contributing his illustrations. It was a great experience working with Berrett-Koehler.

I wish to thank the many companies and organizations that have recognized and supported my work over the years: the East Bay Municipal Utility District, McMillen-Jacobs, Apple, Chevron, Genentech, Novartis, Genomics Health, Kaiser Permanente, the California Regional Water Quality Control Board, the University of California at Berkeley, the University of California at Davis, the National Association of Asian American Professionals, and the San Francisco and Silicon Valley chapters of the Project Management Institute.

Index

ABC Box Model, 160, 175, 176, 224; behavior, 146f; Box A, 147–150, 147f; Box B, 150–153; Box C, 153–157, 154f, 155f, 156t; consequences in, 153–157, 154f, 155f, 156t; motivation and, 166; recognition and, 146; risk taking and, 196; summary, 166–168. *See also* team behavior

ability, 19, 176, 183–189. *See also* ERAM; skills

absenteeism, 18, 21

accountability, 77, 120, 217, 224; low, 164, 208t; in teams, 81–83, 81f, 89

action: disciplinary, 21; fear and, 189; inaction and, 189; plans, 20, 26–27; risk taking and, 184f; self-confidence and, 189. *See also* inaction

active listening, 123–124

agreements, in performance reviews, 134–135

alcohol, 34–35, 38

ambition, team leaders and, 141–146

antecedent, behavior, and consequence. *See* ABC Box Model

antecedents, 146–150, 147f, 167, 177. *See also* ABC Box Model

appreciation, 65, 69, 96–97, 109–110

arrogance, 56

artisan personality type, 68–69, 68t, 69, 70t

assertiveness, 137

attitude, 21, 65; bad, 96, 109–110; behavior and, 71; boss and, 205; can-do, 205; employee, 205; empower-ment and, 105; excitement and, 93–94; levels, 98–99, 99f, 109–110; motivation and, 100; negative, 100–101; perfor-mance and, 93; positive, 100–101; real-life cases of, 91–97; of teams, improving, 101; what drives, 100–101

authenticity, 53, 54–55, 59

authority, 17, 57; delegating, 46; results and, 51–52; sources of, 127; of team leaders, 36, 39; in wedge model of organization, 13f

autonomy, 220

avoidance, 67, 164, 185

background, skills and, 2

behavior, 29, 45; ABC Box Model, 146f; attitude and, 71; bad, 92–93, 95, 111; of boss, 162, 202; boss favors, 207–208, 208t; definition of, 23; of difficult people, 120; as divisive or unifying, 75–76; exclusion and, 70; of high performers, 120; intention and, 137; management of, 141–146; motiva-tion and, 26, 214–215; outcomes and, 102–104, 145–146; performance and, 90; performance problems and, 23; in performance reviews, improvement of, 133–134; real-life cases on, 102–104; rewards and, 93, 97, 102–104; right, 145–146; risk taking as, 174, 184f; of successful teams, inclusive, 78–88, 89; transparency and, 82–83; of underperformers, 120; values and, 28, 145. *See also* CPB;

About the Author

Zachary Wong, PhD, is an accomplished professor, scientist, author, trainer, consultant, and senior manager in business and project management with over thirty-five years of experience. He is an Honored Instructor at the University of California at Berkeley Extension and an adjunct professor at the University of California at Davis. He has held senior management positions at Chevron in research and technology, strategic planning, business analysis, and health, environment, and safety. He is an active management consultant in organizational and personal effectiveness, leadership training, and the development of high-performing teams.

Zachary Wong, PhD

Dr. Wong was born and raised in San Francisco and received his PhD in environmental toxicology and pharmacology from the University of California at Davis. He has served extensively on project teams, executive leadership teams, and decision review boards in public committees, industry associations, and academia. He lives in Alamo, California, with his wife, Elaine, and two daughters, Amy and Sarah.